Battles...

*Vieques is our unsinkable
battleship in the Caribbean.*

—United States Naval Officer

Battleship Vieques

Puerto Rico from World War II to the Korean War

CÉSAR J. AYALA

JOSÉ L. BOLÍVAR

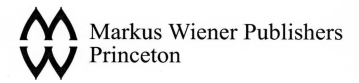 Markus Wiener Publishers
Princeton

This book is made possible in part through a faculty grant from the Institute
of American Cultures and administered through the Chicano Studies
Research Center at the University of California, Los Angeles.

For information, write to: Markus Wiener Publishers
231 Nassau Street, Princeton, NJ 08542
www.markuswiener.com

Library of Congress Cataloging-in-Publication Data

Ayala Casás, César.
  Battleship Vieques : Puerto Rico from World War II to the Korean War / César Ayala
Casás, José Bolívar Fresneda.
    p. cm.
    Includes bibliographical references and index.
    ISBN 978-1-55876-537-5 (hardcover : alk. paper)
    ISBN 978-1-55876-538-2 (pbk. : alk. paper)
  1. Vieques Island (P.R.)—History, Naval—20th century. 2. United States. Navy—
    History—20th century.
  3. Militarism—Puerto Rico—Vieques Island—History—20th century.
  4. Civil-military relations—Puerto Rico—Vieques Island—History—20th century.
  5. Decolonization—Puerto Rico—Vieques Island—History—20th century.
  6. Protest movements—Puerto Rico—Vieques Island—History—20th century.
  7. Social change—Puerto Rico—Vieques Island—History—20th century. 8. Vieques
    Island (P.R.)—History—20th century.
  9. Vieques Island (P.R.)—Social conditions—20th century. 10. Vieques Island (P.R.)—
    Economic conditions—20th century.
  I. Bolívar Fresneda, José. II. Title.
  F1981.V5A95 2011
    972.95'9--dc22
                  2011005532

Markus Wiener Publishers books are printed in the United States of America on
acid-free paper and meet the guidelines for permanence and durability of the Committee
on Production Guidelines for Book Longevity of the Council on Library Resources.

Contents

Abbreviations

A.F.L.M.M.   Archivo de la Fundación Luis Muñoz Marín

A.G.P.R.   Archivo General de Puerto Rico

A.T.S.D.R.   Agency for Toxic Substances and Disease Registry

C.I.H.   Centro de Investigaciones Históricas de la
                  Universidad de Puerto Rico

D.H.   Departamento de Hacienda

H.A.B.P.P.R.   Historial Archive of Banco Popular de Puerto Rico

H.A.P.R.W.R.A.   Historical Archive of the Puerto Rico Water
                  Resources Authority

N.A.   National Archives of the United States

P.A.A.C.   Private Archive of The Arundel Corporation.
                  Documentation under the custody of The Arundel
                  Corporation P.O. Box 5000 Sparks, MD 21152–5000.

P.C.J.P.   Proyecto Caribeño de Justicia y Paz

P.D.P.   Popular Democratic Party

U.S.N.–S.M.A.   U.S. Navy Seabees Museum Archives,
                  Port Hueneme, California

V.H.A.   Vieques Historical Archive

Abbreviations Used in Archival Citations

Art. . . . . Article   Leg. . . . . Legajo
Col. . . . . Collection   R.G. . . . . Record Group
Doc. . . . . Document   Sec. . . . . Section
Ent. . . . . Entry   Ser. . . . . Series
Fdr. . . . . Folder   Tar. . . . . Tarea
Fol. . . . . Folio   Tom. . . . . Tome
Fon. . . . . Fondo

Militarism in Vieques in an Epoch of Decolonization

T he U.S. Navy occupied most of the land of the Puerto Rican island of Vieques from 1941 to 2003. When it finally left, it did so in response to a massive movement of protest and civil disobedience in Vieques, in the island of Puerto Rico, and among communities of Puerto Ricans in the continental United States. There is a growing literature on that movement of protest.[1] In this book, we seek the historical root of the conflict between civilians and the military, which culminated in a massive wave of protests in 1999–2001, in the period of formation of the navy base in Vieques. This work is about the establishment of the U.S. Navy in Vieques, Puerto Rico, from the beginning of World War II to the U.S. war in Korea. It examines the transformation of local society and economy in Vieques under the impact of the acquisition by the navy of roughly two thirds of the land of the island. The land grab by the navy was followed by the relocation of the population to the central part of Vieques, by considerable disruption of the local economy, and by the disconnection of Vieques from the main thrust of the historical changes then taking place in the island Puerto Rico.

For it was precisely during the years when the navy set up its presence in Vieques that profound changes took place in Puerto Rico, starting with a process of agrarian reform initiated in 1940. During the war years, the local government justified land reform as a means to guarantee food production. After the war, it defended the continuation of the agrarian reform with the aim of diminishing Puerto Rico s dependence on one industry, the sugar industry, as its main source of exports. The agrarian reform and the decline of the sugar industry were accompanied by a quick process of industrialization, by fast-paced urbanization, and by the initiation of mass migration from Puerto Rico to the United States. Many of the positive economic changes of the postwar years were given an initial impetus by massive federal military expenditure in Puerto Rico in the decade from 1940 to 1950. At the political level, during this period Puerto Ricans achieved a measure of self-government. This took place in the context of the wave of decolonization sweeping Asia, Africa, and the Caribbean after World War II. In the United States, President Truman's initiative to desegregate the armed forces in 1947 added force to the decolonizing thrust in Puerto Rico. In 1948, the old colonial political system, in which the governor was appointed by the president of the United States, was modified to allow Puerto Ricans to elect their own government. In 1952, the creation of the Commonwealth of Puerto Rico, through a so-called compact of association with the United States and the retention of U.S. citizenship, supposedly expanded local control over political matters, resulting in greater political autonomy.

In Vieques, by contrast, the thrust of change was not toward more local control over political or social life. The irruption of the navy into this Caribbean island actually put its residents at the mercy of larger imperial forces over which they had little influence. We thus examine, for the island of Vieques, but always in the context of the changes taking place in Puerto Rico, the transformation of colonial society and economy during the years of formation of the navy presence. We wish to know which of the old colonial structures survived, which were modified, and which, in turn, emerged as a result of the arrival of the navy. And we wish to place whatever changes happened in the optic of the changes taking place simultaneously in the main island of Puerto Rico.

In 1940, Puerto Rico was considered the poorhouse of the Caribbean, a U.S. colony ruled by governors appointed by the president of the United States in which foreign sugar companies owned much wealth and the local working population suffered chronic economic hardship. In 1953, it was a "commonwealth," which elected its governor. According to the euphoric view of the time, it was on the way to full decolonization and economic advancement through agrarian reform, the dismantling of the old plantation economy, and quick industrialization.[2] As U.S. power increased in the postwar years, and U.S. economic hegemony acquired a planetary dimension, the old colonial empires of the British and French, Dutch and Belgians collapsed, and gave way to a multiplicity of new national states and an international regime of free trade, with the dollar as world currency and New York as the banking center of the world. The U.S. colony of Puerto Rico, acquired during the Spanish-American War of 1898, figured in this scenario as a relic from the past. Indeed, direct colonial rule by presidentially appointed governors progressively appeared as outmoded in the context of the worldwide decolonization movement initiated by the independence of India from British rule in 1947.

A local political movement forged in alliance with the New Deal in the United States in the 1930s achieved unprecedented political prestige in the island after its institutionalization as a party, the Popular Democratic Party (P.D.P.), in 1938. In 1940, its leader, Luis Muñoz Marín, became president of the Puerto Rican Senate, and representatives of his movement challenged the sugar companies, initiated an agrarian reform after a victory in the U.S. Supreme Court in 1940, challenged the power of the sugar barons, and earned in the process the allegiance of the rural population, winning a landslide victory in the elections of 1944. The P.D.P. won all elections for the next twenty-four years. By 1948, this movement had persuaded the U.S. Congress to pass an act allowing Puerto Ricans to elect their own governor, and by 1952, it had created the Commonwealth of Puerto Rico, a supposedly "sovereign" entity.

During those same years, the U.S. Navy established itself in the Puerto Rican island of Vieques. In late 1941, the U.S. federal government expropriated the land of local landowners to build a navy base. This happened, like the agrarian reform of the P.D.P. in Puerto Rico, in the context of the Second World War, at a time when German U-boats were sinking civilian ship after civilian ship in the waters of the Caribbean, impeding trade and threatening the population of Puerto Rico with starvation. By the end of 1943, the United States had repelled the U-boats and was on the offensive both in the Pacific and in the Atlantic and North Africa. The navy base closed down, and land was transferred to the Department of Interior in 1946, which in turn leased it to the government of Puerto Rico. The latter on its part attempted to revive the civilian economy of Vieques through a state-owned agricultural company. In late 1947, with the initiation of the Cold War, the navy reclaimed the land, the operations of the agricultural company closed down, and in early 1948, the navy began utilizing Vieques for military maneuvers. Thus, the establishment of the navy in Vieques coincides with the period of transformation of Puerto Rico from an agrarian society to an induststrial one, and with the change in colonial regime, from direct rule by presidentially appointed governors to locally elected governors, and finally, to the establishment of the Commonwealth of Puerto Rico in 1952.

The transformations wrought by the navy in Vieques ran contrary to the decolonizing thrust of the changes then taking place elsewhere in Puerto Rico. We find that U.S. militarism in Vieques is imbricated with colonial structures, old and new. For the economy and society of Vieques had been hardened in the kiln of Spanish colonialism, which left a deep imprint on the local structure of society. First and foremost, Vieques had been a "sugar island" under the epoch of slavery, and it had remained a sugar island after emancipation, which took place in Peurto Rico in 1873. The end of the slave regime did not translate into the end of the plantation economy. Rather, the plantation survived and transformed itself, retaining many features that rendered it a structure first and foremost of social inequality. The plantation as an institution survived into the twentieth century and was actually strengthened by the incorporation of Puerto Rico into the U.S. trade and tariff structures under the post-1898 colonial regime. Free trade between Puerto Rico and the United States helped to strengthen the traditional sugar industry, to increase the power of the landowners, and to fasten the subordination of the plantation labor force to the big landowners.[3] When the navy entered Vieques in 1941, it encountered this plantation structure. When it transformed the island through the expropriation of land to establish a base, the resulting economic and social configuration was partially formed by the preexisting plantation legacy. Thus, old colonial formations dating from Spanish times and modified during the first half of the "American century" in Puerto Rico, affected the process of transformation initiated by the entrance of the navy.

But the resulting social product was not merely the artifact of old colonial structures. The navy also introduced into Vieques brand-new colonial practices, which issued not from the semi-feudal heritage of the Spanish colonial epoch,[4] but from the very center of modernity in the United States of America. Racial segregation was the main aspect of the new colonial configuration, all other forms being but ancillary features of this main thrust of inequality. The new inequality in Vieques would be structured according to segregationist practices, separate living quarters for different "types" of U.S. citizens, and unequal pay according to ethno-racial criteria.

The resulting scenario presents an interesting paradox. While in the rest of Puerto Rico the transformations of 1940 to 1952 were called by some observers "decolonization," and by others more cautious a positive transformation of the colonial regime, in Vieques the transformation of the years 1941–1953 actually represented a historical regression. The period was characterized by a hardening of colonial inequality, implying a definite feeling of diminishing control of citizens over their own lives. That is, historical change was in the direction of not more, but rather less self-determination. One could argue that the changes introduced by the navy represented, therefore, a coarsening of the colonial bond, rather than the dissolution of colonial structures, whether old or new. Throughout the book, we make comparisons with conditions in the main island of Puerto Rico. For it is the experience of Puerto Rico that informs the citizens of Vieques, and it is to conditions in the larger island that they take recourse when making comparisons. What the situation of Vieques means for Puerto Rico as a whole, and for the supposed dissolution of colonialism that resulted from the creation of the Commonwealth, we leave for the reader to judge.

CHAPTER 1

The German Naval Blockade and the War Economy

In February of 1942, German U-boats advanced westward across the Atlantic and arrived in the Caribbean, signaling the beginning of a remarkable series of attacks on merchant ships, tankers, and navy vessels in the sea corridor between the Caribbean and the U.S. Atlantic coast. Because of the ease and frequency with which they found and destroyed their targets, with almost no resistance, the first eight months of 1942 became known to the German U-boat captains as the "Second Happy Time." The "First Happy Time" (*Die Glückliche Zeit*) had been in 1940–1941 after the fall of France. An unprecedented number of commercial ships and tankers were sunk in the first eight months of 1942, resulting in heavy casualties and material losses. The U-boats severely disrupted trade between the United States and Puerto Rico. In that corridor alone, over 350 American merchant ships and tankers were lost, representing more than double the numbers of American ships lost in any other region during the war, such as in the Northeast Atlantic, including ports in Great Britain and Belgium (155 ships lost), the Philippines (128 ships lost), and in Pacific ports, including Hong Kong (130 ships lost). Altogether, 1,768 U.S. merchant vessels and tankers were lost during the course of World War II, and of the 243,000 merchant marines who served during the war, over 9,000, or 3.94 percent, died, a significantly higher rate of mortality than that of the marines (2.94 percent) or the army (2.04 percent).[1] The assaults began in Aruba on February 16, 1942, and continued relentlessly through August of that year. There was widespread fear that the Puerto Rican economy could collapse under a German naval blockade. While losses continued to mount throughout the rest of the war, the regional losses sharply diminished as the war progressed to other theaters.

The concerns about increasing trading difficulties were compounded by the fact that Puerto Rico had suffered economic contraction during the 1930s. By the time the United States entered the Second World War on December 8, 1941, the economic situation was already dire. The Great Depression had devastated the island, leaving large segments of the rural population lacking in essentials such as a pair of shoes, income for adequate medical care, or a permanent home.[2] During the war, food became scarce and prohibitively expensive, and unemployment was rising exponentially. The U-boat assaults traumatized the population up and down the east coast of the mainland United States and throughout the Caribbean, but the effect of submarine warfare in 1942 was detrimental in specific ways to the economy of Puerto Rico. The expansion of sugar production during the first forty years of the twentieth century had turned the island into a monocultural export economy, whose survival was acutely dependent on food imports and open sea lanes that were threatened by both German naval blockade and U.S.-imposed cargo restrictions in imports. Because the island was dependent upon trade for one third of its staples,[3] open sea lanes were crucial to guaranteeing the food supply. The mainland economy, by contrast, was internally articulated through a vast railroad network that was not easily vulnerable to enemy attacks.

The costs of imported food staples began to spiral out of control as cargo capacity was increasingly dedicated to war materials at the expense of consumer goods. In 1942, when so many merchant ships and tankers were torpedoed and sunk in the Atlantic corridor,[4] the desperation for food rose to a new level. The U.S. military by no means had the U-boat assault under control before the end of 1942, while continuing to build its presence, and to expand its bases, in Puerto Rico and other Caribbean islands. In his memoir, Puerto Rican Governor Rexford Tugwell recalls his desire to see a ship on a day in July, 1942. "In the week since I had got home, no merchant ship had come in. The whole sweep of the horizon had been empty through the long days, save for the patrol boat which crossed and recrossed the entrance to the channel a mile or two at sea."[5] Tugwell recounts that living with a view of the harbor exacerbated his anxiety. He did not dare ask Admiral Hoover for ship movement plans,[6] "thinking no one ought to possess any [information about ship movements] except the very few operations officers whose business it was to protect them."[7] "As protection improved in the North Atlantic," he wrote "the submarines were coming down our way. They were a familiar ghostly phenomenon. We never saw one; but we felt their presence constantly. I will not say that we got used to them; but they were sinking a ship a day or thereabouts in our waters, and the survivors were all over the place. So there was nothing strange any more about the awareness of their presence."[8] The sinkings resulted in the coast guard picking up survivors who then landed in ports in Puerto Rico. For example, the twenty-one crew members from the boat *La Carrière*, sunk seventy miles southwest of Guánica by U-156, landed in the port of Guánica on February 25, 1942. Eight officers and twenty-eight men from the tanker *E. J. Sadler* landed in Mayagüez on June 23, 1942, after a day adrift in lifeboats at sea, following the attack of U-159.[9] News of the attacks and the survivors compounded the sense of emergency created by lack of commercial ships coming to port in San Juan. Governor Tugwell searched in vain for the arriving merchant ships for quite a few months.

From April through December of 1942, tonnage decreased by 55 percent and food imports by 22 percent when compared with 1940 levels. (See Table 1.1.) This situation created a great gap in the food supply and soaring prices, resulting in major social and economic disruption.[10] The overall reduction in imports was primarily felt on the island after March of 1942, as it was during this time that U-boat warfare in the Caribbean started to take a heavy toll on Allied shipping. The first three months of 1942 saw tonnage decrease to 91,153 when compared to the levels of 1940, when monthly figures had averaged 112,933 tons. After March, imports decreased even further, to 50,863 tons. In order to feed the increasingly hungry population, the percentage of foodstuff in each vessel was expanded from 45 percent in January of 1942 to 75 percent by December of the same year. In spite of this effort, there was still a critical shortage of food.

Most of the foodstuff imported to the island was in the form of carbohydrates, and little in the form of protein. Rice accounted for 28 percent of the imports, followed by flour, which made up an additional 10 percent. Beans, pork, and codfish amounted to only 7 percent of the total imported foodstuff. In 1940, imported food accounted for one third of total food consumption. War shortages increased the price of food sold by retailers by 48 percent between December 1941 and December 1942. As if this were not enough, the war caused a concentration of import tonnage into the port of San Juan, resulting in serious distribution problems because of limited truck and railway transportation and fuel shortages. It also created major employment problems for the stevedores located on the southern and eastern ports of the Island.[11]

The reduction in the amount of maritime cargo space allocated to general merchandise created additional hardships, as imports of industrial and commercial materials, such as lumber, cement, steel, construction materials, and fertilizers were greatly curtailed. The amount of maritime cargo space allocated to food imports was increased at the expense of industrial and commercial materials. The shortage of industrial materials stifled the manufacturing, construction and transportation sectors of the economy and contributed heavily to escalating unemployment.

In the continental United States, despite a 24 percent reduction in the production of civilian goods between 1941 and 1943, the economy nonetheless expanded due to a surge in military production. Consequently, the number of people employed increased by more than two million relative to the period before December 1941. While a large proportion of the male population was enlisting in the war effort, four million women were employed in the production of military goods and services by the end of 1943.[12] In the continental United States in 1945, for example, 47.5 percent of the electrical manufacturing labor force were women (347,200 of 778,000 workers), and women comprised 22 percent of the automobile manufacturing labor force (158,100 of 705,800 workers).[13]

The employment situation created in the continent was not replicated in Puerto Rico. Overall, while the United States contemplated labor scarcity, war conditions had the opposite effect of crippling agricultural and industrial production in Puerto Rico, and consequently, unemployment soared. There was no developing war industry in Puerto Rico.[14] The number of unemployed was 99,100 in June 1941, meaning that 16 percent of the total labor force was out of work. By June 1942, the number of people unemployed reached a new height of 165,000. In July, the figure jumped to 210,800, and by September of 1942, the number of unemployed had risen to 237,400, representing 37 percent of the labor force.[15] With no job in sight for their wage earners, the future of many working families looked bleak.

Given this utterly chaotic unemployment situation, Luis Muñoz Marín, president of the Puerto Rican Senate, urgently wrote to William H. Davis, Chairman of the War Labor Board, on September 30, 1942, pleading that "hunger among the employed as well as the unemployed is rapidly reaching a point of serious danger both psychologically and physically. As a representative of my people, I appeal to your good will to help us find part of the solution that must be found to this problem. . . .We are in very desperate need."[16] In a parallel effort, on September 30, 1942, Filipo L. de Hostos, president of the Puerto Rican Chamber of Commerce, wrote to Senator Harry S. Truman, urging immediate action in order to remedy the critical situation facing the island due to the dramatic reduction in maritime transportation. De Hostos argued that federal assistance was imperative in order to avoid total collapse of the Puerto Rican economy.[17] Under the circumstances, the extreme hardships resulting from reduced shipping made it impossible for Puerto Rico to manage the crisis by itself.

Material conditions of scarcity were compounded by the psychological state of uncertainty.[18] The first German attack on Western soil was a U-boat strike against American-owned Standard Oil Co.'s Lago Refinery in Aruba, on February 16, 1942,[19] less than a week after American troops landed to secure the oil refineries of Aruba and Curaçao at the request of the Netherlands government.[20] The Germans chose their first target strategically, as it was the vital supply source of aviation fuel for the British air forces and for the American air force that had now joined the war. Had the Germans been successful in the refinery attack, Allied efforts could have been greatly hampered. The refinery, the largest in the Western Hemisphere, had just announced a $10,000,000 expansion program to refine aviation fuel on site. Formerly petroleum had to be shipped for refining to the United States, Canada, France, and Britain.[21]

The attack on the Aruba facility, the largest oil refinery in the world, was the first Nazi operation "against American soil."[22] The refinery in Aruba was not destroyed by the attack, but three tankers were lost, twenty-three men died, and another eighteen were hospitalized in the incident. Attacking in Caribbean waters was considered at the time "a far bolder foray than the raids on unescorted shipping off the United States and Canadian coasts."[23] Traffic from Lake Maracaibo in Venezuela to the Dutch refinery in Aruba was suspended until U.S. forces cleared the route.[24] The Associated Press reported that Nazi broadcasts beamed to Puerto Rico three weeks before the Aruba attack had addressed islanders with the message "Fellow-countrymen and friends! We'll be there by February 15" and that at the time, "the incident was laughed off as a joke."[26] By February 19, 1942, nine tankers had been sunk.[25] Two million tons of shipping losses were suffered in January and February alone in the Atlantic corridor.

Comparatively few U-boats were sunk as the captains learned the schedules of the antisubmarine destroyers and were able to avoid them. Despite being advised by the British command to take specific precautionary actions, the Americans did not institute coastal blackouts until July. Ships in or near the harbors were neatly outlined by the backlight of the cities, making them easy prey for the U-boats.[27] Likewise British advice to use convoy escorts was not heeded until later in the war. Admiral Ernest J. King, commander in chief of the U.S. Fleet and chief of naval operations, who had resisted the British advice earlier in the year, finally agreed on June 10, 1942, to use a convoy system in the Caribbean.[28]

The situation in the Caribbean became so acute that by May, 1942, the loss rate approximated the building rate for ships. "In making a choice it is considered better to lose merchant ships at a steady rate than to lose transports crowded with supplies and men upon whom months of meticulous preparation depend." Since oil was a critical material for the war effort, it required rationing and became scarce to the consumer. This had adverse effects on all industries, whether related to the war effort directly or not. "The tanker sunk off Cape Hateras with 10,000 tons of crude oil destined for civilian consumption in New York, by this reckoning, is more easily spared than a tanker making the long voyage around Africa with high-test gasoline for bombers which must be grounded if it does not arrive."[29]

Under these severe conditions, the need to supply the war effort required strict adherence to state-imposed standards in the selection of cargo. Ships that in times of peace transported textiles, coffee, and hundreds of other consumer products now had to specialize in transporting munitions and other military cargo, in addition to massive amounts of materials and equipment for the construction of the military bases at Ensenada Honda, San Juan, and Vieques. Likewise, ships arriving stateside in the United States were increasingly dedicated to importing war material such as manganese and other metals. Under these dire circumstances, the consumer needs of people in Puerto Rico were not high on the scale of military priorities. The navy decided what commodities had priority lading.[30] At one point during the food crisis the president of the Senate, Luis Muñoz Marín, angrily argued with Paul Gordon of the Federal Department of the Interior over a decision to leave three hundred precious cases of salted codfish behind in New York in order to transport beer for the increasing numbers of military personnel stationed in Puerto Rico.[31]

The shortage of food in Puerto Rico was an important issue in the internecine political battles within the island. Specifically, it was utilized to defend a program of agrarian reform that was part of a larger package of reforms introduced by the Popular Democratic Party (P.D.P.), established in 1938. Luis Muñoz Marín was the leader of the Puerto Rican Senate in 1941, and the principal leader of the Popular Democratic Party, which implemented a series of reforms in cooperation with liberal governor Rexford Tugwell. Devised in the spirit of the New Deal and promoting state-planning in the economy, the principal aspect of the reforms concerned land tenure. On March 25, 1940, the U.S. Supreme Court opened the way for the implementation of the early twentieth-century law that stipulated that no corporation may own more than five hundred acres of land in Puerto Rico. At the time of its enactment in 1900, the beet-sugar lobby in the United States was pressuring for the restriction of cane sugar production in the newly acquired territories of the Philippines and Puerto Rico. While the law remained on the books, it went unenforced for decades, but in 1935, the insular legislature created the judicial means for enforcing the legislation in favor of stimulating the production of locally grown food. The case of Rubert Hermanos, the first corporation to be prosecuted, challenged the authority of the insular legislature to enforce a federal disposition. The insular Supreme Court upheld the statute, the U.S. Court of Appeals for the First Circuit in Boston revoked that decision in the fall of 1939, and finally, the U.S. Supreme Court upheld it on March 25, 1940. The path was thus open for the agrarian reform long promised by the Popular Democratic Party.[32]

The principal component of agrarian reform was the *parcelas* (land plots) program. Before the agrarian reform, *agregados* or sharecroppers (sometimes referred to as "squatters" by the navy during the expropriations) were subject to the power of eviction of the landlords, because their homes were built on the landowners' properties. Through the agrarian reform policies administered by the Land Authority, created by Law 26 of April 12, 1941, the Insular Government began to distribute *parcelas* of between half an acre and three acres to former *agregados*. Given the all-encompassing nature of plantation life, in which rural workers were both employed by the cane growers and lived on land owned by their employers, the introduction of the *parcelas* program signified an important blow to the politico-economic power of the big landowners in Puerto Rico. The large *colonos* (cane growers) as well as the *centralistas* (sugar mill owners) naturally opposed the implementation of the law. Between the beginning of agrarian reform in 1941 and 1945, 14,000 families were resettled in *parcelas*. The distribution of land continued, and by 1959, 52,287 families had been resettled in *parcelas*.[33] Calculated on a modest family size of five, the *parcelas* program positively affected 70,000 people by the end of World War II and 261,435 by 1959.

The Popular Democratic Party became the dominant party in Puerto Rican politics after 1940 and successfully carried out its program of agrarian reform, industrialization, and creation of the Commonwealth of Puerto Rico (1952), yet during World War II the battle over agrarian reform was still raging, and its outcome was uncertain. On the island, Governor Tugwell and the New Dealers in Puerto Rico were moving forward with land redistribution, while the sugar companies and their allies in the U.S. Congress opposed the measure on the floor of the House. The resident commissioner of Puerto Rico in Washington, Bolívar Pagán from the *Coalición*, an association of parties opposed to the Popular Democratic Party, composed of the Republican and Socialist Parties, led a campaign in the U.S. press denouncing Tugwell and the P.D.P. Pagán, a prominent member of the Socialist Party, went so far as to compare Tugwell to Hitler and Mussolini, stating that Puerto Ricans were "on the verge of revolution" over the land reform controls. He stated that Tugwell created 7,000 "imaginary" jobs for "useless bureaucrats [who] wander through the towns and countryside doing nothing for the Government, but spread political propaganda for Tugwell and the Popular-Communist party."[34]

Prominent employers such as José A. Ferré of Ponce Cement, Antonio Roig, a sugar baron from Humacao, the Chamber of Commerce, and the Association of Sugar producers denounced Tugwell, Muñoz Marín, and the P.D.P. In the United States, a House Committee led by Jasper Bell (Democrat-Missouri), was clearly anti-Tugwell and against the program of reform of the P.D.P. Bills were introduced in Congress in 1943 to unseat Governor Tugwell, to annul legislation creating the Land Authority and other agencies, and to reassign rum-tax funds to federal projects on the island, thus diverting them from the hands of Muñoz Marín and the P.P.D administration. The Fajardo Sugar Company, concurrently, contested the implementation of the five-hundred-acre law in court.

In the context of U-boat attacks, the bombing of Aruba, and the sharp reduction in the number vessels arriving in the island, food shortages were a reality and starvation was considered a real and imminent threat.[35] In this context, Muñoz Marín and the P.D.P. began to defend agrarian reform as a necessary measure to guarantee food production while Puerto Rico faced the threat of naval blockade. The notion of increased food production by local farmers challenged the insistence of the sugar producers that Puerto Rico could do no better than exporting its sugar and importing most of its food. This insistence amounted to validation of the overspecialization of Puerto Rico in sugar production at the expense of food production, forcing an agrarian island with an essentially rural population to rely on food imports. Opposing the sugar companies on the issue of land reform, the P.D.P. skillfully presented itself as the champion of the war effort by guaranteeing subsistence food to a population that had been totally dispossessed and formerly had to buy imported food at company stores in the plantations. At each step between 1941 and 1944, the opposition of the large landowners and sugar companies to the modest land reform of the P.D.P. was characterized as unpatriotic, as sabotaging the war effort, and as exposing the island to potential disaster in the event of total naval blockade.[36]

The scarcity of food deteriorated month by month during the year 1942. In April, the director of the Comisión de Alimentos y Abastecimiento General, Antonio Fernós Isern, requested profit estimates from merchants in order to limit the price margin between wholesale and retail rice, but the merchants argued that they lacked the information requested.[37] There were shortages of bread in San Juan the following month, and protests over the distribution of food erupted. The situation was so severe that the authorities considered importing food by airplane, especially after almost eight hundred importers withdrew their products from the market in reaction to the price controls introduced by the federal authorities in Puerto Rico.[38] In July, Governor Tugwell ordered the rationing of rice.[39] In October of the same year, the Office of Price Administration published in the local press maximum retail prices for basic foods: 8 cents for a pound of rice, the same for a pound of beans, 60 cents for a pound of butter, 10 for a tin of milk. In November, a more extensive list was published.[40] That same month in Ponce, the news that a ship carrying rice had anchored in the port caused civilian unrest requiring police intervention.[41] Meanwhile the Works

Progress Administration was feeding 137,687 children (infants to fourteen years of age) in 1,443 units throughout the island, and Paul Edwards, the administrator, announced that his agency intended to feed 150,000 children in December.[42] In the municipality of Río Piedras, the mayor and the director of the Civil Defense were regulating the distribution of rice to civilians by retailers.[43] On December 12, 1942, the Office of Price Administration established a system of government-issued certificates authorizing wholesalers to sell to retailers, at administered prices, government-specified quantities of rice. All transactions lacking the certificate were declared illegal. Finally on December 15, 1942, the Office of Price Administration established a quota of two pounds of rice per person per week.[44] Rice, the essential staple in the diet, was scarce. In 1941, the island imported 262.2 million pounds of rice, but in 1942 only 198 million pounds were imported, that is, 70 million pounds less than in the preceding year, representing a reduction of 27 percent. According to historian Cruz Miguel Ortiz Cuadra, this set back rice imports to the level of 1925.[45]

Shortages of food were combined with distortion of established prices and the emergence of a black market. Items such as cigarettes and beer destined for the armed forces were sold in the black market to the civilian population. Since these transactions escaped local taxation, the newly created black market adversely affected the coffers of the government of Puerto Rico. The black market products were also cheap and easy to get, adversely affecting sales of locally produced cigarettes and beer.[46] Shortages lasted until the end of the war and continued to affect the well-being of the population. Toward the end of the war, shortages were rampant and the president of the Puerto Rican Senate, Luis Muñoz Marín, wrote to President Truman that black market practices in Puerto Rico resulted "in a lowering of nutrition which is a crime against humanity and constitutes a dangerous threat to public health."[47] The Office of Price Administration had established a campaign to educate the public against black market practices, and enforcement against violators resulted in 801 arrests in June of 1945 and 1,468 in July.[48]

The construction of military bases, an increase in the price of sugar, as well as in the quantity of sugar and rum exported to the United States, provided some economic relief.[49] This was despite the fact that distillers sometimes lacked bottles for their rum and had to resort to exporting rum in barrels.[50] Sugar, as a strategic war material, is indispensable to the production of canned and boxed food, both as a preservative and as a source of calories. Tinned and packaged food, in turn, was part of the lifeline of U.S. troops in Europe and the Pacific. Therefore, the local authorities in Puerto Rico faced the double burden of assuring the production of a strategic war material while trying to avoid social unrest or the collapse of the capacity of the labor force to work in order to produce the required exports.

Paradoxically, this conjuncture of war and scarcity was the beginning of a prosperous time, albeit a brief one, in Vieques. The trauma of mass relocations of citizens resulting from large-scale expropriations of land in Vieques and the resultant demise of the sugar industry on the island was cushioned by the appearance of steady work at a far greater rate of pay than could be earned at the seasonal work in the cane fields. Vieques experienced the principal economic boom in its history, before or since, in 1942–1943, precisely during a construction boom associated with the establishment of the navy there. Due to the dire economic situation on the main island, a steady supply of laborers was available for the huge navy construction project, charged with the mission of building naval bases in Vieques and Ensenada Honda in Puerto Rico and other bases in smaller Caribbean islands.

Puerto Rico Becomes a Military Fortress

Puerto Rico's strategic location was of utmost importance to the United States, which expected that military bases on the island would help to secure the naval and air routes to the United States, the Gulf of Mexico, and the Panama Canal. The protection and defense of the canal had been of great concern to the United States since the start of the war in 1939.[51] No new major base construction had been undertaken in Puerto Rico since 1898. Many of the existing military and naval facilities were inherited from Spain through the Treaty of Paris. The only new major naval presence was the naval base in Culebra that was acquired in 1899 by presidential decree, but it had not been developed or fortified.[52] On October 30, 1939, a month after the start of hostilities in Europe, the U.S. Navy selected the Arundel Corporation and the Consolidated Engineering Company, Inc., two corporations based in Baltimore, after competing successfully with "the most outstanding construction firms in the United States."[53] Puerto Rico lacked an airport infrastructure capable of projecting air power in the region.[54] Due to the remoteness of the work to be performed from the continental United States, the contract was negotiated and awarded on a cost-plus-fixed-fee basis.[55] The Vieques project would be part of the greatly expanded system of bases, and it was projected that it would eventually displace the citizens of Vieques, while the navy would acquire two thirds of the landmass of the entire island. The land used to build the military installations was obtained in a variety of ways, including purchases, donations, but principally expropriations by condemnation under existing eminent domain laws.[56]

Before Vieques

Before the navy embarked on the expropriations in Vieques and on the construction of a military base there, it had been engaged in the construction of a military base in San Juan. There, the navy encountered some of the features that would later characterize its presence in Vieques during the construction phase: human settlers in the land and local firms demanding contracts. The land had so-called "squatters" that had to be removed and sometimes compensated. Secondly, local contractors found themselves excluded from the lucrative work of building for the navy. The contracts were reserved for continentals. The success of the Arundel Corporation in San Juan earned it the contract to build other bases in the Caribbean, including those at Ceiba and Vieques, which together formed what became Roosevelt Roads Naval Station.

As early as 1937, long before the beginning of World War II and the commencement of the huge military construction projects in Puerto Rico, the navy had shown interest in a tract of land within the San Juan Bay. Some of this land was waterfront property, other parts were swamps, and the remainder included a small island within the bay by the name of Miraflores. The navy had decided that this location was ideal for building a naval base.

Law No 32, approved on April 25, 1939, by the Legislative Assembly of Puerto Rico, allowed the U.S. government to occupy and use the lands on Isla Grande and all of the filled lands from Isla Grande to Miraflores Island, for the purchase price of $11,866,836.[57] Law No. 66 was passed on

April 25, 1940, allowing a cluster of ten parcels of mangrove swamps and hard land comprising 1,631 acres and including a land plane runway to be transferred by the People of Puerto Rico.[58]

The Puerto Rican government was compensated just under half a million dollars for this package. In the first few months of 1940, with Arundel Corporation and Consolidated Engineering Corporation in charge of the dredging project, the officer in charge of construction, Commander Johnson, negotiated the removal of "squatters" from the land between Miraflores Island and the acquired dry-dock property. The navy contributed $2,200 to the Insular Treasury, for the Commissioner of the Interior to compensate the fourteen squatters an amount of between "$25 and $200" each "to abandon or remove their houses."[59] Commander H. W. Johnson, the officer in charge of construction of Contract NOy-3680, hoped to persuade Enrique Colom, the commissioner of the interior of Puerto Rico, that filling the mangrove swamps would perform a service to the People of Puerto Rico—who held title to the swamps—by contributing to the control of the mosquitos in the area.[60] Eventually the project was completed by Arundel and Consolidated Corporations "using coral clay and sand from a dredge pump to stabilize the original swamp site."[61] All remnants of Miraflores Island, which had played a vital role in the defense of Puerto Rico against the British attack of 1797 (Battle of San Juan), were thereafter lost to history.[62]

Puerto Rican firms were almost totally excluded from the military contracts. When Arundel took over the project, the subcontracted work of filling the wetlands was begun by Rexach Construction, a local Puerto Rican construction firm, but in March 1940, Arundel declared to its board that the dredging work with Rexach was "not progressing satisfactorily."[63] The contract was abruptly terminated, and the stateside Standard Dredging Co. was immediately hired to do the job. No further mention of Rexach appears in the board notes. From our research it appears that Rexach was perhaps the only local firm involved in military contracts—with the notable exceptions of Puerto Rico Cement and Ponce Cement, which supplied cement for virtually all of the military projects—and their participation in the project was short-lived.

The lucrative cost-plus-fixed-fee contract basis posed little to no financial risk to the contractors, and it even allowed them to advance the projects ahead of schedule, because the additional cost of doing business in Puerto

Rico—for example, the cost of importing machinery to the island—was covered by the terms of the contract. Continental companies were better positioned to acquire these contracts than local companies, assuring that profits went stateside. Construction of the naval base in San Juan began on October 31, 1939, and was completed on December 31, 1940, sixteen months ahead of the estimated schedule, allowing Arundel to secure further contracts for construction of military facilities, including those of Vieques, Puerto Rico.

Arundel in Ceiba and Vieques

On March 17, 1941, the Navy Department again expanded the scope of the contract with Arundel and Consolidated to include the construction of officers' quarters and roads at San Gerónimo Naval Reservation and housing quarters for enlisted personnel at San Patricio. Preliminary work was begun in April of 1941, when the Navy Department officially approved construction of a naval base in Vieques. Shortly thereafter, another larger base began to be built,[64] located on 37,000 acres across the Vieques sound at Ensenada Honda in the municipality of Ceiba in eastern Puerto Rico. Ultimately, the entire expanded base, in Ceiba and Vieques, on both sides of Vieques Sound, became known as Roosevelt Roads.[65]

The naval base in Vieques was completed on July 1, 1943, and all remaining military construction was completed by November 26 of that year. A final audit of the project revealed that the total amount contracted by the Navy Department, which included not only Vieques, Roosevelt Roads, the naval air base at San Juan but other related constructions in San Juan and the eastern Caribbean Islands, had increased to $110,494,008,[66] resulting in a profit of $1,159,535 each for the Arundel Corporation and Consolidated Engineering. The Hardaway Contracting Co., added later in the venture, earned $409,027.[67] Simultaneous to the naval contracts, other military installations were built across the island. In Aguadilla, for example, 1,877 acres were expropriated in order to build Borinquen Army Airfield and Fort Buchanan was expanded to 1,514 acres.[68]

The Economic Effects of World War II
on Puerto Rico and on Vieques

Historians have emphasized the role of the Insular Government in the transformation of Puerto Rico from a sugar-producing, plantation-based economy before World War II to one based on rapid industrialization in the postwar period. In the established view, the agrarian-reform program initiated by the Partido Popular Democrático, in combination with a willingness on the part of the Insular Government to establish state-owned industries under a program of import substitution to produce cement, glass bottles for the rum industry, corrugated cardboard, textiles, and shoes, laid the foundation for the industrial transformation that typified Puerto Rico's development in the postwar period. However, recent research has shown that as important as these changes were, federal expenditure in the island during the years of the war and immediately after had a profound transformative effect. Between 1939 and 1950, the federal government spent in Puerto Rico the staggering figure of 1.2 billion dollars. To place this figure in perspective, the U.S. government spent 13 billion dollars in the Marshall Plan for the reconstruction of the much larger economy and population of Europe between 1947 and 1951.[69]

The construction of bases represented just one component of the multifaceted massive federal economic intervention. Road construction represented another. The Insular Treasury benefited from the increased federal expenditures in Puerto Rico, particularly during 1940–1943, the heyday of the construction period. Rafael Carrión Pacheco, vice president and stockholder of Banco Popular, one of the largest locally owned banks in Puerto Rico, clearly articulated the sense of the times when he stated that the hopes of the country rested on the investments made by the federal government on the military fortification of the island. These investments represented critical economic activity during a time when the commercial, construction, and industrial segments of the economy were severely affected by the war. Carrión Pacheco added that the large contingent of continentals associated with the armed forces who lived in Puerto Rico increased the demand for goods and services. Consequently, in spite of the restrictions caused by the war, many businesses were actually experiencing a period of great prosperity. However, Carrión Pacheco cautioned that the source of the island's current wealth—the military build-up—was in the hands of the federal government, and that change in policy would severely affect the local economy.[70]

The construction of military bases required the bulk of all locally produced cement, thereby limiting its availability for other activities. During 1942, the peak of the construction activity, federal projects consumed 89 percent of the production of one of the two cement factories on the island, the state-owned Puerto Rico Cement.[71] The scarcity of cement lasted until after the end of the war in 1945, since the limitations placed by federal agencies during this time restricted the ability of these companies to purchase equipment necessary to increase production.[72] Puerto Rico Cement's privately owned competitor, Ponce Cement, used this opportunity to raise its prices.[73] (See Table 1.2.)

Once the military bases became operational, they required 20 percent of the electrical capacity generated by the state-owned Puerto Rico Water Resources Authority, the only state-owned power plant on the island. At the time, there were two privately owned power plants in Puerto Rico, the Porto Rico Railway, Power, and Light Company and the Mayagüez Light, Power, and Ice Company, both in the process of being purchased by the government of Puerto Rico. Because of the unexpected surge in demand required by the military bases, the power plants could not supply additional needs for local clients. In addition, the War Production Board severely limited the purchase of the materials and supplies required to maintain the power plants in optimal condition, resulting in limited capabilities. Electrical power became scarce resulting in 1944 in a sixty–day rationing period during a severe drought in the island. The state-owned power plant was able to purchase a limited amount of power from the naval base at Roosevelt Roads, which had its own independent power plant. However, this limited supply of power did not alter the need for additional capacity. The Puerto Rico Water Resources Authority, which at the time was the only available source of power on the island, had to wait until the end of the war, for restrictions to be lifted in order to increase its output.[74] For a while, demand kept some local companies running at top capacity but unable to increase output.

On the positive side of the scorecard, the impact of the war was not limited to federal expenditure. Opening markets were part of the picture also.

By 1944, construction work in the military bases slowed to a crawl, accompanied by a significant reduction in the amount of federal expenditures. This reduction was offset by a dramatic increase in the quantity of Puerto Rican rum sold in the mainland. Rum exports soared in the context of shortages of imported whiskey from Britain, due to shipping difficulties, and due to the diversion of alcohol produced in the mainland to industrial uses rather than human consumption. This situation presented a unique opportunity for the distillers of Puerto Rican rum, as they could sell all of their production to the mainland with little or no competition from other liquors. Even in the face of the difficulties faced by the Puerto Rican distillers in obtaining equipment, they managed to increase output during the war.[75] Since federal taxes collected on this product were returned to Puerto Rico, the export of rum proved a second bonanza for the Insular Government, accounting for up 49 percent of its income in 1944.[76] (See Table 1.3.)

The transformation of the local economy of Puerto Rico from sugar monoculture to industrialization brought significant progress to the residents of Puerto Rico so that retrospectively, the period of World War II can be seen as the foundation of the postwar prosperity of the island. While this prosperity had its downside, including the inability of the local economy to absorb the surplus labor available, resulting in massive emigration to the United States, the three decades after 1945 were nevertheless characterized by increasing standards of living and overall improvement in the material and social conditions of Puerto Ricans. The transformations brought about during the war in Vieques, however, did not lay the foundation for any growth in the postwar period. On the contrary, as we shall see, the existing sugar-plantation economy was dealt a severe blow and was further constricted in the 1950s but without alternative economic paths such as were being opened in Puerto Rico becoming available to the residents of Vieques. In short, just as the economic effects of World War II were very different in the continental United States and Puerto Rico—neither full employment nor the massive incorporation of women to the labor force were achieved in Puerto Rico—the lingering economic after-effects of the war were radically different in Puerto Rico and Vieques. The road infrastructure of Puerto Rico was transformed, and a significant transfer of technology skills to the local construction industry took place, initially in the form of the training of managers and workers employed in U.S. firms.

In Puerto Rico, federal expenditure had the effect of laying the infra-structural foundation for further industrial growth—through the building of highways and electrification, for example—whereas in Vieques no such positive effects were observable. Whereas Vieques had been pretty much a typical municipality of Puerto Rico during the first half of the twentieth century, and like so many other municipalities had undergone its own cycle of expansion and bust of the sugar industry, after World War II, with the construction of the base, its economic and social fate would begin to di-verge from that of the rest of the island. Because the residents of Vieques form part of a larger Puerto Rican community, their reference point in con-sidering their own well-being is the island of Puerto Rico. To understand the differential effects of World War II, federal expenditure, and base con-struction on Vieques and Puerto Rico, we now turn to the peculiarities of Vieques' historical development before the arrival of the navy. For, while it was on the one hand very much a part of Puerto Rico, the island of Vieques nevertheless had its own unique history.

CHAPTER 2

Vieques:
From Frontier to
Plantation Society

W hen the navy began to build a base in Vieques in 1941, it encountered a society with a social structure that had been formed in the course of the Spanish colonial epoch (1492–1898). Because the interaction between armed forces and society requires some understanding of both parties in the process, we now turn to the specifics of local economy and society in Vieques. Under pressure from German submarine warfare, the navy had other concerns, but these inherited social structures nevertheless conditioned the way in which the building of the base affected the local population, with long-lasting consequences. Land tenure, relations between landowners and workers, the industries in which the workers participated, and traditional rights over the use and the fruit of the land, had been defined traditionally by agrarian relations that had evolved over a century in Vieques. The degree to which local rural society was similar to Puerto Rico, or to the societies of the Eastern Caribbean, is the question this chapter seeks to answer. For, while the island of Vieques belongs to the larger island of Puerto Rico historically, its location for centuries at the edge of Spanish settlement in the Caribbean, in proximity to the British, Danish, and French Caribbean islands, made it unique in some ways, and different, from the larger island of Puerto Rico. The location of Vieques in the Spanish imperial frontier gave it some specific characteristics that help to explain the extreme social inequality prevalent at the time of contact with the U.S. Navy. The specificities of economy and society in Vieques, affected the way in which the local population experienced, and reacted to, the expropriations of the navy and the building of the base.

A Caribbean Frontier

The east of Puerto Rico and the neighboring island of Vieques represent a geographical and political frontier in the Caribbean. In pre-Columbian times, Vieques was supposedly at the intersection between Taino and Carib peoples. Although some Caribbean scholars question whether there were in fact distinct "Carib" and "Taino" peoples, Vieques is rich in archaeological evidence about the life of pre-Columbian peoples in the Caribbean, indicating that it was an important transit point for pre-Columbian migrations.[1]

During Spanish colonial times (1492–1898), Vieques was located in the frontier between Spanish power on the one hand, and British, French, Danish, and Dutch power on the other. The island was too close to Puerto Rico for the Spanish to allow the British to settle there, and too close to the British-ruled islands to be settled by the Spanish. Thus, during most of the Spanish colonial period, Vieques remained uninhabited. It was only settled under the Spanish regime in the 1830s. This happened at a time when Puerto Rico was experiencing a sugar-plantation boom and the slave trade was flourishing. The lateness of the colonial settlement of Vieques under the Spanish regime had an effect on its social structure. Whereas eighteenth-century Puerto Rico had a well-established peasant culture that predates the plantation boom of the early nineteenth century, Vieques lacked this peasant substratum. It was settled, in fact, during the plantation boom of the nineteenth century, by sugar planters of French ancestry who introduced slavery into the island, making Vieques a more pure case of "plantation economy" than the island of Puerto Rico as a whole, where plantation agriculture was never able to completely supplant peasant agriculture, and the two coexisted well into the twentieth century.

Although Vieques was probably visited in Columbus's second voyage, Cristóbal de Mendoza, governor of Puerto Rico, first claimed Spanish dominion over the island in 1524.[2] From the early stages of the conquest, the islands of the eastern Caribbean and Vieques were pretty much abandoned by the Spanish until the seventeenth century, when the English and the French first began to settle them. In 1685, Governor Martínez de Andino wrote to the Crown reporting that a runaway slave from Saint Thomas had brought news that there were limestone ovens ready to make bricks for houses in Vieques and that the English had gone to Nevis to gather settlers to populate the island. The following year, upon royal orders, the governor made a reconnaissance of Vieques. His findings indicated that the island had been previously occupied and that the inhabitants of the nearby islands spent time in Vieques hunting for turtles. In 1690, the governor of Puerto Rico sent an expedition to remove three hundred settlers and destroy their

fortifications in Vieques.[3] In 1691, the Spanish government once again issued orders to raze to the ground any settlements, and in 1693, the Windward Armada was ordered to defend Vieques. Vieques was the frontier
between the British and the Spanish, a sort of contested terrain that
remained unsettled by either colonial power.

An expedition to Vieques was organized by the governor of Puerto Rico
in 1718. With the assistance of Puerto Rican corsair Miguel Enríquez, who
allocated two schooners, four artillery men, seven infantry men, 289 militia
men, among them sixty-five blacks from Cangrejos, the expeditionary force
destroyed the fortifications of the English and chased and captured thirty-
five English settlers, their families, and ninety-five slaves they owned. They
also seized six cannon, three small sloops, one schooner, cattle, and agricultural implements. The Spanish captured commander Abraham Wells,
who testified that he had been placed in charge of Vieques, known to the
English as Crab Island, by Baltasar Hamilton, captain general and commander of the English Windward Islands. The report sent to the Spanish
Crown by José Rocher de la Peña, commander of the Spanish Windward
Fleet, argued that the expedition prevented further settlement of the island,
and that in the absence of this expedition, the English could have settled
two thousand families in Vieques in just four months.[4]

In 1753, the governor and captain general of Puerto Rico, Felipe
Ramírez de Estenoz, wrote that the island of Vieques was continually full
of foreigners who went there to cut precious woods, principally *guayacán*,
mora, and *coyagua*. In the governor's view, these sporadic forays into
Vieques threatened to become settlements and, due to the proximity of
Vieques to the main island, potential settlements there would be tantamount
to condoning non-Spanish settlements in Puerto Rico itself. Throughout
the eighteenth century, the Spanish repeatedly sent expeditions to clear
Vieques of English settlers.[5] In 1765, a *Real Cédula* (Royal Edict) petitioned the viceroy of New Spain to send the *Armada de Barlovento* (Windward Armada) to Vieques for that purpose. Because of its location between
the Greater Antilles, dominated largely by the Spanish, and the eastern
Caribbean, dominated by the British, French, and Dutch, Vieques had
strategic importance to the balance between the colonial powers.

Vieques remained unpopulated until the nineteenth century. Insofar as
the Spanish were able to draw a line between what belonged to the Spanish

state and the possessions of the British, French, and Dutch, Vieques was the line itself. This gave Vieques a special place in the history of the Spanish Caribbean. Before the plantation boom of the nineteenth century, the island of Vieques remained uninhabited, representing a hiatus between the food-producing island of Puerto Rico and the sugar-producing islands of the Eastern Caribbean. Vieques was neither a peasant-dominated economy of the Spanish Caribbean, nor a plantation-dominated society of the Eastern Caribbean, typical of the so called "sugar islands" of the British and French. Rather, it remained unpopulated, for geopolitical reasons. When it was settled in the nineteenth century, it was the plantation, and not the peasant, that won the day. Thus, Vieques was settled as a slave-based society, and it never had the free peasantry that characterized the Spanish islands. In Puerto Rico, by contrast, after the decline of the initial sugar plantation boom in the first half of the sixteenth century, there followed over two hundred years where peasant agriculture predominated, until the resumption of plantation growth in the last quarter of the eighteenth century. All of the Spanish islands had a strong, free-peasant sector between roughly 1550 and 1762, the date of the British occupation of Havana during the Seven Years War—a date that marks the resumption of plantation growth in the Spanish islands. Vieques, by contrast, remained uninhabited throughout this entire phase of peasant-based economic development in the Spanish Caribbean. Thus, its social structure, unlike that of Puerto Rico, was not formed by the superimposition of a plantation sector over a preexisting peasant economy. Instead, like the sugar islands of the Eastern Caribbean, the social structure was constituted from the start as a slave-based, sugar-plantation economy.

In the eighteenth century, the big producers of sugar in the Caribbean were the British and French islands, whereas the Spanish islands, including Cuba and Santo Domingo, had a clearly underdeveloped plantation sector and a much stronger free peasantry than the British or French islands.[6] As the plantation economies of the British and French islands of the Eastern Caribbean had developed in the seventeenth century, they had become dependent on food imports, prompting the emergence of an inter-Caribbean division of labor. British Jamaica and French Saint Domingue (present-day Haiti) followed the same pattern in the eighteenth century, in that they were plantation economies that relied increasingly on food imports. The Spanish islands provided foodstuffs produced by free peasants, which were exchanged through contraband trade with the British and French. The British and French provided manufactured goods to the peasants and purchased foodstuffs and raw materials that were not sufficiently available locally to feed the slave populations of their "sugar islands" and to supply some of the other inputs required by the plantations.

Plantation economies that specialized in the production of a profitable export crop such as sugar typically rely on imported food. This is seemingly paradoxical, in that it implies that an agricultural society where the bulk of the population works on the land relies on imported food for sustenance. Nevertheless, in the profit calculus of the planters, it was rational to dedicate as much land as possible to the production of the lucrative export crops at the expense of food crops. This was especially so in the smaller islands of the Eastern Caribbean, where land was scarce. Throughout the Caribbean, in all plantation societies, the slaves nevertheless fought for the right to keep small plots of land, to cultivate some subsistence crops, and to raise some domestic animals. Despite the efforts of those who tilled the soil, the economy over which the planters ruled was dedicated to the production of export crops and such food production as did exist represented a hard-won, and often elusive, victory of the subsistence-oriented slave populations over the profit-oriented planters.[7]

In the eighteenth century, in the Spanish part of Hispaniola, Santo Domingo, the dominant economic sector was composed of *hateros* (ranchers) who transported cattle overland to the plantation economy of Haiti. Similarly, the *hateros* of the province of Camagüey in Cuba exported cattle to the neighboring Jamaican plantation economy. Puerto Rico had the same role of food-provider in relation to the plantation islands of the Eastern Caribbean. Indeed, Caribbean interdependence developed on the basis of a nexus between plantation economies producing sugar for export with coerced slaves in the British and French islands, and free peasant producers in the Spanish islands providing food, cattle, and timber to the plantation islands. This happened at all times against the restrictive interdicts on commerce of the Spanish state. In the eighteenth century, the contraband trade with the Eastern Caribbean was the economic backbone of the Puerto Rican peasant economy.[8]

As a result of the Revolution of 1791–1804 in the French colony of Saint

Domingue, which then changed its name to Haiti, many white and mulatto planters fled to Louisiana and Puerto Rico. These "French" planters constituted an important segment of the planter class that flourished in Puerto Rico after the Haitian revolution shut down the principal sugar producer of the Caribbean. In the municipality of Ponce, for example, the largest group of "foreign" planters was French.[9] The establishment of foreign planters, and especially the French, in Puerto Rico, was assisted by a royal edict of 1815 called *Cédula de Gracias*, which permitted the settlement of non-Spanish individuals, so long as they were of the Catholic religion. This edict granted special tax exemptions on the importation of equipment for sugar mills and slaves, and was aimed at restoring the productive capacity of Puerto Rico and reintegrating it into the Spanish orbit.

In the eighteenth century, the dominant contraband trade with the British and French had practically pulled Puerto Rico from the sphere of Spanish power in economic terms. Indeed, the main finding of Marshall Alejandro O'Reilly in his famous memoir of 1765 had been the extent of the contraband trade and the lack of loyalty of the residents of Puerto Rico to the Spanish Crown, due to the trading restrictions imposed by the imperial state.[10] In the last quarter of the eighteenth century, the Crown made special efforts to reintegrate the Spanish colonies of Cuba and Puerto Rico to the imperial trading system. In the first quarter of the nineteenth century, when the Spanish were losing their continental empire to the independence movements of the Spanish colonies, the two remaining loyal colonies of Cuba and Puerto Rico received special attention. The *Cédula de Gracias* of 1815 was an imperial device designed to boost the economy of Puerto Rico and to promote loyalty to the Crown among the subjects of the Spanish monarchy in that island. Settlement by friendly colonists of the Catholic religion was meant to revive trade, to enhance the economy of the island, to keep the residents in the Spanish imperial orbit, and to prevent them from joining the insurrections then sweeping all of continental Spanish America.

The period between 1800 and 1850 in Puerto Rico was characterized by a revival of the plantation as an institution, by increasing imports of slaves, and naturally, by increasing exports of sugar. The boom of sugar plantations in Puerto Rico was closely linked to the rise of the Danish island of St. Thomas as a commercial clearinghouse for plantation products and as a source of financing for the plantations.[11] It was in the context of the sugar-plantation boom of Puerto Rico that Vieques was settled. Plantation-oriented settlement was initiated by an enterprising Frenchman by the name of Teophile Jaime José María Le Guillou, who is considered the "founder" of Vieques. Born on May 4, 1790, in Quemperle, a region in the north of France, Le Guillou originally came to Vieques in 1823 to purchase lumber. He established himself in Vieques, and during the following twenty years, he amassed wealth and political power to an extent never before seen on the island. The town of Isabel Segunda was established on lands he donated. Le Guillou was appointed military and political governor of Vieques during its formative years and occupied this position from 1832 until his death in 1843. The "French Connection" established by Le Guillou contributed to the creation of a colony of French landowners that dominated the sugar industry during the remainder of the nineteenth century.[12] But the history of slavery and the planter class of Vieques has not yet been thoroughly studied. We know that a number of sugar mills functioned in the nineteenth century, that the planters were principally of French origin, and that the labor force was composed of slaves. The transformation of Vieques from a frontier demarcating one colonial power from another, into a productive colony inserted into the trading networks of the Atlantic world took place during the period of ascendancy of Puerto Rico's sugar-plantation economy (1800–1850). From the start, Vieques was a plantation society, not a society of free peasants such as existed in other parts of Puerto Rico in the eighteenth century. Land concentration and social polarization, together with extremes of wealth and poverty, were thus structural features of Vieques from its inception. This colonial legacy lasted in Vieques into the twentieth century, and it conditioned the economic evolution of Vieques in the period of U.S. colonialism after 1898.

Many of the landless workers of Vieques in the twentieth century were descendants of the slaves of the nineteenth century. Still others were descendants of a population of black workers from the eastern Caribbean, who had migrated to Vieques in the nineteenth century and had formed a sugar proletariat in the plantations. In 1874, barely a year after the abolition of slavery in Puerto Rico, English-speaking West Indian workers rioted in Vieques in response to maltreatment from the planters and the government. The civil guard killed a worker and wounded several others, initiating a period of burnings of cane fields that lasted several weeks. Dozens of work-

ers were jailed in Count Mirasol Fort, in Isabel Segunda.[13] Slavery was
abolished in Puerto Rico in 1873, but in the British West Indies, it had been
abolished in 1834. The kind of coercion that the planters of Vieques
deployed against the British West Indian workers was fiercely resisted by
the free workers, who were at least two generations removed from the
experience of bondage. Thus, the extremes of social polarization and the
power of the planters prompted workers' resistance and violent class
struggles. In Vieques, the plantation proletariat continued this tradition of
resistance into the twentieth century.

Land Concentration in Vieques in the Early Twentieth Century

At the beginning of the twentieth century, Vieques had four sugar *centrales*:
Santa María, Arcadia, Esperanza, also known as Puerto Real, and Playa
Grande.[14] In 1910, these mills produced fewer than 5,000 tons of sugar,
and by 1920, the total output of Vieques' sugar plantations reached 13,000
tons yearly. The amount was not insignificant, but compared with the production output from the *centrales* of the great corporations established in
Puerto Rico after the U.S. occupation, the volume was relatively modest.
The Guánica mill of the U.S.-owned South Porto Rico Sugar Company, for
instance, reached an output of over 100,000 tons of sugar yearly, while
Central Cambalache, a locally owned mill in Arecibo, Puerto Rico, produced more than 40,000 tons.

The Puerto Real sugar mill emerged out of a fusion between the sugar
hacienda of Víctor Mourraille in Puerto Ferro and the Hacienda Martineau
in Barrio Mosquito. Jointly, Messrs. Mourraille and Martineau formed the
Mourraille-Martineau Society. Upon the death of Martineau, Mourraille
took charge. The *central* was then transferred from Víctor Mourraille to
his son Gustave. A sugar cane workers strike of 1915, that caused several
deaths in violent clashes between the police and the strikers, influenced
Gustave Mourraille to sell the Puerto Real mill to the heirs of Enrique Bird
Arias, the head of a group of sugar investors linked to the Fajardo Sugar
Company.[15] The incidents of 1915 were linked personally to Mr. Gustave
Mourraille, an ill-reputed employer in Vieques whose differences with the
workers produced rioting during the strike. Rev. Justo Pastor Ruiz de-
scribed Mourraille (also known as Murray) as follows:

It should be stated here that the system which Don Gustavo [Gustave Mouraille, C. A.] had established in his cane farms was far from satisfactory. He had a style in which he was the prosecutor, the judge, and the collector of fines. It was a disciplinary system of his own making and we think that it originated in the French colonies but not in republican France, where the rights of man are so well respected. He used to fine the workers or leave them without work or confiscate their wages. . . .

There was also something between Murray and the other employers, because Murray took on certain rights and the others did not challenge him. Murray would take the police precinct to his own house. There he had the Judge and the Chief of Police. Whenever he wanted. I don't know the extent of truth in the phrase, but I have heard that Murray and his cronies were abusive with the people that worked for them.[16]

The Heirs of Enrique Bird Arias, the entity that acquired the Puerto Real mill, were in turn foreclosed by the firm of L. W. P. Armstrong and Company, lawyers of the Fajardo Sugar Company, after the death of Enrique Bird Arias. But the Puerto Real mill did not end up in the hands of the Fajardo Sugar Company. It was instead sold to the United Porto Rico Sugar Company, and then it was transferred to the Eastern Sugar Associates. It ground its last crop in 1927. After that date, the cane was ground at the Playa Grande mill.[17]

If the Armstrong firm represented the Fajardo Sugar Company, why did the Puerto Real end up in the hands of the United Puerto Rico Company instead? L. W. Armstrong and Company were part of a complex web of New York sugar interests that controlled, through holding companies, the Fajardo, the Aguirre, and the United Porto Rico companies, and they were in addition linked to the National Sugar Refining Company, the principal sugar refining interest represented in the board of directors of sugar enterprises in Puerto Rico.[18] James Howell Post, on the boards of directors of both Fajardo and Aguirre companies, was president of the National Sugar Refining Company and a member of the board of directors of City Bank that controlled the United Porto Rico Company. The web of U.S. sugar interests was densely woven. Many apparently independent enterprises controlled by investors in the United States were in fact owned in common by tightly knit groups of investors controlling other sugar companies in Puerto Rico, Cuba, and the Dominican Republic. The enterprises in the Caribbean, in turn, were vertically integrated through links of common ownership to the oligopolistic sugar refining industry in the United States. The Fajardo and United Porto Rico companies in Puerto Rico, for example, belonged to the same group of sugar investors that controlled the Chaparra Sugar Company in Cuba and the West India Company in the Dominican Republic, each of these companies in turn owning several sugar mills in their respective islands. The group controlling the Fajardo, Aguirre, and United Porto Rico plantations in the Caribbean sold its raw sugar output to its sugar refineries in the United States, organized as the National Sugar Refining Company. Plantations and refineries were thus owned in common, although each enterprise was individually incorporated, and the entire complex was headquartered in 29 Front Street, New York. In the space of two decades after the U.S. occupation of Puerto Rico in 1898, the sugar industry experienced a transition from traditional family ownership to corporate control and integration with U.S. sugar-refining interests. Vieques was typical in this respect. Like the rest of Puerto Rico, its sugar industry was controlled in approximately equal shares by local Puerto Rican capitalists and by U.S. corporations. Specifically, the Benítez family was the biggest sugar producer in Vieques, while the United Porto Rico/Eastern Sugar Associates were the principal U.S. corporate landowners.

The United Porto Rico Company closed its Puerto Real mill, known as *Central Vieques* or *Central Esperanza*, in 1927 but continued to produce cane on its lands. The sugar cane was shipped from the port of Esperanza in Vieques toward Humacao in the main island of Puerto Rico, where it was ground in Central Pasto Viejo. This mill was founded in 1926, and it was also owned by the United Porto Rico Sugar Company. The United Porto Rico Company had established itself in the 1920s to serve as a holding company for local mills that had gone bankrupt or were foreclosed. When a drop in sugar prices put a number of locally owned sugar mills in dire straits, the United Porto Rico Company acquired them. This company thus mirrored the operations of New York–based Citi Bank in Cuba, in that it acquired preexisting local companies. It thus operated somewhat differently from the other three large U.S. sugar enterprises that established themselves at the beginning of the century in Puerto Rico (South Porto Rico, Aguirre, and Fajardo), which had built their own mills as opposed to acquiring local ones. United Porto Rico produced large quantities of sugar, but it did so in a variety of smaller mills, including Pasto Viejo, which ground cane from Vieques. At the beginning of the 1930s, United Puerto Rico changed its name to Eastern Sugar Associates in a corporate reorganization, and the titles to both the Puerto Real lands in Vieques and the Pasto Viejo mill in Humacao were transferred from United Porto Rico to Eastern Sugar Associates.

The sugar business in the Spanish Caribbean in the first half of the twentieth century was a truly multinational enterprise. There was nothing extraordinary about shipping cane from Vieques to Humacao. The South Porto Rico Sugar Company, which had lands planted in La Romana in the Dominican Republic, also shipped its cane early in the century toward Central Guánica in Puerto Rico. The crossing of the Mona Passage—which is located between the Dominican Republic and Puerto Rico—is a much longer trip than the skip from Vieques to Humacao, which has a distance of only six miles. Nevertheless, for the South Porto Rico Company, the endeavor was profitable as a result of the duty-free entrance of all sugars from Puerto Rico into the U.S. market, a tariff advantage that gave sugar producers in Puerto Rico a significant edge over the competition in Cuba and the Dominican Republic. This tariff advantage explains the immense interest of U.S. capital in enterprises of a relatively small size, such as the Puerto Real mill in Vieques, and it also explains the profitability of the enterprise even after accounting for shipping costs to Humacao from Vieques. Puerto Rico's incorporation into the U.S. tariff system explains the spread of cane cultivation throughout the island. Relative to its size, Puerto Rico became the most overspecialized sugar producer of the Caribbean. Vieques, which already had a sugar economy in the nineteenth century, also experienced the spread of sugar monoculture in the twentieth century. (See Table 2.1.) Thus, the transition from Spanish to U.S. colonialism in Vieques resulted in the strengthening of the sugar industry and of the old landowning class that had controlled Vieques from the days of slavery. The property of the great landowners became even more concentrated as the number of sugar mills decreased.

Central Arkadia produced sugar in the years 1907–1910, and probably stopped grinding cane in 1911. The Santa María mill was operated until 1923, registering small sugar outputs. It produced in its distillery a now-extinct brand of rum, Ron Santa María.[19] The Puerto Real mill operated until 1927. By 1930, the Playa Grande enjoyed "the distinction of being the surviving sugar factory on the island of Vieques."[20] Economic concentration eliminated the smaller cane-grinding units and replaced them with larger ones. Industrial concentration, however, did not entail the disappearance of the landowning class. Landowners continued to produce cane, which they sold to the larger central sugar mills as the industrial phase of sugar production was centralized into fewer but larger units.

The Great Depression of the 1930s sent the sugar industry of Vieques into sharp decline. The number of *cuerdas*[21] planted in cane decreased from 7,621 in 1935 to 4,586 in 1940. Cane yields dropped from twenty-four tons of cane per *cuerda* in 1924 to twenty-two in 1935 and nineteen in 1940.[22] Of the four sugar mills that existed in Vieques at the beginning of the century, only Playa Grande survived into 1933–1934, which were the worst slump years for sugar industry prices. The Great Depression caused economic dislocation and sparked social and political unrest. Militant union struggles took place during a general strike of the sugar cane workers in Puerto Rico in 1934, following the general strike in Cuba that overthrew Dictator Gerardo Machado in August of 1933, in the context of a worldwide slump in sugar prices during the Great Depression. The Puerto Rican strike started in December of 1933 and became an island-wide work stoppage in January of 1934. Workers in Vieques were in the forefront of this industry-wide movement.[23]

Land concentration in Vieques was not a phenomenon generated under U.S. rule after 1898. The structure of property ownership was by and large established under the Spanish regime in the nineteenth century, in the context of a plantation boom based on slave labor. During the 1930s the control of the great landowners over land resources reached its peak. The Eastern Sugar Associates owned 11,000 acres of land, with 1,500 acres planted in cane. Like the United Porto Rico Corporation before it, Eastern Sugar Associates shipped the cane to the Pasto Viejo mill in Humacao, Puerto Rico.[24] More than two thirds of the land planted in cane in Vieques was in the hands of two firms, the Benítez Sugar Company, owner of the Playa Grande mill, and the Eastern Sugar Associates. Thus "the evils of land concentration and absentee ownership, prevailing in most sugar cane lands in Puerto Rico, were deeply intensified in Vieques. The bulk of the population was landless, a part of the 'peon' class."[25] In short, Vieques was one of the municipalities in Puerto Rico most afflicted by the problems of land concentration and social inequality typical of plantation economies.

The preexistence and continuity of the sugar plantation economy and culture from the nineteenth century was largely responsible for the state of land concentration which the navy encountered in Vieques at the time of the expropriations in the 1940s. Slave emancipation in Puerto Rico had happened in 1873, in a gradual process administered by the Spanish colonial state. As hard as the slaves fought to gain their freedom, the land of the big proprietors remained untouched and, because the process was promoted from above and lacked the revolutionary fervor of other historical processes in the Americas such as the Haitian Revolution or the U.S. civil war, there was never even a proposal seriously considered for "forty acres and a mule" for the freedmen along the lines promoted by the radicals of Lincoln's Republican Party in the United States.[26] Emancipation was a conservative affair, and the ex-slaves never received land, although they did organize for better working conditions, wages, and benefits immediately after emancipation.[27] The fact that Vieques lacked a preexisting peasant economy, in contrast to Puerto Rico, produced higher indexes of land concentration than in Puerto Rico. Concentration of land ownership is typical of all sugar plantation regions in the Caribbean, but in the main island of Puerto Rico, the preexisting peasant economy brought average farm size down. In this respect Vieques was much more like the "pure plantation economies" of the Eastern Caribbean than Puerto Rico.[28] Widespread landlessness among the rural population was the flip side of land concentration in the hands of the plantation owners. In this respect, Vieques was among the municipalities with the largest proportion of landless people. This was already true at the moment of the U.S. invasion of Puerto Rico in 1898. In the U.S. colonial period, land concentration increased slightly, from an already concentrated state at the end of the Spanish regime. (See Table 2.2.)

The combination of preexisting landlessness and economic crisis in the 1930s rendered the situation of the rural proletariat dire. The 1930s were years of terrible crisis in the sugar industry in the entire Caribbean.[29] By 1940, the sugar industry of Vieques was in sharp decline. The number of *cuerdas* planted in cane had decreased, cane yields had dropped, unemployment was massive, and Viequenses had begun to emigrate to St. Croix in search of employment. The population of Vieques peaked in 1920 and declined thereafter, a signal that by the time of the expropriations of the U.S. Navy in 1940, the sugar economy was already in decline and outmigration had begun.

The Playa Grande sugar mill owned by the Benítez family went bankrupt in 1936 and was under receivership to the Bank of Nova Scotia until September, 1939, when the mill and over 10,000 acres of land were purchased by Juan Angel Tio. In the tax assessments of 1940, however, the Benítez family still appears as the principal owner of the lands. The taxes charged were small compared to those paid by the Eastern Sugar Associates, probably on account of the state of bankruptcy of the Playa Grande Corporation, perhaps on account of its doubtful legal standing, or perhaps due to litigation in court and competing claims by the bank and the new owners. Despite the fact that Tio started to operate the Playa Grande mill in 1939, in the tax records of 1940, the members of the Benítez family were still listed as the principal landowners of Vieques, owning almost half of the land in the island municipality. Dolores Benítez, Carlota Benítez, and others, Carmen Aurelia Benítez Bithorn and María Bithorn Benítez, each appear as the owner of 3,636 *cuerdas*, while Francisco and J. Benítez Santiago are listed as the owners of a tract of 1,191 *cuerdas*. In aggregate, the abovementioned members of the Benítez family owned 15,735 *cuerdas* of land out of a total of 36,032 *cuerdas* assessed for taxation, or 44 percent of the land of Vieques.[30] (See Table 2.3.) These 15,375 *cuerdas* assessed at $47,410 for tax purpose in 1940, or $3.01 per *cuerda*. In contrast to the situation of the lands of the Benítez family, the 10,043 *cuerdas* of the Eastern Sugar Associates were assessed in the same year at $661,400, or $63.95 per *cuerda*, that is, their assessed value was twenty times more per *cuerda* than the assessed value of the lands of the Benítez estates.

According to the Census of 1930, just two owners of more than 1,000 acres controlled 71 percent of the farmland in the municipality of Vieques. On the main island of Puerto Rico, only two municipalities had structures of land concentration more unbalanced than that of Vieques. They were: Santa Isabel, a municipality where much land was owned by the Aguirre Sugar Company, and where just one farm of over 1,000 acres owned 87 percent of the farmland, and Guánica, a municipality controlled by the South Porto Rico Sugar Company. The South Porto Rico and the Aguirre were the largest and most profitable enterprises producing sugar in Puerto Rico, respectively. They were thus frequently mentioned in the 1930s when the crisis of the sugar industry and rampant rural poverty prompted much criticism of the overspecialization of Puerto Rico in sugar production among intellectual circles.[31] In Vieques, eight farms of over 100 acres occupied 93 percent of the area, in comparison to Santa Isabel, where three farms occupied 98 percent of the area. Vieques stands out as one of the three municipalities of Puerto Rico with the highest indexes of land concentration. The other two municipalities were as dominated by the sugar industry as Vieques.

When compared to the indexes of land concentration in Puerto Rico as a whole, Vieques appears to be an extreme case. According to the *Census of the Puerto Rico Reconstruction Administration*, the average farm in Vieques spanned 393 acres, while in all of Puerto Rico the average farm size was 36 acres. While much land in Puerto Rico was devoted to the sugar industry and land concentration was high in the municipalities most specialized in sugar production, the expansion of tobacco cultivation in the twentieth century, which promoted the growth of small-scale farming, translated into much lower farm sizes. In fact, during the first twenty years of the twentieth century, small farms proliferated, especially in the tobacco-growing municipalities, and the Gini index of land concentration decreased, slightly.[32] In more than 70 percent of Puerto Rico's municipalities, average farm size was below 50 acres, and there were only eight municipalities with average farm sizes larger than 100 acres.[33] Vieques ranked third among Puerto Rico's *municipios* in terms of land concentration. There is no doubt that the problem of land concentration dominated the social and economic landscape of Vieques, to a much greater degree than in the most of the *municipios* of Puerto Rico.

The state of extreme land concentration in Vieques was based on the fact that unlike Puerto Rico, Vieques remained undeveloped during the period when a strong peasant economy flourished (1550–1762), that its development had taken place as a pure plantation economy, and that in the twentieth century its principal cash crop was sugar cane, and not tobacco. Preexisting colonial structures had thus left a legacy that the U.S. Navy en-

countered when it began building a navy base in the 1940s. U.S. Navy accounts of the expropriations generally emphasize that most of the land was
acquired from a handful of owners:

> Of the 21,000 acres, 10,000 acres or nearly half were acquired
> from Juan Tio, owner of Playa Grande mill and sugarcane lands
> in the western, central, and eastern sectors. Another substantial
> portion, nearly 8,000 acres, was acquired from Eastern Sugar
> Associates who had owned and operated the Esperanza sugar
> mill and lands in the east central sector. Lands of two other major
> families, Benitez and Rieckehoff, brought the total to over
> 19,000 acres or 90% of this first series of acquisitions.[34]

The acquisition of large tracts of property through expropriations required few transactions and was facilitated by the concentrated structure of
land tenure that was inherited from the Spanish colonial epoch and continued into the period of U.S. colonialism. Thus, the navy faced inherited social structures whose roots went back to the nineteenth century. Specifically,
most of the rural population settled on the land actually lacked land titles,
making the expropriations and removals a somewhat simpler matter for the
navy. The unprotected population felt the impact of the expropriation most
severely, paradoxically, because they owned nothing to begin with. They
were mostly workers who lived in the farms owned by others, under a traditional arrangement known as *agrego*. The workers who lived on the land
of the landowners, known as *agregados*, nevertheless had enjoyed some
traditionally defined usufruct rights. The *agregados* were legally defined
as "any family residing in the rural zone whose home is erected on lands
belonging to another person or to a private or public entity, and whose only
means of livelihood is labor for a wage."[35] When a new landowner purchased the land, he or she inherited the *agregados* settled there as well as
the mutual obligations between landowner and tenant typical of the *agrego*
contracts. The transfer to the navy was different. While the big landowners
who had to transfer their lands to the navy received compensation, the landless population, that is the majority of those affected by the process, were
simply expelled from the land. How these processes of expropriation and
expulsion unfolded is the topic of the next two chapters.

CHAPTER 3

Expropriations
and Evictions

U nited States planners had been preparing for the possibility of war since the 1930s. From September 1939 to November 1940, Fleet Admiral William D. Leahy served as governor of Puerto Rico, where he oversaw the military preparations for the war. Prior to becoming governor of Puerto Rico, Leahy was chief of naval operations, that is, the senior officer in the U.S. Navy. After serving as ambassador to France (1940–1942) Leahy served as chief of staff to President Franklin D. Roosevelt throughout World War II, and continued under President Harry S. Truman, until he retired in 1949. His appointment to Puerto Rico in 1939–1940 indicates the importance assigned to the island by U.S. naval planners.[1] When Germany declared war on the United States on December 11, 1941,[2] four days after Pearl Harbor, building the bases in the Caribbean for protection of U.S. imperial interests against German U-boats acquired extreme urgency.

Land ownership in Vieques was concentrated in a few hands. The majority of the rural population was title-less, but enjoyed usufruct rights as part of their contracts as *agregados* in the farms of the landowners. When the navy decided to build a base in Vieques, it forced the landowners to sell their lands at fixed prices. This process affected a relatively small number of people, many of them well-off property owners. However, the workers residing in the lands of these landowners, who received no compensation for the breaking of the traditional contracts of *agrego*, were nevertheless evicted from the land. This process of eviction of title-less families affected a much larger sector of the population of Vieques than the expropriation of the landowners. Thus, two groups of people were affected, in different ways. Landowners lost their farms but were compensated. *Agregados* lost their jobs, their houses, and their subsistence plots, but received no compensation. For purposes of the expropriations, the navy did not recognize the reciprocal duties and obligations of each party in an *agrego* contract.

Expropriation of the Landowners

The social structure of Vieques inherited from Spanish colonial times and consolidated during the first forty years of the U.S. colonial regime was characterized by the concentration of land in the hands of a few families or enterprises, on the one hand, and widespread lack of ownership of land by most rural families on the other. The expropriation of land by the navy proceeded on the basis of a limited number of civil actions in court against a small number of landowners. (See Table 3.1.) The property tax records for the municipality of Vieques offer a glimpse into rural life in a colonial plantation society dominated by a few landowning families. For example, the farm of "Carlota Benítez and others" located in the barrio named Punta Arenas, spanned 3,082 acres. There were "62 houses" among the improvements listed in 1940. The farm of Francisco and J. Benítez Santiago in Punta Arenas, which spanned 558 acres, contained sixty houses. The Eastern Sugar Associates had sixty-two houses in one of its properties. Another farm owned by Carlota Benítez in Barrio Llave, spanning 54 acres, had a cockpit in addition to a number of houses.[3] Some of these structures were *ranchones or barracones* that housed some of the poorest workers. Even cockfights, which were an important part of rural community life, took place on the land of the great landowners. The land and the houses were listed in the tax records as belonging to the landowners, who paid the corresponding taxes. The workers, having no titles, were removed without legal obstacles when the large landowners sold their properties. The ease of eviction was due, to a large degree, to the degree of rural landlessness among a rural population.[4]

Tax records provide no insight, however, into how the big landowners experienced the expropriations or how this process differed from the plight of small farm owners and *agregados*. The large landowners of Vieques were also reeling from the sugar crisis.[5] The sugar economy of Vieques was in a critical condition by 1941. Juan Angel Tio, owner of the Central Playa Grande—the only mill still grinding sugar cane in Vieques at the time—had only been operating it for three harvests prior to the entrance of the United States into the Second World War. Playa Grande had been acquired by the Tio family from the Bank of Nova Scotia just two years earlier, in 1939. The bank had, in turn, foreclosed the property of the Benítez family.

The Tios acquired not only the lands and the mill from the bank, but they also inherited the *agregado* system, which was "already established in the land at the time of purchase."[6] This means, in short, that when the Tios purchased the land, they inherited a relation with the rural population that was already settled in it. Thus, *agregados* were in a sense part the landscape, almost legally ascribed to the land, to the point that purchasers of land retained these rural workers and inherited the established relations of *agrego* from previous owners. The navy, however, did not accept the claims of *agregados* to usufruct rights over the land when it acquired the holdings of the Tios. Instead, it referred to the *agregados* as "squatters."

Agregados were rural workers who lived on the plantations and exchanged labor services for usufruct rights over the land. The *agregado* system existed in Puerto Rico since the nineteenth century and developed initially in the interior highland region that specialized in coffee production.[7] In its origins, *agrego* relations served landowners as a means of securing workers in a context of labor scarcity by offering land, sometimes a house to live in, cows for milk, and so on. As the landless population and the supply of labor increased in the nineteenth century, the terms of *agrego* deteriorated for the workers, and by the twentieth century, many *agregados* were in practice undistinguishable from rural workers. But often workers living on the land of landowners did enjoy the use of one or two acres of land to grow food crops—plantains, malanga, *yautía, ñame, yuca*, squash—which were essential to the survival of families during the *tiempo muerto* or dead season of approximately five months during which there was very little employment in cane agriculture.

The fate of these *agregados* changed dramatically in Puerto Rico after the Popular Democratic Party (P.D.P.) initiated its program of land reform in 1941. Historically, *agregados* had been subject to the combined politico-economic power of the landowners, but the redistribution of small plots of land through the agrarian reform program initiated by the P.D.P. allowed many to get enough land to build their houses, raise garden crops, and keep some animals, independently of the power of the landowners. In 1941, a new *Land Law* created the *Land Authority*. A program of distribution of small plots of land or *parcelas* of up to three acres (most were smaller) impacted the rural population. *Agregados* received the land in usufruct. Children could inherit usufruct rights, but the *parcelas* could not be sold or mortgaged. The acquisition of small plots of land by former *agregados* sig-nified the creation of a living space not subject to the authority, or power of eviction, of the landowners. Plantation life had a kind of "total" character regulating not only labor time but also the space in which workers experi-enced their "household" life. The acquisition of a *parcela,* therefore, signified freedom from the all-encompassing world of plantation life. By 1945, 14,000 families had already been settled in *parcelas* in the main island of Puerto Rico. The *parcelas* program continued after the war. By 1959, 52,287 families had been resettled in *parcelas* forming rural com-munities. Approximately 10 percent of the Puerto Rican population bene-fited from the agrarian reform.[8]

The agrarian reform in Puerto Rico was accompanied by a political cam-paign organized by the P.D.P. emphasizing the power of the vote aimed at boosting political participation among a rural population that had in the past been politically apathetic at best, if not disenfranchised. The changes in rural relations in Puerto Rico contributed to the modernization of the is-land and to the process of industrialization. But in Vieques this process was arrested because there, the acquisition of land by the navy prevented the agrarian reform from advancing as in the rest of Puerto Rico. This produced a different course of events, especially for the *agregados*, who did not re-ceive land and did not experience "enfranchisement" through participation in the political process. Instead, the rural population of Vieques experienced forced relocation into minute plots reserved by the navy. Politically, *agre-gados* did not experience "enfranchisement" but rather the overwhelming political power of the navy as a total and arbitrary outside force over which they had absolutely no influence. While the thrust of the reforms of the P.D.P. in the main island of Puerto Rico leaned in the direction of enfran-chisement and political and civic participation by the hitherto dispossessed rural population, the transformation wrought in Vieques by the navy treated the local residents not as citizens but as "squatters" without any rights. In these two senses—the economic as expressed in the agrarian reform, and the political as expressed by the campaign of the P.D.P. to get the vote out among the rural population—the direction of events in Vieques was dia-metrically opposed to that in the rest of Puerto Rico. Thus, the expropria-tions set Vieques on a divergent course of development from the rest of Puerto Rico.

The expropriation process began several months before Pearl Harbor, but the attack was the event that made landowners accept the events without further litigation. As traditional usufruct rights were not taken into account during the expropriations, the navy compensated the owners of the properties without being concerned about the fate of the *agregados* or other rural workers who were settled on the land. According to Tio's recollections, a marshal from the Federal Court brought a notification to his family that explained that the navy was expropriating most of their lands and had already deposited in the Federal Court the amount of money deemed as reasonable compensation for their property. Initially, the Tios tried to defend their assets by contesting the condemnation decree and trying to prove in court that the allocated compensation did not correspond to the real market value of their property. But the pace of the process was too rapid to allow them to organize a better defense. War was looming, and in times of conflict, sugar is a strategic war material, fetching high prices.

Tio remembers how immediately after the notification, the navy asked for permission to start the construction of military installations in Monte Pirata, the highest elevation of Vieques, located within Tio's fields. Subtle intimidation of the family by the commander in chief of the base followed. The expertise of Aurelio Tio, an engineer, was sought by the navy to assemble a map of the island's properties and their legal owners. According to Aurelio Tio, Juan Angel's son, his cooperation was secured in this manner:

> Commander Johnson, chief of the base, came to talk with Tio. He already had in place several study brigades to measure the island of Vieques. He asked Tio to draw for him a landholding map, as best as he could, and to have it ready in 30 days. The only way to accomplish this task was to take some measurements, and by putting into a bigger map all of the already existing maps of the island. Tio replied to Johnson that, how was he going to do this if they were going to use this map to expropriate him? The commander told him that if he didn't do it he was going to recruit him, make him a lieutenant and then order him to do it. This was said half-jokingly and half seriously, but more seriously than jokingly. This was a few days before Pearl Harbor

and when the attack occurred, he went to the federal court, settled the case and finished with everything. He did the map, as
best as he could, exactly enough.[9]

Tio remarked that his family did not participate in any way in the process
of notifying or removing the *agregados* from the property. The navy took
charge of everything. The principal way in which his family was affected
was economic, as the navy was expropriating a sugar mill that was expected
to turn a tidy profit in times of war and soaring sugar prices. The navy paid
the Tios an average price of $37 per acre, while the average price paid for
the remainder of the land expropriated during this time frame was $60 per
acre. (See Table 3.1.) During a second round of expropriations, after World
War II, the navy paid $122 per acre, 238 per cent above the price paid to
the Tios.

The authorities expropriated most of the lands of the Tio family but not
the sugar-mill itself nor the land on which it was built. The properties of
the Tio family thus became fragmented. They now owned a sugar mill but
did not have sufficient cane lands to operate it. Additionally, they also had
2,000 head of cattle but not enough grazing lands to sustain them. The Tios
operated the mill as best they could, buying cane from some cane growers
who still remained in Vieques, until 1944, when they finally closed it. The
machinery was sold to a corporation from Mayagüez, Puerto Rico, led by
sugar investor Miguel Angel García Méndez. This corporation in turn sold
the machinery to the Okeelanta Sugar Company, in Belle Glade, Florida.
Okeelanta went into bankruptcy and the machinery ended up in Central
Manatí in Cuba.[10] The mill machinery was sold at a discounted price and
the cattle were sold in a hurry. Since they did not have enough lands to
keep the animals, they had to accept whatever price was offered by the purchasers. The family concluded that pursuing their case in the Federal Court
would not increase their final compensation substantially, and therefore,
they could not justify putting up a struggle during the war emergency.

Eviction of *Agregados* and Workers

The existence of a plantation economy and society in Vieques had important repercussions during the expropriations. As in many other plantation

regions, there was no geographic separation between workplace and place of residence. The workers lived and worked on the land of the large landowners. This gives plantation life a kind of "total" character that is different from the situation of most urban wage workers.[11] When the expropriation of the large landowners took place, workers lost in one single blow both their jobs and their houses. To urban workers, this would be the equivalent of being fired from the job and evicted by the landlord on the same day. Additionally, *agregados* also lost their subsistence plots and farm animals.

Workers who lived on the land of the landowners typically had subsistence plots, as part of the usufruct rights characteristic of the traditional arrangement known as *agrego*. In Vieques the small amounts of land for planting available to those who described themselves as *agregados* indicate that the function of the plots was principally the production of subsistence garden crops rather than commercial agriculture. Matilde Bonaro, a Vieques resident at the time of the expropriations, indicated that she was an *agregada* in Playa Grande who had at her disposal half a *cuerda* of land. Francisco Colón López, another *agregado*, had two *cuerdas* available in Barrio Mosquito, Ventura Feliciano Corrillo had one, while Teodora Velázquez and Juan Sherman each had one and a half *cuerdas*.[12]

On this scale it is not possible to make a living without recourse to wage labor in the sugar fields at harvest time. Clearly, the function of usufruct rights was to facilitate the reproduction of labor power while guaranteeing a supply of laborers to the landowners. For many rural households, survival during the *tiempo muerto* of cane agriculture depended on these usufruct rights. The frontier between *agrego* as a sort of tenancy or sharecropping arrangement, and rural proletarianization is therefore blurred, so it is not possible to speak clearly of "tenants" on the one hand and "workers" on the other. Among the forty-one *agregados* from Vieques interviewed by Proyecto Caribeño de Justicia y Paz, the median size of the plots held in usufruct was two *cuerdas*.

Subsistence plots were particularly important during the idle season of the sugar industry, which lasted from June to November. During these months of *tiempo muerto,* most sugar-cane workers were unemployed. In Vieques, people who lived during the epoch of the sugar plantations refer to the dead season as *la bruja* ("the witch"), and the term *pasar la bruja* means "to survive the idle season." In other areas of Puerto Rico, the relation of rural peasant/proletarian communities to the ecology has been amply documented.[13] In Vieques, this aspect has yet to be studied, but it has undoubtedly conditioned the claims of the communities that, based on traditional rights of *agrego* relationships, understood that they had certain rights of possession and usufruct over the land. This explains the double reality of lack of titles, on the one hand, and the widespread feeling of rural dispossession after the houses, built by the workers themselves, were leveled during the expropriations. The U.S. Navy itself acknowledges, concerning the land title issues extant in the resettlement areas of Vieques, that traditional usufruct rights associated with Puerto Rican *agrego* relations have conditioned the expectations of the civilian population regarding their right to have a place to live:

> For those who now live in Vieques and who once lived on Navy land, a sense of "ownership" and therefore desires for return pertains to their former rights of access and use of land.[14]

The existence of usufruct rights also affected the expelled populations, who could not count on subsistence crops in the resettlement plots provided by the navy and whose means of subsistence were thus radically curtailed. These subsistence plots had helped to support families during the idle season in cane agriculture, when households lacked the wages paid during the harvest season. One *agregada* reported, for example, that her family had to let go of the farm animals they had because in the relocation plots there was no place to raise them. She also reported being notified of the eviction by the owner of the land and receiving no compensation: "As we were *agregados* they just told us to leave."[15]

Nazario Cruz Viera remembered that before the expropriations, "there were farms and the landowners needed many people to work them. They even gave you a place to live. We had everything. We lacked nothing."[16] Severina Guadalupe, who was thirteen years old when the bulldozers razed her family's home in Vieques, remembered the transition from the rural economy where food was abundant, to the squalor of life on the Santa María resettlement tract.[17] The transition from *agregado* settled on the land to urban dweller settled on a navy resettlement tract in Montesanto or Santa

María produced an increase in the number of families living in poverty and a deterioration of living conditions. The Rev. Justo Pastor Ruiz described the transition experienced by the dispossessed as follows: "Those who had garden plots or lived happily on the landowners land surrounded by farmland and fruit trees, live today in overcrowded conditions . . ."[18]

Thus the impact of the navy's expropriations was much broader than one might suppose, considering only the property owners of the island who were evicted through the navy's condemnation proceedings. In addition to landowners large and small, the families of the *agregados* and rural workers who lived in the land of the property owners were affected by the evictions. They were expelled from the land and relocated to the central parts of Vieques. The expropriation of the landowners in turn generated a much wider process of evictions (*desalojos*) that affected *agregados* and rural workers as well. Forty-one of the fifty-three individuals interviewed by the Proyecto Caribeño de Justicia y Paz stated that at the time of the expropriations they were *agregados*.[19]

Traditionally, landowners had honored *agrego* contracts to the point that the sale of land from one landowner to another implied that the new landowner inherited the resident *agregado* population on the land. This was the case of the Tio family, who retained the *agregados* who were settled in the land that the Tios purchased from the Benítez family. The workers in turn, were expected to work for wages for the landowner during the harvest. The navy did not honor the usufruct rights of the *agregados* when it purchased the land. It expelled them. However, when it did need workers for construction projects, it required that the males from families relocated to navy lands work for the navy, exactly as had been required under traditional *agrego* relations. "All able bodied males residing on the naval reservation were forced to work for the NOy-3680 or move off navy land."[20] This is a remarkable statement underscoring the forced nature of the work. Extraeconomic coercion of the labor force had disappeared in the Caribbean, by and large, decades before. Indentured servitude in the region had ended in 1918, when the British had abolished it in their colonies.[21]

In measuring the social impact of the expropriations, the fate of the landowners who received compensation must be sorted out from the situation of the *agregados* who generally did not receive any compensation.[22] The navy's own conservative estimate is that altogether, "Navy land acquisitions dislocated an estimated 4,250 to 5,000 people, or 40 to 50 percent of the total population. Of these, approximately 27 percent was resettled with navy assistance. This traumatic upheaval created havoc among the residents of the island, altering both the social structure and the economy for generations to come."[23]

Condemnation Proceedings

The navy has not always acknowledged that it expropriated lands in Vieques and has sometimes openly denied it.[24] The editor of *Sea Power Magazine*, for example, once argued that the United States did not "expropriate any property on Vieques." The navy, continued the argument, "purchased" the land over a nine-year period.[25] However, a scholarly study produced by the navy at about the same time talks of "expropriations," "displacement," and mentions that the urgency of the war situation necessitated "condemnation proceedings" to move the civilian population. According to the study commissioned by the navy, "condemnation was the method of acquisition at this time and was utilized because of the haste necessitated by wartime conditions."[26] What is at stake is not whether property owners received some compensation, but the element of compulsion in the sale.[27]

The initial stage in the eviction of the Vieques population from their land took place between 1941 and 1942 and began in the western section of the island, the region closest to Puerto Rico, for which the navy had immediate occupation plans. Three quarters of all families were notified by a letter written by the Naval Station officer in charge of construction, informing them that the United States had acquired the house and land occupied by the tenant's family, and that the property had to be abandoned within ten days after receiving the notification. Still, a quarter of those interviewed reported that this written notification was delivered only twenty-four to forty-eight hours in advance of their actual eviction.

According to one interviewee, the former manager of the Central Playa Grande—immediately employed as field manager by the navy—delivered most of the letters. He was accompanied by "an American or soldier," which served to further intimidate those receiving the notice. The *agregados* living closer to the eastern section of Vieques were given, according to those interviewed, more time to move out in the second expropriations of 1947–1948.[28] In case the family had nowhere else to go, the navy offered to relocate them on a plot of land, provided they agreed to abandon this place again with only twenty-four hours of advanced notification, and surrendering any future claims. According to the navy instructions recalled by our informants, no cement dwellings were to be constructed in these plots. This condition increased the insecurity felt by most families, then and over the years, since no matter how long they had been living in the navy resettlements, or the improvements they had made to their houses as time went by, they felt they could again be evicted from one day to the next without any legal rights to protect them.[29]

The navy relocated these families in a sugar cane *colonia* in Santa María, in lots of fifty feet by forty feet, thus creating the first slum of Vieques. The other families were transferred to lands purchased by the navy, outside the restricted zones. The municipality of Vieques would be left in virtual bankruptcy, due to the decrease in property-tax revenue, which, according to the report, would mean a loss of $20,346 out of a budget of $52,903, that is, a reduction of 38.5 percent.

The tearing down of houses caused considerable trauma. In the words of one resident: "A truck was sent with a carpenter in charge of tearing down the dwelling. Our things were thrown into the assigned plot." Those who had more than a twenty-four-hour notice recalled: "We gathered our animals and began to tear down the house." "Our things were thrown out in the new lot, and we had to begin to clear out the brush." Another family remembers that after tearing the house down, the truck did not arrive that day, and they had to sleep in the open. After others were informed that their houses were torn down, they were taken to the assigned lots, given a tarpaulin, and they lived under those conditions for three months until the navy brought them their wood planks to the new place.

The situation of women-headed households with their children, and of expecting mothers in the community, was singled out by our interviewees as particularly pitiful: "Women with their children were brought here under the rain and were left with just a zinc plank above." "Many gave birth under those zinc boards." "My sister was pregnant and ill. She got wet during the eviction and died soon after." The fields that were converted into residential plots lacked any previous conditioning, water, or basic sanitary provisions.

"They were bitten by scorpions and rats. Water and food were lacking. Their skin was swollen." "We arrived during the rainy season. Many contracted the flu. They were carried in hammocks to the hospital."[30]

The massive eviction evoked feelings of sadness, bitterness, and impotence in the majority of those interviewed. "My mother cried and cried. She arrived in Santa María with her face covered with a towel." "I was heartbroken." "I thought I was not going to be able to survive." "Even a hurricane would have been better than the expropriations." Others, however, believed their situation was not too different from before, and in fact, improved in the short term. "In the Tio farm [where they lived as *agregados*] there was no water. Besides, a house was given to us in the new plot." "We were sad, but they promised so much lasting work." "When the navy arrived in Vieques, the sugar mill stopped grinding cane. The construction of the base created at least some jobs."

The colonial plantation system established in Vieques had provided subsistence plots to the farm workers, and employment part of the year in the sugar harvest. The acquisition of land by the navy affected the local population in specific ways according to these preexisting arrangements. Because the majority of the rural population had no titles to land, eviction became a relatively easy process, in that it entailed only a few large transactions for the navy, as opposed to a farm-by-farm process involving hundreds of rural households, which would have been the case had Vieques been characterized by a more equitable distribution of land. There was, therefore, practically no active opposition to the expropriations on the part of the landless population. The urgency of the war emergency and a certain level of consciousness that the struggle against Hitler's Germany required some sacrifices also contributed to the mood of the population. Nazario Cruz Viera, a ninety-year-old resident of Vieques interviewed in 2002, remembers the sense of emergency: "War emergency, and we were side by side with the American nation. Because we were afraid—Germany, Hitler, it was dangerous."[31]

Generalized distress was not translated into resistance. Many reported talks among their neighbors of refusing to leave, but their determination was weakened by several conditions: they were *agregados*, not the owners of the land, and felt that if their landlord was willing to comply and received money, there was little they could do. This sense of resignation was expressed in the interviews conducted by the Proyecto Caribeño de Justicia y Paz: [32]

> "People were afraid of the navy and scared of being jailed."
> "They were *agregados* and respected the federal government. They believed the Americans would send them to Devil's Island."

The bulldozers used to clear the expropriated lands scared the population and became an effective deterrent to any action.

> "I was afraid of the bulldozers. The marines were evil."
> "We had seven children, they threatened us with the bulldozers . . ."
> "The law was more stringent then, you had to obey. I was scared of the bulldozers."

Yet, equally important was perhaps the general understanding among *agregados* that they were ill equipped to face forces too superior for them, and that they would be alone in any type of struggle chosen.

> "There was nobody backing us. There was fear because of the language (English). It was mandatory (to leave)."
> "We were disoriented. Those who could offer any help were in favor of the navy. Nobody paid any attention if anyone protested."

Reflecting on the question of the lack of resistance, one last interviewee summarized the general outlook as follows:

> "There was a lot of opposition, but people were afraid to express themselves openly. The government and all the powerful were Americans. We had no support. We were slaves."
> "We had no rights."

A sense of the conditions in the resettlement tracts is conveyed by the language used by a committee appointed by the Senate of Puerto Rico in 1943 to study conditions in Vieques, which referred to the location of the resettled population as "the reservation" and as "the slum community of Santa María."[33]

The Disappearance of the Barrios

The two successive processes of expropriation in Vieques affected the western barrios first, and then the eastern barrios. The condemnation proceedings that began in late 1941 affected all of Punta Arenas, Llave, Mosquito, and some of the lands of Puerto Ferro, Puerto Diablo, and Florida. (See Maps 1, 2, and 3.) The navy acquired by its own reckoning 21,020 acres, or approximately two thirds of the island between 1941 and 1943. In a second wave of expropriations, between 1947 and 1948, the navy acquired an additional 4,340 acres in the eastern portion of Vieques, principally in Puerto Diablo.[34] According to the municipal taxation records, the municipality of Vieques lost all of its taxpayers in barrio Punta Arenas during the first wave of the expropriations of the navy.[35] (See Table 3.2.)

Llave lost 95 percent of its assessed, tax-paying land and Mosquito lost 91 percent, while 76 percent of the lands of Puerto Ferro stopped paying taxes at this time. Due to the high degree of land concentration, the largest haciendas spanned two or more barrios, and for this reason it is difficult to establish with precision what percentage of the large farms belonged to which barrio. For example, in 1940–1941 the tax records list 5,856 *cuerdas* of land as belonging jointly to the barrios of Puerto Real and Puerto Ferro, without listing what part of the land belonged to which barrio. In 1945, as a result of the expropriation of the lands of Puerto Ferro, some of the land that had previously been listed jointly now appeared as belonging solely to Puerto Real, where it was taxed. Due to this statistical effect, Puerto Real appears as having more land under taxation in 1945 than in 1940. In the entire island of Vieques, the Department of the Treasury of Puerto Rico assessed for taxation purposes 36,032 *cuerdas* of land in 1940–1941, but only 9,935 in 1945. The difference of 26, 097 *cuerdas* (72 percent of the land of Vieques) is greater than the figure cited by J. Pastor Ruiz of 22,000 *cuerdas* expropriated by the U.S. Navy during this period (the Navy figure is 21,020 acres or 21,415 *cuerdas*).[36]

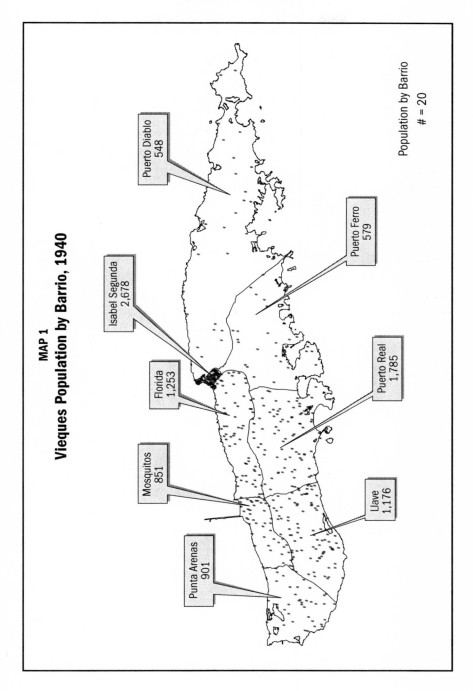

MAP 1
Vieques Population by Barrio, 1940

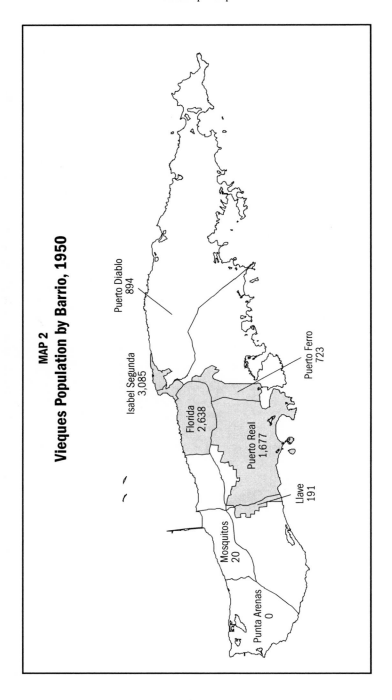

MAP 2
Vieques Population by Barrio, 1950

Puerto Diablo
894

Isabel Segunda
3,085

Florida
2,638

Puerto Ferro
723

Puerto Real
1,677

Llave
191

Mosquitos
20

Punta Arenas
0

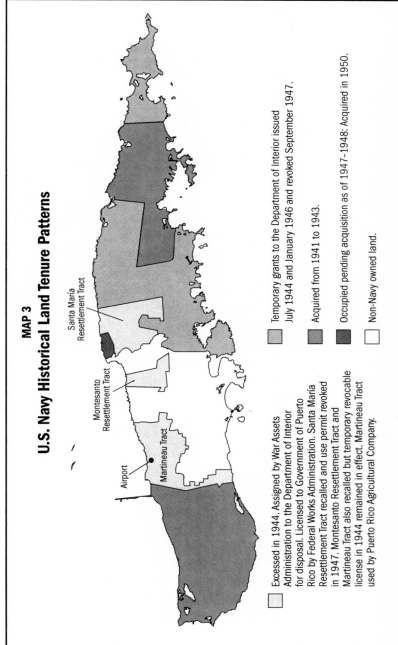

MAP 3

U.S. Navy Historical Land Tenure Patterns

Santa María
Resettlement Tract

Montesanto
Resettlement Tract

Airport

Martineau Tract

Temporary grants to the Department of Interior issued July 1944 and January 1946 and revoked September 1947.

Acquired from 1941 to 1943.

Occupied pending acquisition as of 1947–1948: Acquired in 1950.

Non-Navy owned land.

Excessed in 1944. Assigned by War Assets Administration to the Department of Interior for disposal. Licensed to Government of Puerto Rico by Federal Works Administration. Santa María Resettlement Tract recalled and use permit revoked in 1947. Montesanto Resettlement Tract and Martineau Tract also recalled but temporary revocable license in 1944 remained in effect. Martineau Tract used by Puerto Rico Agricultural Company.

Source: Department of the Navy. 1979. *Continued Use of the Atlantic Fleet Weapons Training Facility Inner Range (Vieques): Draft Environmental Impact Statement*. N.p., Tippetts-Abbett-McCarthy-Stratton: Ecology and Environment.

Between 1945 and 1950, the number of *cuerdas* registered in the municipal taxation records decreased from 1,204 to 369 in Florida, a decrease of 69 percent. In Puerto Diablo, the corresponding decrease was from 3,921 to 2,791 *cuerdas* (a 29 percent decrease) and in Puerto Real, the number of *cuerdas* taxed by the municipality decreased from 4,238 to 1,689 (a 60 percent decrease). In Vieques as a whole, the total area under civilian control according to the taxation records decreased from 9,934 *cuerdas* in 1945 to 5,685 in 1950, a 43 percent decrease from the land area available in 1945. If we consider the original taxation figure of 36,032 *cuerdas* in 1940, before the first wave of expropriations, and 5,685 in 1950, the municipality of Vieques was taxing only 16 percent as much land in 1950 as in 1940. This is a dramatic decrease in the civilian land area, and even allowing for some error in the municipal taxation figures of 1940, this means that in 1950, civilians had in the best of cases one fifth of the land they had in 1940. This is a remarkable figure if one considers that the population of Vieques did not decline proportionally. In 1950 there were 9,228 persons in Vieques, compared to 10,037 in 1940. In other words, 89 percent of the civilian population remained on the island during the 1940–1950 decade, but civilians retained only 16 percent as much land in 1950 as in 1940. (See Table 3.3.) Land available to civilians decreased from 3.6 *cuerdas* per person in 1940 to 0.6 in 1950. It does not take much of an imagination to visualize the effects of this change on a society that had been fundamentally rural and agrarian in 1940. (See Maps 1 and 2: Vieques, Population by Barrio, 1940 and 1950, respectively.)

The fifty-three persons interviewed came from all parts of Vieques. Most, however, lived in the western barrios, which were the most populous before the expropriations. Only eight of the fifty-three lived in the eastern sectors. Many were *agregados*, and they listed as their place of residence communities whose names are difficult to locate in today's maps. In the interviews, Viequenses who experienced expulsions from the land were asked not only where they lived before the expropriations, but also where they went after the expropriations. Fifteen were relocated to Montesanto and twenty-one to Santa María, the rest moving to various other places in Vieques and even to the main island of Puerto Rico. The navy's version of events concedes that the population of *agregados* and workers, that is, those who were not property owners, was larger than that of the property owners.

This is what one would expect given the degree of concentration of landed property in Vieques and the rates of rural landlessness.

> A larger population living on the acquired lands, who were not property owners, were resettled to Montesanto (a tract isolated from the other acquisitions) and to Santa María (a tract at the northeastern edge of the Eastern Sugar Associates acquisition and close to Isabel Segunda). Resettlement to these areas was proposed and accomplished in a relatively short period of time. Records indicate that a proposal of December 1942 to relocate "aggregados" [sic] from the Naval Ammunition Facility to Montesanto was a reality by August 1943 and that the Santa María tract had also been established. Those now in Vieques who were among the resettled recall an extremely rapid resettlement. Although recollections of the types of Navy assistance vary widely, the moves appear to have been accomplished with some Navy assistance. The numbers of tenant families affected range from about 500 at a minimum to 1300 at a maximum with 800 the most frequently cited number.[37]

With an average family size of approximately 4.5 persons in Vieques, 500 families translates into 2,250 individuals, or one quarter of the population of Vieques. The figure of 1,300 families translates into 5,850 or 59 percent of the population of Vieques. Between these two extremes, the "most frequently cited" number of 800 families means 3,650 individuals, or 37 percent of the population of Vieques. The number of those affected by the evictions ranges between a quarter and 58 percent of the population of the island. Thus, the evictions had a much greater social impact than the expropriations per se, which affected only the minority property-owning population of Vieques.

Displacement

Most of the population of Vieques was relocated, after the old neighborhoods were razed to the ground. Within days, *barrios*—sections of the island that had been the homes to Viequenses for decades—disappeared, vanishing as if they had never existed. Other areas of Vieques, despite the lack of appropriate infrastructure to support this dramatic increase of population, became overpopulated. The population of Florida, a central barrio of Vieques, doubled during the decade of 1940–1950 due to the settlement, in the vicinity of Isabel Segunda, of the population expelled from Punta Arenas, Mosquito, and Llave. However, the population of Florida was already on the rise at the time of the expropriations and had increased in the period 1935–1940 due to a 1937 resettlement project of the Puerto Rico Reconstruction Administration, which provided plots of 2 *cuerdas* to 199 homesteaders.[38] In Punta Arenas the population declined by 100 percent, in Mosquito it dropped 98 percent, while Llave lost 89 percent of its population during 1940–1950. The increase in the central sector of Vieques is the counterpart to the decrease in the barrios affected by the expropriations. According to Rev. Justo Pastor Ruiz, "The barrios of Tapón, Mosquito, and Llave disappeared. All the neighbors and small owners disappeared and formed new barrios in Moscú and Montesanto."[39] The navy's version of events is not very different.

> Both personal recollections of the relocation and naval records substantiate that those who lived in barrio Llave (including the Playa Grande settlement), Resolución, the Monte Pirata area, and Punta Arenas were moved to Montesanto. The records of lot assignments to Montesanto reveal that of 383 tenant families who lived in the western and southern sector, 284 resettled in Montesanto and the remaining 99 chose to go elsewhere. The 17 tenants who had lived in Montesano prior to the establishment of the resettlement tract were also assigned lots. Records and recollection confirm that families who lived in the Mosquito area (Barrio Mosquito and portions of Florida) on land associated with the Benitez sugar family were moved to Santa Maria. Tenants in the eastern sector lands owned by Eastern Sugar Associates and by Juan Tio were also apparently relocated to Santa Maria. Estimates of the number relocated there range from 180 to 200 families but estimates of the number who may have lived on the affected lands would be considerably higher. A 1943 investigating Committee places the total number of affected families in both tracts as high as 825.[40]

A study carried out by the Agricultural Experiment Station of the University of Puerto Rico in 1943 stated that the total number of families affected was undoubtedly larger than 825.[41]

The effects of the expropriations on the population were conditioned by the social structure of Vieques. Before the arrival of the U.S. Navy, the majority of the population was poor and depended on employment in sugarcane agriculture. Widespread rural landlessness had been a feature of this colonial plantation society since the nineteenth century. Society evolved in the twentieth century, the sugar industry prospered, but rural landlessness remained the norm in the first forty years of the U.S. colonial period. Rev. Justo Pastor Ruiz described the situation in the 1930s, before the expropriations, with the following images of the cane fields and the sea: "Surrounded by the beauty of the ocean and the green cane fields, a man starved to death. The ocean, rich in mysteries and hidden wealth, could not help him. The soft and whispering cane field was a sight to behold. But that was all. . . . The ocean and the cane-field have no heart."[42] Pastor Ruiz reminds us that before the expropriations Vieques was no paradise. Rural landlessness and poverty were rampant, as in the rest of Puerto Rico. Yet retrospectively, those expelled remembered life before the expropriations as having been better than after.

For most, eviction from the land meant deteriorating living conditions due to the loss of usufruct rights. The expropriations had a profound and devastating effect on the standard of living of most of the population. The residents of Vieques were forced to live on 16 percent of island. Even decades after the initial expropriations, the memory of these events lingers. The sugar landowners, compensated by the navy, eventually left Vieques. Many *agregados* stayed. As the sugar industry, the most importance source of jobs on the island, evaporated, the islanders were forced to look elsewhere for jobs. With only a small portion of land in which to live, and the main source of employment gone, the outlook for Viequenses eventually became bleak, as reflected in the memories of the evictions presented in this chapter, all of which were collected many years after the events. However, in the immediate aftermath of the evictions, construction of the base and the pier in Vieques generated an employment boom that for a while dimmed the impact of the expropriations and evictions. In 1941–1943, in fact, Vieques experienced the greatest economic boom in its history.

CHAPTER 4

Interlude

From November 1941 to mid-1943 the economy of Vieques experienced the greatest economic boom in its history due to the number of jobs generated by the military construction of the base and a pier in the *barrio* of Mosquito. These construction jobs typically paid 40 percent more than those in the sugar industry, and employment was continuous, not seasonal, as in the sugar industry. After the summer of 1943, a period of true misery followed as military construction ceased, displacing almost 1,500 workers. A third period began when the Puerto Rico Agricultural Company (PRACO), a government-owned corporation, attempted to revive the economy of Vieques. During this third period, the PRACO employed over 1,000 workers in Vieques, and it made considerable (although not sufficient) investments. The situation after the first expropriations, therefore, was not homogeneously disastrous for Viequenses. The expropriations, the construction of the base, the end of military construction, and state intervention in the form of PRACO investments each had an immense impact over this small island and its inhabitants, who were caught in the ups and downs of an economy that remained, at all times, subject to the decisions of the U.S. Navy. Thus between 1942 and 1948, the economy of Vieques went through three distinct periods. Contrary to the commonplace assumption of an invariably disastrous situation in Vieques, the inhabitants of the island lived through a period of prosperity, a disastrous period, and a period of partial recovery.

The Initial Expropriations

Juan Angel Tio, the Eastern Sugar Associates, and the Benítez-Rieckehoff family were among the principal property owners expropriated in 1942. Because of these expropriations, the navy ended up with close to 22,000 *cuerda*s, approximately two thirds of the Island. This first round of acquisition of land by the navy disastrously reduced the revenue of the municipal government of Vieques. Mayor, Dr. Leoncio T. Davis (who was the only medical doctor on the Island), complained that the municipality would no longer receive the taxes paid by the best sugar lands of Vieques. Property-tax revenue amounted to $18,700 out of a municipal budget of $46,244 in fiscal year 1941–1942, that is 40 percent of municipal revenue, before the expropriation of the Eastern Sugar Company. The mayor projected that once the Eastern Sugar stopped paying taxes, Vieques would be left without any income from property on land.[1] (See Table 4.1.)

How did the inhabitants of a small agricultural island survive after los-ing, according to the least damaging estimate, 64 percent of the land? Dur-ing the period immediately following the expulsions, Viequenses not only were able to survive, but contrary to what intuition might tell us, they did rather well. The island went through a construction boom. According to Rev. Justo Pastor Ruiz, Episcopal Minister of Vieques, "the town swam in gold for a couple of years."[2] According to Puerto Rican geographer Rafael Picó, who observed the situation directly in the summer of 1943, "there is today a boom in Vieques such as the Island has not experienced for 100 years."[3] The construction of the Military Base in Mosquito, between late 1941 and the summer of 1943 employed 1,700 Viequenses, 1,000 workers from Puerto Rico, and 250 workers from the continental United States, thus diminishing the negative economic impact of the expropriations on those who were expelled from the land and resettled. The population of Vieques reached its highest point ever, growing from 10,400 in 1940 to 14,000 in 1943. Construction activities paid wages of $2.25 daily,[4] approximately 40 percent more than the daily wage in the sugar industry. In contrast to the sugar industry, construction offered employment without the interruption of the dead season. Working eleven months instead of seven, with a daily wage 40 percent higher, the yearly income of a worker was more than dou-ble than during the period of the sugar plantation economy.

"People worked twenty-four hours a day. There was no rest, there was no limit to the circulation of American dollars." Of course, this panorama of economic activity and prosperity needs to be tempered by the increase in the cost of living and the shortages of consumer goods generated by the war economy. Even then, the situation was one of "boom in cash, the period of the fat cows." Despite the hyperbole of the following description by Rev. Justo Pastor Ruiz, which was no doubt influenced by the Christian outlook a minister emphasizing temperance and moderation, the following description of Vieques nevertheless suggests the magnitude of the economic boom.

> Rents increased threefold and fourfold, people purchased good clothes and treated them carelessly, alcoholic beverages were consumed without measure. There were those who washed their floors with beer, and those who purchased a thirty-five-dollar suit on Saturday and ruined it on Monday after two hours of work mixing cement! People said: "The base is there, and it provides more."[5]

Central Playa Grande still provided some employment, as it continued to grind cane until its last harvest, which ended in the summer of 1943. During the period immediately following the expropriations, the long-term impact was not yet visible. Instead, Vieques seemed poised for smooth sailing into a future of prosperity, thanks to the navy.

Despite the damaging effects of German submarines, which were by no means under control in 1942, the U.S. Navy was already shifting gears and relocating assets to the Pacific. The war situation was changing dramatically. Since 1942, the U.S. Navy had decided to shift resources to the naval war in the Pacific. A decision to reduce construction at Roosevelt Roads and Vieques was reached after a review of the "present and potential enemy naval forces in the Atlantic, the type of naval warfare conducted by the Axis in this area, the necessity of maintaining a large portion of the U.S. major naval units in the Pacific, the shortage of shipping and critical materials." The navy had concluded that "the proposed requirements of the Roosevelt Roads project should be restudied, with the view of reducing, eliminating, or deferring certain projected items." This meant a 50 percent reduction of the work in Ceiba and Vieques, based on the notion that "only such work be proceeded with at Roosevelt Roads as necessary to provide services to 30% of the Fleet instead of 60%."[6]

The navy command knew in 1942 of the forthcoming reductions in construction activity and employment. Exactly when the government of Puerto Rico was informed is unknown, but by February of 1943, it was taking measures to dampen the impact of the future closing of the base and the loss of construction jobs in Vieques. On February 23, 1943, after a meeting between the president of the Puerto Rican Senate, Luis Muñoz Marín, and a delegation of leaders from Vieques, a committee was appointed to study the situation in Vieques and make recommendations to buffer the impact of the closing of the base.[7] This committee was known as the Comisión Picó.[8]

The Picó Committee

On February 26, 1943, three days after the meeting with the representatives from Vieques, Luis Muñoz Marín sent a telegram to those present at the meeting indicating the creation of a committee to study the Vieques situation. The telegram listed the names of the people charged with "visiting the small island" next Wednesday, March 3, to remain there until Thursday afternoon to study the matter and come up with recommendations."[9] Muñoz Marín sent a telegram to Mayor Leoncio T. Davis, on March 1, revealing the names of the members and asking the mayor to help organize public hearings on March 3 at 8:00 p.m. in the Town Hall. The president of the Puerto Rican Senate asked the mayor for assistance to ensure large attendance at the hearings.[10] On March 1, Muñoz Marín informed Dr. Rafael Picó, president of the Puerto Rico Planning Board, that, in a meeting with the members of the committee, "it was agreed to appoint you President of the Committee."[11]

The Report of the Committee was delivered to Luis Muñoz Marín on March 18, 1943. The most urgent concerns of the committee were: the reduced finances of the municipality of Vieques due to the reduction in taxable property caused by the expropriations of the navy and the looming unemployment crisis once construction stopped. The report argued that unless measures were taken to diminish the impact, the closure of the base would generate layoffs of 1,475 workers representing 1,187 families. The first expropriations had caused the expulsion of 700 families who lived in the 8,000 *cuerda*s belonging to the Playa Grande mill.[12]

The Picó Committee Report tried to minimize the impact of the navy expropriations by arguing that "even before Navy had hired a single worker on Vieques the economic situation of the island was pretty desperate."[13] It also pointed out that upon the cessation of the construction in the base Vieques "will face the severest crisis in its history" and that "there is no evidence that the workers are saving their unusually high salaries."[14]

The report recommended asking the navy to find out if the 13,000 acres expropriated without military restrictions could be transferred to the Interior Department of the United States and to find out if they could be used for agriculture and for resettlement of the displaced families. Additionally, the report argued that the navy should compensate the municipality of Vieques for the loss of tax income related to the shrinkage of the property-tax base in the expropriated lands.[15] Luis Muñoz Marín sent a copy of this report to Governor Rexford G. Tugwell.[16] He also sent copies to multiple federal and insular agencies, on April 6, 1943.[17] On April 13, Muñoz Marín wrote to Teodoro Moscoso, general administrator of the Puerto Rico Industrial Development Company (PRIDCO), who was at the time attempting to launch state-owned import substitution industries, asking him to review the recommendations of the Picó Committee regarding the establishment of small industries in Vieques, and to report his findings to Dr. Picó.[18]

In the spirit of the Popular Democratic Party, the local incarnation of the New Deal in Puerto Rico, the Report of the Picó Committee contemplated the redistribution of land parcels of between 1¾ and 2 *cuerda*s following the model of the Puerto Rico Reconstruction Administration (P.R.R.A.), which would entail the permanent settlement of areas which the navy had already expropriated. The P.D.P. program of land redistribution was active in the main island of Puerto Rico at this point. In Vieques, the Picó Committee recommended the resettlement of up to 700 families. This solution would not merely imply the redistribution of land from sugar cane to food crops, but also the conversion of grazing lands to small farm agriculture, which would result in the improvement of the land as a result of the labor of the resettled families. "The intensive work of these 700 resettlers, or as many of them as can be accommodated, should thus produce a net addition to the production of land outside the 8,000 acres tract. This increased production could actually provide the increased economic base for a large number of the dispossessed 825 families. A thorough technical investigation should reveal the exact number to be thus settled on this land."[19] The proposed land redistribution to small holders never took place.

Reacting to the urgency portrayed in the committee's *Report*, on May 11, 1943, the Insular Government approved Law Number 83, appropriating $50,000 in order to compensate those municipalities whose incomes had been adversely affected by the expropriations of taxable land and property

by the federal or insular governments.[20] Not surprisingly, the totality of
these appropriations ended up in Vieques, since it was the municipality
most severely affected by the expropriations. Between fiscal years 1944–
1945 and 1948–1949, the Insular Government subsidized the Municipality
of Vieques to the tune of $50,000, approximately $10,000 per year. However, this amount did not make up for the cumulative loss in revenue that
affected the municipality during these years. As a result of a steep decrease
in property valuations—from $2,472,614 in fiscal year 1941–1942 to
$970,180 in fiscal year 1948–1949—the municipality lost $108,234 when
compared to the income the municipality derived before the expropriations.
Therefore, even with the subsidies from the Insular Government, the municipality experienced a loss of $58,234 between fiscal years 1942–1943
and 1948–1949.[21] (See Table 4.2.)

Muñoz Marín followed up on the findings of the committee, writing to
Dr. Picó on December 24, 1943, inquiring about the state of the recommendations and mentioning that he wanted to be informed as soon as
possible.[22] Four days later, on December 28, Muñoz Marín received correspondence from Vicente Géigel Polanco, then secretary to the president
of the Senate, stating that he had talked with Lieutenant Kiarsten who had
informed him that "the governor received a letter from Mr. Thoron, in
which he informed that the matter was under study, to determine if the
transfer of Navy lands can be carried out by the Government through an
executive order without Congressional intervention."[23] In spite of these efforts by Muñoz Marín and the Popular Democratic Party, the redistribution
of *parcelas* in Vieques did not happen as in the rest of Puerto Rico, where,
under the banner of *Pan, Tierra y Libertad* (Bread, Land, and Liberty), the
party had won the massive support of the rural population on account of
its land-reform program. The P.D.P. lost Vieques in the 1944 general elections. Elsewhere in Puerto Rico, the party won a landslide victory in 1944,
capturing 65 percent of the vote, an absolute majority in the House of Representatives and in the Senate, and winning the races for mayors in all the
seventy-eight municipalities of the island except Vieques, Culebras, Aguas
Buenas, and San Lorenzo.[24] The residents of Vieques had sent a clear message to the P.D.P.: its efforts to help the island population were not enough.

Second Period

Construction activity ceased in July of 1943, and extreme poverty set in. In the summer of 1943, the second largest employer of Vieques, the Playa Grande sugar mill, also shut down. The period of the "fat cows" during which the base "provided more" came to a close. Unemployment blanketed the island of Vieques. During the summer of 1943 there were "demonstrations carrying black flags demanding employment and attention to the working masses of Vieques."[25] In July of 1943, after visiting Vieques, the director of the Federal Works Agency, Puerto Rico, and Virgin Islands Headquarters, wrote to Luis Muñoz Marín describing the situation:

> In my opinion, conditions are really worse over there than they were at that time [March, 1943, C. A. and J. B.]. This is occasioned primarily because the then private contract work being done for the Navy has all ceased, and nothing new has been opened to take its place. With that condition, and with the sugar cane industry being so handicapped through the purchase of lands formerly planted in cane, the outlook is indeed very dismal. . . .
>
> Of course, we could not take care of all of the unemployed, but we could put some people to work on fixing the main streets and maybe some road work and particularly malaria control.[26]

Rafael Picó, on his part, estimated in July of 1943 that "without question, the problem of unemployment which we foresaw in our report of last March is already a reality in Vieques. It is necessary to insist with the Navy to allow us to use the 13,000 *cuerda*s which it owns, and are presently idle, which could provide income to around 800 families that lost their means of subsistence with the expropriation of Central Playa Grande and its cane lands. . . . Soon a plan will be formulated to submit it to the Navy as the basis for the petition to use those lands for agricultural purposes."[27]

From the closing of the Mosquito base to the creation of the Puerto Rico Agricultural Company in April of 1945, almost two years elapsed. But in fact the effects of PRACO only began to be felt in January of 1946, when the navy finally transferred its lands to the Interior Department and this agency in turn transferred them to the government of Puerto Rico, which in turn leased the land to PRACO. This means that the period of extreme misery lasted from mid-1943 to January of 1946, when a partial recovery based on the investments of PRACO and the employment thus generated began to be felt in Vieques.

During these two and a half years, the legislature of Puerto Rico assigned funds to buffer the crisis in Vieques, but these funds were not utilized. The contrast between the diligence in the phase of decision-making and the slowness of implementation is startling. The Picó Committee filed its reports with recommendations on March 18, 1943, before the crisis was unleashed, precisely with the aim of preventing the social disaster looming on account of the coming closure of the Mosquito Base. Laws 89 and 90, which were aimed at restoring sugar production in Vieques with state assistance, were approved in March of 1944, one year after the recommendations of the Picó Commission. This is remarkable, in that the Popular Democratic Party, which was elsewhere promoting land reform and defending a program of economic diversification aimed at reducing the dependence of Puerto Rico on the sugar industry, nevertheless promoted the restoration of the sugar mill in Vieques as the best means to generate employment. But the funds assigned to these laws were never used, and it was not until the creation of PRACO that the funds assigned in laws 89 and 90 were reassigned to the new government corporation. In January of 1946 the navy yielded the lands, and it was only then that the work of PRACO began, properly speaking.

Laws 89 and 90 of March 11 of 1944 assigned $500,000 to PRIDCO and $1,500,000 to the Land Authority to purchase: (a) the machinery of the Playa Grande Sugar Mill (b) the equipment necessary to build a distillery and (c) the 8,000 *cuerda*s of the Eastern Sugar Associates that had been expropriated by the navy.[28] These efforts did not yield any results despite the fact that the government of Puerto Rico was willing to pay 375 percent more per *cuerda* than the navy had paid two years earlier. The sense of emergency was incorporated into the text of Law 89: "There is a state of emergency and therefore this law, by virtue of being of an urgent nature, will become applicable immediately after its approval."

However, PRIDCO did not purchase the machinery of Central Playa Grande nor the equipment for the distillery. Governor Tugwell resisted signing Laws 89 and 90, and it was necessary to send "a great number of telegrams and messages and other activities to get the Honorable Governor to sign that legislation." The president of PRIDCO, Teodoro Moscoso, called a meeting with a group of Viequenses where the implementation of the law was discussed. Moscoso argued that he had to proceed cautiously "due to the political situation and the risk that the enterprise might not be successful." Moscoso argued that the unfit state of Playa Grande and the war situation, which impeded the acquisition of new equipment, prevented PRIDCO from moving ahead. He suggested the possibility of acquiring a small mill such as that of the Godreau family in Guayama, who were at the time dismantling the Caribe mill. In any case, the installation of a small sugar mill would contribute to lengthening the harvest, and allow the work of cutting cane to last most of the year. Installing the sugar mill would take at least twelve months. When the Vieques delegation asked when they could start working in the cane lands so as to have cane for grinding by the time the mill was installed, Moscoso referred them to the director of the Land Authority, José Acosta Velarde. According to Pastor Ruiz, who was part of the meeting, the Vieques delegation went at once to meet with Acosta Velarde, it was only then that they discovered that first, lands would need to be purchased or leased from the federal government and that this would take time.[29] Neither Moscoso in PRIDCO nor Acosta Velarde in the Land Authority could make any investments without assurances that lands would be available.

It was not until January of 1946, that the Interior Department of the United States ceded 13,000 *cuerdas* of land previously utilized by the navy to the government of Puerto Rico, and the latter in turn leased them to the Puerto Rico Agricultural Company (PRACO). The Agricultural Company invested $1.9 million in Vieques between 1945 and the end of 1947—in cattle, purchase of private lands and buildings—but it was unable to purchase the navy lands. This means that from the beginning of the crisis in July of 1943 until January of 1946, the economy of Vieques was practically paralyzed. When the PRACO stepped in to create jobs after almost three years of massive unemployment in the island, it started its operations under cloudy skies, due to the uncertainties concerning land titles. The federal government temporarily ceded lands to the government of Puerto Rico, but it retained the title to the land, and it was understood that it could revoke any and all arrangements at any time.

Formation of PRACO

The Puerto Rico Agricultural Corporation (PRACO) was created by Law No. 31 of April 24, 1945. It was chartered to expand agrarian activities, exploit the fishing industry, and to develop facilities to sell both agricultural products and seafood in Puerto Rico. The official objective of its program was to better the economy of Puerto Rico and benefit all its inhabitants. In reality, most of the economic resources employed by the Company were devoted to Vieques.

The capitalization of the company was established in articles 8, 9, 10, and 27 of the Law. Article 8 assigned to it the remaining funds originally assigned by Law No. 89 of May 11, 1944 to PRIDCO, for the sugar mill and distillery. The remaining amount according to the Audit Report for Fiscal year 1946 was $497,118.24, that is, practically the entire amount originally assigned to PRIDCO, which Moscoso had not invested. Likewise, PRACO was assigned the remaining funds originally assigned for the Land Authority, amounting to $1,457,029. Of the $1.5 million assigned, the Land Authority had only invested $42,971 during one year, less than 3 percent of the funds.[30]

PRACO was assigned an initial capital of $12,233,954 (equivalent to about $148,397,862 in dollars of the year 2010) to fulfill its objectives. (See Table 4.3.) The mission of PRACO was defined as "doing scientific research and experimentation; establishing preferred practices of cultivation, classification, labeling, marketing, advertising, and packing of agricultural products," and "exploiting and possessing any property or commercial or industrial enterprises related to agriculture or its derivative products." The company was also "in charge exclusively of governmental authority in the economic development and administration of Vieques, Culebra, Mona, and Monito." These objectives were broader than those of the preceding laws.[31]

Strategies of the Insular Government to Generate Employment

The third period after the first expropriations in Vieques was defined by the creation of the PRACO, signaling an exceptional level of government intervention in the economy of the small island. PRACO soon became the largest landowner and the principal employer in Vieques. State initiative was replacing private initiative, given the extreme conditions of Vieques. The concept of a state-owned agricultural corporation along the lines of a New Deal agency is visible, for example, in the list of agencies to which Muñoz Marín sent the Picó Committee Report,[32] and in his correspondence with the Federal Works Agency.[33] Both companies were the product of state intervention in the context of a war. PRIDCO, for example, purchased the Puerto Rico Cement Corporation from the Puerto Rico Reconstruction Administration, and created the Puerto Rico Clay Products Corporation, the Puerto Rico Shoe and Leather Corporation, a textile company called *Telares de Puerto Rico*, the Puerto Rico Glass Corporation, which manufactured bottles for Puerto Rico's rum distilleries, and the Puerto Rico Pulp and Paper Corporation, which used the bagasse of the cane and locally recycled materials to make cardboard and paper. State ownership was a function of the needs of the war economy.[34] But by 1947, PRIDCO was privatizing its state-owned enterprises, and shifting gear to a program of industrialization aimed at attracting private U.S. investors to set up shop in Puerto Rico.[35] PRACO, on the other hand, never transitioned to a private ownership, profit-oriented mode, as its development was arrested by the reopening of the base in Vieques and a new round of expropriations in 1947–1948.

The salient recommendation of the Picó Committee, on March 18, 1943, was to request the transfer of 13,000 acres expropriated in Vieques to the Interior Department, without military restrictions. In January of 1946, the Department of the Navy eliminated all military restrictions over 12,806.7 *cuerdas* of land by transferring them to the federal Department of the Interior. All these lands had been expropriated during 1941–1942.[36] The land was transferred to the government of Puerto Rico, which in turn leased it to PRACO in January of 1946.[37]

In addition to leasing navy lands to create jobs for the population of Vieques, PRACO purchased lands from private owners. It paid fabulous prices, well above those paid by the navy during the first expropriations, and well above the assessed value of the lands for taxation purpose. This shows the urgency of PRACO's mission and its New Deal orientation. For example, in 1946 the PRACO purchased 2,500 *cuerda*s in Vieques. Of these, 722 belonged to Tomás González. They were assessed at $42,440, that is to say $59 per *cuerda*. PRACO purchased them from González at a price of $110,123, that is to say $153 per *cuerda*.[38] Similarly, the last land purchases of PRACO display its determination to solve a social problem in Vieques, something which no doubt benefited the local property owners who sold lands. In 1945, the average assessed value of a *cuerda* of land in Vieques was $58.[39] In 1947, PRACO purchased the last 1,373 *cuerda*s belonging to the Eastern Sugar Associates for a price of $386,500 or $282 per *cuerda*.[40] It paid 47 percent above the assessment carried out by the Land Authority in August 1944[41] and almost five times the average assessed value of a *cuerda* of land in Vieques. With the purchase of these lands, PRACO became the largest landowner of Vieques and the manager of 16,680 *cuerda*s—51 percent of the land of the Island. (See Table 4.4.)

Lands purchased from the Eastern Sugar Associates were not the only ones paid above assessed value. The lands shown in Table 4.5 were purchased at prices that averaged 41 percent above assessed value, so that PRACO paid $205,400 more than what the lands were "worth." The auditors asked the president of PRACO, Thomas Fennel, about the company's real estate transactions, and he justified the purchases by saying that "the going value to the Agricultural Company had to be taken into consideration" and arguing that the program of PRACO had to be implemented as soon as possible.[42] In other words, the unemployment problem in Vieques had to be solved urgently, and if this goal cost additional money, the government was willing to invest it. PRACO paid prices 41 percent above assessed value in Vieques, in contrast to other areas of Puerto Rico, where it paid 16 percent above assessed value. (See Table 4.5.)

PRACO: The Cost of Job Creation

The New Deal nature of PRACO is reflected not only in the urgency of the land purchases and the prices paid, but also in its annual losses as revealed in the auditing reports. PRACO began its operations with annual losses of $350,000 in 1946. In its last year as a public corporation (1950), it accumulated losses of $2.4 million.[43] It purchased lands above price, AND lost money, but it fulfilled the function of job creation in Vieques, which was of extreme importance to survival of the civilian population of the island. Out of the total 2,150 jobs that PRACO generated in Puerto Rico, 1,113 or 52 percent were concentrated in Vieques in 1947.[44] The cost of keeping a person working during fiscal year 1947 was $465—an amount that the government of Puerto Rico was willing to tackle.[45] (See Table 4.6.) This figure was more than double the personal income in Vieques.

The jobs created by PRACO in Vieques helped to reactivate the local economy. According to a report of the period July–October 1947, PRACO paid average salaries of $0.25/hour or $2.00/day, which was less than the $2.25 in effect during the construction of the Mosquito base, but still more than the $1.50 of the sugar economy. With an average of 868 workers, the weekly payroll of PRACO reached $8,846.73.[46] In addition to the jobs created directly, PRACO invested $1.9 million in the purchase of private lands, buildings, and cattle.[47] Certainly these investments must have had some multiplying effect in terms of job creation.

The period during which PRACO was functioning represented a relief from the conditions of 1944–1945. (See Table 4.7.) The PRACO fulfilled yet other functions that made it resemble an agency of the New Deal more than a profit-oriented enterprise. It opened a number of supermarkets that sold their goods in competition with local commerce. According to Muñoz Marín, private commerce was generating excessive profits and manipulating the prices of basic necessities. By selling articles at lower prices, PRACO forced local commerce to reduce their prices, benefiting consumers, particularly those with the lowest incomes.[48] This may have been so, but on paper, PRIDCO looked like a much more promising enterprise than PRACO. While the agricultural company registered sales of $185 per employee, its industrial counterpart towered above it at sales of $5,506 per employee.[49] (See Table 4.8.)

Whether this difference is due to insufficient time to develop the agricultural operations of PRACO to a point of profitability is an open question. Unlike PRIDCO, PRACO did not have the opportunity to transition to a private investment, profit-oriented mode. At the time the industrial company changed gears to a model of private investment of industrialization by invitation, a model which completely transformed the economy of Puerto Rico, the navy decided to reopen Roosevelt Roads and to relaunch and expand its operations in Vieques, putting an end to the activities of the state-owned agricultural company. In late 1947, the navy reclaimed the lands leased to PRACO, and in January of 1948, it began to utilize Vieques as a site for large-scale maneuvers. Additional lands were expropriated, foreclosing until the present the possibility of agrarian development in Vieques. The story of the second expropriations, and their legacy of poverty, is the object of chapter 6. What remained of PRACO after 1948 no longer had a significant impact on the economy of Vieques. The third period after the first expropriations ended, then, with a new round of expropriations by the U.S. Navy and the beginning of the bombing of the eastern target range.

The hope of the population that employment would return to Vieques by reviving the sugar industry was based on the almost total stillness of the base and of Roosevelt Roads across the Vieques sound after 1943. The effects of the expropriations were first felt in 1941, during the eviction and relocation of the civilian population. The process impacted the *residential* life of the civilians negatively, but in the meantime the *productive* life of the population actually improved, due to high demand for labor and higher wages. It was only in mid-1943 that the full impact of the expropriations was felt, because relocation to the Santa María and Monte Santo "slums" was compounded by massive unemployment. The dark period that followed lasted until 1946, when massive government intervention in the economy through the Puerto Rico Agricultural Company restored some jobs and alleviated some of the extreme poverty of 1943-1946. However, this stage in the economic trajectory of Vieques, in turn, was soon overtaken by the return of the navy, now demanding even more land than before.

CHAPTER 5

Cold War and Return of the Navy, 1947–1948

In 1947, the navy announced that it was interested in controlling more than half of the island of Vieques for amphibious training. The navy revealed its intentions of recovering 13,000 acres previously expropriated and currently under the management of Puerto Rico Agricultural Company. PRACO had a lease on this property, which was owned by the Department of the Interior. The terms of this lease stipulated that the Department of the Interior could break the lease unilaterally with little prior notification. The lease also documented that the Department of the Interior would not assume responsibility for the economic hardship that this clause, when executed, would most likely generate.[1]

At the time, PRACO was employing 1,113 people—40 percent of the available workforce on the island—in pineapple production and cattle grazing. In addition, the navy announced plans to expropriate another 4,500 acres. Therefore, the 8,000 acres currently under navy ownership, plus the 13,000 acres it planned to retake from PRACO, and the additional 4,500 acres it planned to expropriate would amount to navy ownership of 25,500 acres—77 percent of the island. The population of around 10,000 U.S. citizens would be forced to live on 23 percent of the remaining land, sharply curtailing their chances for economic prosperity.

The Navy Battles the Government of Puerto Rico

The government of Puerto Rico complained that the economy of Vieques was already in terrible shape and that further takeover of land by the navy would be disastrous to the islanders. Between Fiscal Year 1941–1942 and Fiscal Year 1948–1949, the expropriations reduced the municipality's income by 41 percent. In order to sustain municipal services, the Insular Government provided subsidies totaling $50,000 during these years. However, the municipality's income was still severely reduced, experiencing a loss of 22 percent when compared to the period prior to the expropriations.[2]

In 1946, Governor Jesús T. Piñero declared to the press that Puerto Rico had a sufficiently high population density and a problem of overpopulation. This meant that any loss of land currently used productively would be detrimental to the island as a whole. The governor was aware that the navy was carrying out a study of Vieques for use as an amphibious training site, and he discussed the issue with the secretary of the navy, John. L. Sullivan. The position of Governor Piñero was that the navy should keep the lands it was using in western Vieques but should not acquire any more land.[3] The opposition of Piñero to the navy's further acquisition of land in Vieques took place in an interesting context: the resident commissioner of Puerto Rico in Washington, Antonio Fernós Isern, was lobbying for a bill to allow Puerto Ricans to elect their own governor, and the island needed to renegotiate the sugar quotas that had regulated overproduction in the industry since 1934. Piñero was the last governor of Puerto Rico to be appointed by a U.S. president as opposed to elected by the people of Puerto Rico. He was also the only Puerto Rican ever appointed to that post by a U.S. president.[4]

On March 13, 1947, Luis Muñoz Marín, president of the Senate in Puerto Rico, wrote to Julius A. Krug, secretary of the Interior Department, concerned that the navy might revoke the lease whereby 13,000 acres previously expropriated where returned to the government of Puerto Rico. These lands where currently being used for agricultural purposes. Muñoz Marín pleaded with Krug to intervene with the navy in order to avoid these expropriations unless it was "absolutely necessary to the national security."[5]

An article published in the local newspaper *El Mundo*, November, 23, 1947, documents a meeting between vice admiral Daniel E. Barbey, Governor Jesús T. Piñero, the executive director of the Puerto Rican housing authority, César Cordero, and the coordinator for insular affairs, Elmer M. Ellsworth. The meeting produced the following results:

> The navy would recuperate the lands loaned to the Department of the Interior.
>
> The navy would expropriate 4,500 additional acres currently owned by private landowners.
>
> The Housing Authority was authorized to purchase 84 acres as soon as possible so the navy could commence operations at the beginning of 1948 with the 21,000 acres expropriated between 1941 and 1942.[6]

Between June and November, the objections of Governor Jesus T. Piñero were overcome. The navy's officials, stationed in the battleship *Iowa,* summoned the governor to a meeting on July 19, along with other state governors.[7] The navy officers did not come to San Juan for the meeting. Instead, the governor was required to board the ship to discuss the expropriations with the navy representatives, a clear symbolic representation of the power structure in these negotiations.

In the course of the negotiations, the public statements of the navy reflected their perception of the place of Puerto Rico in the federal polity: Piñero was asked what would be Puerto Rico's position on the sugar quotas, an issue of major concern to the island's main export industry. Evidently, he was being reminded that the U.S. Congress had ultimate economic power over the island's economic fate. Governor Piñero, on his part, pointed out to the press that Puerto Ricans were in fact barred from joining the U.S. navy, because there was no recruiting station in the island, but that he was hopeful that the navy would soon open its doors to Puerto Ricans.[8] Evidently, Piñero was pointing to the colonial paradox of the navy wanting the land of a people it was not eager to admit into its own ranks. The navy's exclusion of Puerto Ricans during Second World War, according to Governor Tugwell, who preceded Piñero, "was understood for exactly what it was, and was deeply resented. Sailors from the States were now all over Puerto Rico, and each of them was a reminder that Puerto Ricans were considered to be an inferior people." Tugwell reports discussing this issue with President Roosevelt, who replied that "he had been having trouble with the navy over Negroes—to have them rated as anything but mess boys—in which, so far, the Admirals had refused to obey."[9] The colonial context of the late 1940s, it must be remembered, included racial segregation in the United States itself.

Navy Vice Admiral Daniel E. Barbey expressed concern that the opposition of the local government to the proposed training zone could derail the development of an immense naval and military training zone in Vieques, which was projected to allow maneuvers by 25,000 troops. Roosevelt Roads, the naval base in Ensenada Honda in eastern Puerto Rico, which represented an investment of $90,000,000, would reopen. Barbey mentioned that the navy's preference was Vieques, but Guantánamo, Cuba, and an unspecified location in Trinidad were also under consideration. The government of Puerto Rico, on the other hand, expressed disapproval of the idea of relocating entire families from the proposed training zone and having to return land that was owned by the U.S. federal government but currently used by the Puerto Rico Agricultural Company .

The Navy and PRACO: Conflicting Visions

In 1947, when the navy announced that it wanted to use Vieques for training exercises, the management of PRACO naturally opposed having to return the lands to the navy, as this would entail the liquidation of their projects. While no sugar *centrales* remained in Vieques, there were still in the island a considerable number of heads of cattle in the hands of local ranchers. The proposal to revoke the lease between the U.S. Interior Department and PRACO immediately opened a phase of dispute between the cattle ranchers and PRACO, on the one hand, and between PRACO and the navy, on the other. Beginning in mid-1947, the battle of the second expropriations began, with the navy arguing that it would only reopen Roosevelt Roads if it had Vieques, while the government of Puerto Rico opposed the acquisition of further lands in Vieques but expressed optimism at the idea of re-opening Roosevelt Roads, which would presumably create employment. Vice Admiral Barbey declared to the press that the reopening of Roosevelt Roads was contingent on the utilization of Vieques as a training ground. Vieques was sought to carry out training exercises similar to those practiced in the islands off the coast of California.[10] Thus, multiple interests were conjured to battle by the navy's initiation of the second expropriations. The local Puerto Rican government, under the de-facto leadership of Luis Muñoz Marín, was struggling to gain the right for Puerto Ricans to elect their own governor. At the same time, the insular authorities had to rene-gotiate the sugar quota, which determined the amount of sugar that could enter the United States free of duty.[11] Therefore, it was hard-pressed to op-pose the federal authorities. PRACO faced the opposition of the cattle ranchers, as they were not content with their existing contract with PRACO. The navy faced both the opposition of the Insular Government and the po-tential opposition of a social movement of the displaced ranchers of Vieques. All of these conflicts were unfolding under the rapidly changing political climate in Washington, which instead of continuing the expected policy of disarmament, was beginning to rearm for the Cold War.

Vice Admiral Barbey laid out the new Cold War policies of the United States, as seen by his own branch of the armed forces at the weekly luncheon meeting of the Lions Club held at the Condado Hotel in San Juan, October, 15, 1947. There was "dangerous communist infiltration" in the world. The Atlantic was a possible future theater of conflict. The resurgence of the Communist International, which Barbey erroneously identified as the "Fourth International," was hindering the progress of the Marshall Plan in Europe. The Russians had plans to extend their rule to Western Europe, Africa, and eventually the Western Hemisphere. This delicate situation called for preparation for a "possible attack from overseas." Barbey expressed his own disagreement with those who thought there would be no danger of invasion in the next seven to ten years, adding that this danger required readiness in the Caribbean. He assured his audience that he had received telegrams from many citizens who were supposedly displaced by the navy in Vieques, and that these citizens were encouraged by the economic prospects of having a navy base there. The navy would benefit Vieques economically, but even if both PRACO and the economy of Vieques were affected, "above all else there is the issue of our security in the face of the serious situation in which we are living."[12]

Barbey was well aware that as a result of the 1941–1942 expropriations, 1,350 Viequenses lost their jobs—over 40 percent of the available work force. In addition, the 30 percent of the population that lost their houses and their belongings were not compensated for any losses.[13] A report by the Picó Committee had documented the economically disastrous consequences of the first expropriations. These findings were public, and they had prompted the Insular Government to create PRACO in 1945 to alleviate poverty in Vieques. The admiral therefore appealed to issues of national security and to the fact that the navy invested $15,000,000 yearly on the island.[14] It was clear that the navy's proposed plans for Vieques were the product of larger strategic considerations against which local concerns carried only minor weight. Still, the citizens of Vieques attempted to assert their rights.

Viequenses Get Involved

Mayor Antonio Dávila of Vieques favored the construction of a base. According to him, 99 percent of the population of Vieques favored the installation of the naval base as soon as possible.[15] He challenged a group of local citizens who opposed it, Asociación de Hijos de Vieques, to a public debate on the matter. Germán Rieckehoff, a local landowner, editor of *El Eco de Vieques*, and the president of the Asociación de Hijos de Vieques, called a public meeting in the town plaza and debated the mayor on the issue of the military base. Avila complained that in the previous four years, sugar-mill employment had disappeared, and he described the inhabitants of Vieques in a "pre-agonic state wandering the streets with black flags looking for employment."[16] The base would benefit the island economically. Rieckehoff of the Asociación de Hijos de Vieques claimed he did not necessarily oppose the base, but that Viequenses had to get clear and concrete answers from the navy about just how the base was supposed to benefit the local economy. If indeed the base was going to benefit the economy of the island, they should support it. If there were no clear signs of economic benefits to the population, Viequenses should oppose it. The town assembly voted to send a delegation to meet with Vice Admiral Barbey to inquire into the economic consequences of the base.[17]

Late that evening, after the public debate between the mayor and the Asociación de Hijos de Vieques, representatives of the Puerto Rican Communist Party took the stand and spoke of the political consequences of the despoliation of Vieques. They were followed by a student delegation from the University of Puerto Rico who took the stand after the Communist Party.[18] In the press, there were some local expressions in favor of the construction of the base, all based on the current economic plight of Vieques and the assumption that the base was going to remedy that situation.[19]

The Expropriation Expenses: Who Should Pay?

At the time that Viequenses were publicly assembling their delegation to meet Vice Admiral Barbey, the matter of the construction of the base had already been settled. As of October 1, for example, the press reported that the talks between Governor Piñero and the Secretary of the Navy John L.

Sullivan were focused on how to transfer the population that lived in the area to be repossessed by the navy. According to the governor, only a third of Vieques would remain open to civilians, and he had questions about how "eleven or twelve thousand inhabitants may end up sandwiched in that narrow strip." The governor wanted the navy to pay for the expenses of relocating the civilians, but the navy insisted that the government of Puerto Rico pay for the relocations. At the time the press reported that "the transfer to the Navy is already settled and the only point under discussion is how to bring it about, especially the issue of the relocation of the families which have to be resettled in another place in Vieques or in Puerto Rico." At issue were the transfer of 150 families out of the area to be occupied by the navy and the transfer of jurisdiction over that area from the Department of the Interior to the navy. The return of lands to the navy would entail the cancellation of the leases to PRACO, which was using the land for cattle ranching and pineapple production. The navy wanted to consolidate its holdings in the eastern zone of Vieques through expropriation of additional lands. This additional purchase was going to affect only six landowners who, according to the press, had already come to terms with the navy's offer of compensation.[20]

The issue of who would pay for the costs of relocation of the families lingered. The navy insisted that the Insular Government should bear the costs. Governor Piñero objected to the government of Puerto Rico paying all the cost of relocation and further argued that the navy should set up a compensation fund to pay the municipal government of Vieques for the loss in property-tax revenue when economic activity ceased after the expropriation of lands. The closure of the sugar mills had reduced the tax revenue of the municipality by 39 percent. Now the forthcoming reductions in cattle ranching and pineapple production threatened to further diminish municipal tax receipts. The government of Puerto Rico had to step in to subsidize the municipality of Vieques in order to keep basic municipal services in operation.[21] The navy, however, flatly rejected Piñero's proposal for compensation of loss of tax revenues.[22]

However, the navy did provide wood and construction materials to build houses for seventy-five families displaced by the expropriations.[23] The navy insisted on having all families cleared from the land by January 5, 1948, to proceed with maneuvers projected for that month. This entailed the acquisition of 13,000 acres of land from the Interior Department and the expropriation of 4,500 acres under private ownership as soon as possible. The government of Puerto Rico acquired land near Isabel Segunda to resettle the seventy-five families. The roads were to be built by the government of Puerto Rico with crushed stone provided by the navy. After January 5, 1948, according to the navy, remaining in the cleared zone would become dangerous due to aerial bombardments and artillery fire.[24]

Additional Expropriations

On November 21, the navy filed a petition in the Federal Court in San Juan requesting possession under lease of an area encompassing 4,370.04 acres of land. The owners would remain proprietors of the lands forcibly leased to the navy, while the navy retained the right to sue for full ownership at a later date. The owners of the land were Alberto Biascochea, Ignacio López Colón, Enrique Cayere, Esteban Díaz, Jovito González, Tomás Ramírez, and the government of Puerto Rico.[25] The petition asked the court to determine the amount of compensation to be paid to the property owners of Vieques.[26] Soon after the filing of this petition, Vice Admiral Daniel E. Barbey announced that other countries would be invited to the military maneuvers in Vieques. During the visit of a Colombian ship to the harbor in San Juan, Vice Admiral Barbey took the opportunity to pose for the press with the commander of the ship and to announce that joint maneuvers would take place in Vieques with friendly Latin American nations.[27]

The Cattle Ranchers

The U.S. Federal Court in San Juan soon granted the petition of the navy and the PRACO was required to return to the navy 13,000 acres of land that it had been using mostly for raising cattle.[28] The lease between the Department of the Interior and PRACO clearly stipulated that the former had the right to terminate the lease without liability. Thus, the fact that the navy had to go to court to seek an order of eviction indicates that PRACO and the ranchers who grazed their cattle on that land were opposed to the economic displacement that would ensue from the transfer of the land to the navy. A number of ranchers in Vieques to whom PRACO had leased lands to graze their cattle petitioned the Federal Court in San Juan to grant them an additional forty-five days to remove their cattle from the area. The cattle ranchers, in addition, organized an association, negotiated with PRACO and the Puerto Rican government, and with the navy.

The principal effect of the first round of expropriation in Vieques in 1941–1942 was the dismantling of the last remaining sugar mill in the island, Central Playa Grande, and therefore the steep decline of cane agriculture, the principal economic activity of Vieques from the 1830s until the Second World War. Some of the resources previously invested in the sugar industry went into cattle ranching, an activity that continued throughout the war. The number of cattle ranchers in Vieques increased between 1940 and 1945, and cattle ownership became somewhat more common. This is probably a reflection of a transition from cane growing into cattle grazing on the part of some of the *colonos*[29] of Vieques who were forced to seek alternate ways of making a living after the closure of the sugar mills. In 1940, the largest owner of cattle in Vieques was the Eastern Sugar Associates, controlling 93 percent of the total livestock. In 1945, it was Juan Angel Tio, with 74 percent. Cattle ownership appears a bit more dispersed in 1950. Official figures do not reflect the many smaller owners who grazed their cattle in Vieques.[30] (See Table 5.1 and Figure 5.1.) When they constituted themselves into an association to negotiate with PRACO, the Puerto Rican government, the navy, and the Federal Court in San Juan, the cattle ranchers, including smaller ones, numbered 175. Although ownership of cattle was concentrated in a few hands, the number of families affected by the decision to establish a base in Vieques in 1947 was not merely a handful of large owners. From the economic point of view, the expropriations of 1947 affected principally PRACO, which had $1,900,000 invested in Vieques and employed 40 percent of the workforce, and the cattle ranching interests, who argued their assets were worth $300,000.[31] In the struggle against the navy and PRACO, the large owners were able to rally the smaller cattle ranchers to their side in their negotiations with the authorities as the area of available land in Vieques shrunk and as grass and water resources became insufficient to support the cattle population of the island.

Paul Edwards—representing Thomas Fennell as general manager of PRACO—wrote to James P. Davis, director of the Division of Territories and Possessions of the Federal Department of the Interior in December of

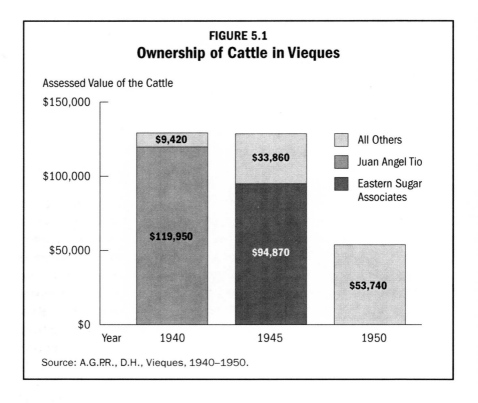

FIGURE 5.1
Ownership of Cattle in Vieques

Assessed Value of the Cattle

Source: A.G.P.R., D.H., Vieques, 1940–1950.

1947 complaining of the difficulties that PRACO was having with the navy in trying to obtain land for the 2,500 heads of cattle currently under its care. He also notified Davis that PRACO was preparing the necessary documentation in order to request a court injunction against the navy.[32] The objective of the injunction was to allow PRACO enough time to dispose of the cattle in an orderly fashion.

The ranchers, deciding that PRACO's actions were insufficient and had, so far, showed no signs of success, hired Attorney Benicio Sánchez Castaño to represent them. A group of ranchers, who owned more than 300 head of cattle each,[33] argued that they needed additional time to dispose of their cattle, lest they suffer irreparable damage because there was nowhere else in Vieques to graze it. The navy asked the court to deny the petition and brought Colonel J. P. Brown to testify that its first contingent of men for maneuvers was scheduled to arrive in Vieques on January 5, 1948. Brown expected that this first contingent of men would soon be joined by others until the navy had the requisite number to carry out the maneuvers. Despite this testimony by the navy, the court granted the ranchers until January 30, 1948, to move their cattle. As to the private landowners, the expropriation for use by the navy was effective until June 30, 1948, with the stipulation that if the U.S. government did not sue for full ownership by that date, the land would return to its current owners.[34]

PRACO Enrages the Cattle Ranchers

The shrinkage of the area previously available to PRACO brought to the fore the issue of what to do with all the heads of cattle grazing in the lands of Vieques. The prevailing agreement was one in which PRACO subleased land from the Interior Department and in turn allowed ranchers to graze the cattle in their land for a fee. Typically, the PRACO was entitled to one half of the increase in weight of the cattle and to one half of all the calves born in its lands. PRACO thus proposed a massive weighing session at its scales in Campaña, where all accounts with the ranchers would be settled. PRACO had plans to take its share of the cattle to the main island of Puerto Rico by barge, but the cattlemen of Vieques, especially the smaller ones, could not so easily dispose of their own cattle.

The month of January 1948 was supposed to mark the initiation of artillery and naval fire upon Vieques. Instead, in the capital city of San Juan the cattle ranchers of Vieques fired their initial salvos in a battle fought in the court of public opinion. The Asociación de Ganaderos Menores de Vieques, representing the cattle ranchers, took their case to the press and entered into direct negotiations with the navy. On January 6, the day after the initial deadline requested by the navy for takeover of the eastern lands of Vieques, the PRACO announced that it would liquidate its accounts with the cattle ranchers. This meant that the company would weigh the cattle and hand over to the ranchers their part, while keeping its share of the cattle, according to the contracts signed with the individual ranchers. The company declared to the press that it had sufficient lands for its own cattle, numbering 1,400, but was not in a position to increase its herd. The return of the land to the navy, of which 13,000 acres were used for grazing, had forced PRACO to cancel plans for a slaughterhouse in Vieques and to cancel plans for dairy production in the island. The company claimed that the situation of the small owners of cattle was "more difficult," since they were grazing their herds in an area of 3,000 acres, which the navy had temporarily granted, but that extension of land could only support at most half the number presently grazing. The intentions of the PRACO were to take care of its own problems, supporting its own cattle in its remaining land, or even taking some to Puerto Rico by barge, while forcing a liquidation of the cattle of the private ranchers.[35] PRACO declared its intentions publicly to the press after a three-hour meeting of its board of directors. The meeting was presided over by the governor of Puerto Rico.

Meanwhile, the cattle ranchers of Vieques were meeting directly with the navy. Juan Gómez, representing a group of 193 small ranchers who claimed to own a total of 2,700 heads of cattle valued at $300,000, met with Vice Admiral Barbey. The delegation was composed of the mayor of Vieques, Antonio Avila; Dr. Leoncio T. Davis[36] as spokesperson for the ranchers; and Juan a Gómez, Pedro Félix, Rafael Sáez, and Federico Aguiar, private ranchers. Present at the meeting were Elmer Ellsworth[37] representing Governor Piñero, and Dr. Carlos E. Muñiz representing PRACO. The ranchers claimed that PRACO knew about the forthcoming eviction by the navy since September but had notified the ranchers only on December 31, not giving them sufficient time to make alternative plans. Davis argued that the grazing rights were granted by the navy to PRACO "to help in the rehabilitation of Vieques and not to make excessive profits at our expense." The ranchers opposed PRACO's claim that they owed the company $70,000. Barbey, sensing the deep division between the government of Puerto Rico and PRACO on the one hand, and the ranchers on the other, assured the cattle ranchers that he would solve their problem by allowing them to graze their cattle on navy land. The ranchers left the meeting very pleased with the vice admiral.[38] They now shifted their aims at PRACO, determined to make the company pay for all the losses caused by the navy.

The next day PRACO announced that it did not have sufficient lands for its own cattle in Vieques. It would therefore liquidate its accounts with the ranchers "within 48 hours," take its 50 percent in cattle, not in money, and transport it to Puerto Rico.[39] The company was trying to be fiscally responsible, arguing that its capital was owned by "the people of Puerto Rico" and that it could not release the cattle ranchers from their contracts, which stipulated liquidation at 50 percent. To do so would entail disposing of the resources of the people of Puerto Rico irresponsibly, in favor of private interests.

On January 10, the PRACO announced that instead of taking its 50 percent in cattle, it would weight all the cattle in the presence of the individual ranchers and debit the ranchers with the price of the increase in weight belonging to the company. Thus, it would settle in cash with ranchers.[40] This probably reflected an attempt by PRACO to avoid the cost of transportation of the cattle to the main island of Puerto Rico. Dr. Carlos Muñiz would represent PRACO in the weighing process, which would take place "within a week." It appeared that PRACO could not carry out the weighing sessions as it had announced: the cattlemen of Vieques did not show up to weigh the cattle and liquidate.

As the negotiations between PRACO and the cattlemen became more difficult due to the common constriction of their resources by the navy, both parties moved further in the direction of making the other pay for the bulk of the losses. The cattlemen did not want to liquidate under the terms of their contracts with PRACO, as this would probably flood the local market and depress the price. PRACO, on the other hand, needed to hold the cattlemen to the terms of the leases, to avoid massive losses in the operation. The navy, which had caused this war of desperation between a Puerto Rican public corporation and the cattle ranchers of Vieques, calculated that its best interest would be served by siding with the ranchers against the government of Puerto Rico. After all, the Puerto Rican governor had opposed the acquisition of land by the navy in Vieques. Thus, Vice Admiral Barbey came forth with a magnanimous offer to the cattlemen.

In further negotiations with the cattle ranchers, who apparently had nowhere to take their cattle, the navy agreed to let them use lands in the western part of Vieques. It transferred as a loan 150 rolls of barbed wire to build fences and authorized the ranchers to cut down wood for posts to fence in their cattle in the western zone. The agreement signed by the ranchers and the navy stipulated that if the fences were not finished by January 15, the navy would allow the ranchers to bring their cattle to a farm of approximately 2,000 acres in Santa María, on the periphery of Isabel Segunda. The cattlemen, on their part, agreed to hand over the eastern lands before

January 30, not to build any houses on navy land, and, due to the proximity of their cattle to the navy's ammunition depot in the western zone, they further agreed that the cattle ranchers and their workmen were to be bound by the rules of the navy concerning transit in navy lands.[41] Whereas PRACO operated under the profit principle and charged the cattlemen a rent of 50 percent by weight to graze its cattle, the magnanimous navy was offering to let the ranchers graze their cattle on its land for free. Of course, this was a unilateral agreement in which the navy had no obligations whatsoever to continue offering land services to the ranchers, but, faced with economic ruin, how could the cattlemen of Vieques contemplate refusing the terms offered by Barbey? PRACO, a public corporation of the government of Puerto Rico, was trying to collect $70,000 or half the cattle from them. The United States Navy was offering free grazing lands for their cattle, and the offer came adorned with free barbed wire and permission to cut posts. The choice was not very hard for the cattlemen to make.

Faced with the looming losses, the cattlemen decided to break their contract with the PRACO and refused to liquidate the cattle according to the terms agreed in their contracts. The Asociación de Ganaderos Menores argued that PRACO was no longer able to provide them land for grazing cattle, and that this represented a breach of contract that freed the cattle ranchers from the other terms of the agreement. The cattlemen thus refused to show up to weigh the cattle and instead hired a lawyer to represent them and elected a leading body to their association: Dr. Leoncio T. Davis as president; Manuel Portela Rivera as vice president; Juan A. Gómez as secretary; and Justino López as treasurer. The representatives of PRACO argued, to the contrary, that the leases to the ranchers clearly stipulated that in case of cancellation of the lease to PRACO, the company would not be liable to the ranchers for any losses.[42] The contract was eventually broken, causing losses of more than $70,000 to PRACO—an amount that was never recovered.[43]

* * *

Reality seemed to turn upside down. The navy, which was the ultimate cause of the constriction of the cattle industry of Vieques, now appeared as the magnanimous savior of the cattle ranchers. The government of Puerto

Rico, which had opposed the expropriations, and which footed the bill for the relocations, now appeared as the villain of the story. The maneuvers were delayed a bit for the navy but overall, Vice Admiral Barbey had achieved considerable sympathies in the local community. In August of 1948, during a visit by Governor Piñero to Vieques in which he met with officers from PRACO, an assembly of two hundred ranchers expressed their deep opposition to PRACO reacquiring lands in Vieques.[44]

In February of 1948, for the first maneuvers in Vieques territory, the navy brought to the island the 65th Infantry of the U.S. Army, a Puerto Rican force of seasoned veterans from World War II, to participate in joint maneuvers with the Marines. The local press then reported on the excellent work done by the 65th Infantry during the maneuvers. The first reports of the press highlighted a problem that would henceforth plague Vieques residents for decades: the proximity of the explosions and their effect on the civilian population. An immense explosion in Vieques during the maneuvers caused a stir in the town of Isabel Segunda: "The tremendous explosion caused such a great shudder in the surrounding zone, and the boom was so strong that many people in the town of Isabel Segunda thought an atomic bomb had been detonated."[45]

Having defused the alliance between those affected by the expropriations and the Insular Government, and after three years of maneuvers in which up to 80,000 men had come to Vieques at one time, by 1951 the navy was in a position to drop its arrangement with the cattle ranchers. It discontinued the arrangement through which the navy informally allowed the ranchers to graze their lands for free in navy territory and leased the land to a Puerto Rican public corporation, the PRACO.[46]

The arrangement through which the navy allowed the small cattle ranchers of Vieques to graze their cattle on its land suited the navy at the moment of the expropriations. The ranchers extricated themselves from payment to PRACO and broke their contracts, and they were able to do so thanks to the navy's offer of free land for grazing. This arrangement came to an end in 1951 when the navy subleased again to the PRACO the grazing lands of western Vieques. Leoncio T. Davis, an ex-mayor and the president of the Asociación de Pequeños Ganaderos de Vieques, protested that the lease was offered to PRACO in violation of procedural requirement that the navy rent the lands after open bidding.

But in 1951, with Vieques secure and after three years of maneuvers, the navy did not feel pressure to defuse a social movement of small ranchers. The navy answered through a spokesperson that PRACO had offered a higher sum than the Asociación de Pequeños Ganaderos de Vieques[47] and that, in any case, the navy "was not in the business of grazing cattle" and furthermore that it had determined that "temporary agreements with a private association had to be renegotiated with a government agency."[48]

The navy paid yearly leases to the private owners of the 4,170 acres of land in the east, and it finally bought the land in 1953 for $500,000, or $120 per acre, after litigation.[49] The small cattle ranchers were another matter. They continued to protest the leasing of navy land to PRACO, which was dissolved and transferred its assets to the Land Authority of Puerto Rico.

During the second expropriations, the navy was heavy handed with the Insular Government, threatening to use its lobbying power in Washington against insular interests, especially on the issue of the sugar quota for Puerto Rico. This became one of the sources of colonial resentment against the navy. Additionally, the presence of large numbers of continentals, both civilian and military, during World War II in Vieques introduced new colonial structures. Unlike land concentration, the unequal distribution of wealth, or the *agrego* system, these structures were not part of the Spanish colonial legacy. The new colonial structures, as we shall see in the next chapter, were fully made in the United States of America.

CHAPTER 6

Colonial Segregation

In 1948, Jesús T. Piñero, governor of Puerto Rico, complained to the local press of the island that the navy wanted to take more land from Puerto Ricans for further military build-up, but that it did not care to recruit Puerto Ricans into its ranks and had failed to set up a recruiting station in Puerto Rico during World War II. The complaints of the governor signal one of the most intractable issues in the relations between the navy and the Puerto Ricans: racism. Racial segregation was part and parcel of military culture during World War II. The armed forces of the United States only began to desegregate after Truman's Committee on Civil Rights recommended in 1947 legislation and administrative action "to end immediately all discrimination and segregation based on race, color, creed, or national origin in . . . all branches of the Armed Services." And yet, it took decades for desegregation to advance in the armed forces. The navy was probably the most reluctant of all the branches of the military to integrate. During World War II, despite Roosevelt's insistence that it recruit African Americans, it was understood that this would be for kitchen jobs and the like, as it was unthinkable to impose on U.S. white soldiers the burden of cohabitation with blacks in ships or submarines. By mid–1944, over 38,000 blacks were serving as mess stewards, cooks, and bakers. These jobs remained in the eyes of every African American "a symbol of his second-class citizenship in the naval establishment."[1]

In the aftermath of World War II, as desegregation advanced, the navy's percentage of black men and women actually dropped from 4.7 in 1949 to 3.6 in 1954 (compared to 12.4 percent and 13.7 percent for the army, respectively on those dates). While the percentage of blacks in the army approximated closely their percentage in the national population, that was not the case for the navy. Segregation in the navy was not only more entrenched than in the other branches of the armed services, but its dissolution advanced at slower speed and with greater reluctance on the part of the leaders of that service. (See Table 6.1.)

The consequence of U.S. racial segregation for the interaction of the

navy with Puerto Ricans is hard to underestimate. Yet it is also hard to measure as the numbers of Puerto Ricans in that branch of the services was very,
very limited, despite some notable exceptions. The navy was only the most
recalcitrant of all the services in terms of segregation and its persistence,
but it was not alone. Racism and segregation not only were part and parcel
of the functioning of all the branches of the armed forces, they also affected
civilian life, especially for the continentals and Puerto Ricans working on
U.S. military construction projects.

The construction records for the Caribbean projects of the navy listed the
number of workers hired and specified different nationalities, distinguishing
for example U.S. citizens from aliens from the British West Indies. Additionally, the typology used by the state authorities drew distinctions between
different kinds of U.S. citizens, distinguishing "continentals" from Puerto
Ricans and U.S. Virgin Islanders. Thus, for example, 220 continentals and
7,580 Puerto Ricans worked in construction in the San Juan area. In Ensenada Honda, the reports distinguish the 9,365 Puerto Ricans working there
from the 625 continentals. In St. Thomas, the report lists four kinds of workers: (1) 950 Virgin Islanders, that is, 900 locals and 50 workers from St.
Croix; (2) 200 Puerto Ricans; (3) 1,000 "Aliens (Tortolans, Anguilians,
etc.)"; and 50 "continentals."[2] By itself, the fact that the state drew distinctions between different kinds of U.S. citizens was not necessarily problem-
atic. These distinctions were useful in calculating the impact of a project on
local employment, for example. But this was not their primary purpose. The
typology differentiating different kinds of U.S. citizens also reflected unequal treatment by race or ethnicity, especially in housing and pay scales.

Housing for workers on the navy project included separate quarters for
Puerto Rican and continental workers. Some of the housing for continental
civilians and officers was designed for families. In the case of Puerto Ricans,
no provision was made for families, only for single male workers. In Ensenada Honda, for example, the housing for Puerto Ricans was designed to
house 208 men per barrack, whereas facilities for continentals were designed to house 42 persons per barrack. The Puerto Rican workmen's camp
had four 208-man barracks and a cafeteria-style mess hall with a total volume of 333,000 cubic feet. The continental camp consisted of ten 42–man
barracks, four 12–man barracks, six Type-A houses of two bedrooms, 120
Type-B houses of two bedrooms, with a mess hall, recreation building, and

laundry totaling of 2,412,000 cubic feet of space. Thus, the 972 continentals, assuming the camp were full, would enjoy dining and recreational facilities designed to provide 2,481 cubic feet of space per person, whereas the facilities for Puerto Ricans provided 400 cubic feet of space per person, or about a sixth as much as for continentals.[3]

The Puerto Rican mess hall cooked a noon meal for several thousand men in the field and sold it for 25 cents to workers on the job. This hot meal resulted in a definite increase in production among an otherwise undernourished group of workmen. This meal must have represented a further incentive for local men to work on the navy projects, since food was scarce and employment was otherwise non-existent. This facility actually "resulted in a small profit to the navy."[4]

Across the sound from Ensenada Honda, in the island of Vieques, the continental camp consisted of eight 42–man barracks, three 12–man barracks, one 96–man barrack and mess hall for the marines. For families there were six Type–A houses of two bedrooms, twenty Type–B houses of two bedrooms, forty Type–C houses of one bedroom, one 336-man mess hall, and one recreation building. The combined volume of all buildings was 1,483,600 cubic feet. The 652 continentals that the complex was designed to house would enjoy, at full capacity, 2,275 cubic feet of space per continental. The Puerto Rican camp consisted of four 96–man barracks, a mess hall and a recreation building with a combined volume of 300,700 cubic feet. There was no housing for families. The 783 cubic feet of space per person provided for the Puerto Ricans was about a third of the space provided per continental.[5] The fact that dining and recreational facilities were separate means that they were designed not to encourage, but rather to impede socialization between continentals and Puerto Ricans.

Wages were disparate for continentals and Puerto Ricans. For example, a report on the labor situation in military construction projects in Puerto Rico and Vieques recognized that "laborers at 20¢ and carpenters at 50¢ produced an amount of work equal or greater in dollar value to that obtained from similar trades in Eastern States." Puerto Rican electricians, plumbers and truck drivers struck for higher wages. Laborers struck in February 1942 and obtained a raise from 16.5 to 20 cents per hour, "which was the rate paid by the U.S.E.D."[6] Both skilled and unskilled workers sought parity with U.S. wages.

The effects of the racial culture of the armed forces on its interactions with Puerto Ricans were also felt as the military presence of continental troops in the island increased during the course of World War II. As the contact between U.S. military personnel and civilians in Puerto Rico increased, so did the number of violent incidents, leaving behind a residue of hostility on the part of the population of this Caribbean Island. Like all islands of the Caribbean, Puerto Rico has a racially mixed population. The boundaries between white and black were configured differently, as the island possessed since Spanish times a large, racially mixed intermediate population in which color discrimination functioned in a sort of continuum without clear demarcations between white, brown, and black. This is not to say that the island did not have its own racist history and culture. The fact that this racist culture was configured differently from the U.S. standard, and the fact that legal segregation did not exist, nor had the black population been disenfranchised from the vote, created a clash of racial systems, and generated quite a bit of hostility between locals and continentals.

There were clashes between the military personnel stationed in Puerto Rico and civilians during the initial stages of the Second World War. The draft as it was carried out in the island was highly racialized. Puerto Rican troops were looked upon by their commanding officers as either unfit for service, or as exemplary soldiers that should be treated equally, depending on the commanding officers. Once they were deployed, initial perceptions changed. The U.S. armed forces sanitized versions of the conflicts between continental officers and local recruits. Puerto Ricans were not treated by the armed forces as their counterparts in the continental United States. We show that the rejection rates among Puerto Ricans were higher than those of the continental Americans, and higher than the rejection rate of African Americans. We also show, however, that once the Puerto Ricans were allowed to serve, their performance was consistently praised by their commanding officers in all theaters of the war.

U.S. Military and Civilians Clash in San Juan

In his 1919 letter to the chief of naval operations, Virgil Baker, lieutenant-commander of the District Communication Center in Puerto Rico, stated that even though the United States had yet to fix the location of the naval base whose area of operation would be the West Indies and the Caribbean Sea, the only area under the U.S. control that met all requirements was the western part of the Vieques Sound. Fortunately, according to Baker, the "white native labor of Porto Rico is loyal, much of it is skilled and intelligent, and much more of it is capable of being developed, under proper instruction and training, and under better living and social conditions, into skilled mechanics and all other skilled trades necessary to a naval base." Regarding Samaná Bay in the neighboring Dominican Republic, Baker stated that "the only labor available is of the most ignorant negro type which is not skilled or trained nor it is capable of being trained . . . the surrounding population is unfriendly and will probably remain so for a long time to come."[7] These early racist comments by a U.S. officers show that perceptions of the ability of the local population were influenced by the racist cognitive map that the continentals imported from the United States. Baker's comments were made two decades before the naval build-up of Puerto Rico, but reflect the navy's racial and racist stance in 1919. The navy was still a racially segregated institution by the time it established itself in Vieques. The respective racial compositions of the Caribbean Islands formerly under Spain's dominion (Cuba, Dominican Republic, Puerto Rico) were similar. Baker's comments about Negro Dominicans would certainly apply to black Puerto Ricans. Contact between the racially segregated, English-speaking armed forces and a local population with significant portions of black and brown Spanish-speakers generated racial conflict.

The American military bases represented a major source of employment, precisely at a time when the German submarines were strangling the economy of Puerto Rico and other Caribbean Islands. For example, at the base that was being built in St. Lucia, 1,000 workers were employed. In St. Thomas, 1,170 people worked in building a foundation for submarines, a hospital, accommodation facilities, hangars for seaplanes and communication centers. In Antigua, 418 workers were employed, while the Roosevelt Roads Base in Ceiba, Puerto Rico, employed up to 3,474 workers. Vieques, whose works included the construction of temporary camps, cafeterias, a hospital, and a railroad from Punta Arenas to the breakwater and quarry, also employed up to 2,050 workers.[8]

The presence of the military personnel that assisted in the construction phases and later lived on the base led to frequent personal encounters between the civil population and the armed forces. This was particularly felt by end of 1940 as the construction of the naval base at Isla Grande headed toward completion and the base became operational. On December 18, 1940, an incident took place at the dry dock under construction involving a Puerto Rican worker and a navy sentry. The Puerto Rican was employed as a night watchman on the property. The sentry, who had just come on duty, asked the Puerto Rican worker for his identification badge. The worker tried to explain to the sentry that he had left his badge in his coat a short distance away. However, not understanding Spanish, the sentry grappled with the worker in order to take away his machete. The Puerto Rican resisted, and a tussle ensued. The sentry then struck the Puerto Rican several times with his club and afterward drew his revolver. It was only due to the intervention of bystanders that this incident did not continue to escalate. The Tenth Naval District issued a statement to the press indicating that the incident was "very unfortunate." The reports published in the local press, which gave prominent coverage to this incident, were more critical of the incident.

The following day, another incident occurred at the naval base that produced a great deal of resentment and unanimous editorial condemnation from the two leading local newspapers, *El Mundo* and *El Imparcial*. According to the navy's version, at about 6:45 in the morning, Marine B.L. Daus of the Marine Corps was directing traffic on the road in front of the administration building of the Arundel Corporation and the office of the officer in charge of the construction of the base. A car driven by the brothers Salomón and Gaspar Vázquez, electricians working for the Arundel Corporation, approached the location and objected to the traffic directions given by Marine Daus.

The naval report states that both brothers then got out of the car, seized the club from the hands of Daus, and struck him in the head. This caused a severe wound that bled profusely. As Daus attempted to draw his pistol, the other brother grabbed it from him. Daus latter stated that he did not wish to fire as there were a considerable number of spectators in the area. The brothers Vázquez were then arrested by a squad of marines with the assistance of some of the spectators and were placed under custody until formal charges were brought against them in the Federal Court in Old San

Juan. The story given by the Vázquez brothers to the local press varies considerably from this sanitized version. According to them, as they arrived at the gate, Marine Daus interpreted a conversation between them as an insult, and Daus struck Gaspar Vázquez with a club. When Daus attempted to strike Gaspar a second time, Gaspar sized his club. Having lost his club, Daus reached for his gun with the apparent intent of firing it, but Gaspar took it away from him. In the ensuing struggle, Gaspar struck Daus in the head.

After this incident, the Vazquez brothers were locked at the guard house where they were clubbed by other marines and soundly beaten before they were brought to the officer in charge. When they asked for water, and claimed that as American citizens they were entitled to better treatment, the marine responded: "You are not American citizens. You are our slaves."[9]

As a result of the frequent encounters between the members of the armed forces and the civilian population, on Friday morning, December 27, the president of the Senate, Luis Muñoz Marín, the prosecutor of the Federal Court, A. Cecil Snyder, and the associate judge of the Supreme Court, Martín Travieso, met with Rear Admiral Raymond A. Spruance, commander of the Tenth Naval District at the naval base in Isla Grande. The meeting sought to prevent similar incidents from happening in the future. Rear Admiral Spruance assured the Puerto Rican delegation that members of armed forces were tried by a court martial that is open to the public and that sentences imposed by the military court were usually more severe than those imposed by the ordinary courts. The meeting concluded with a joint press conference that pointed out that all crimes committed by members of the armed forces in Puerto Rico were judged publicly and quickly and punished severely, in processes similar to what the armed forces policies utilized in the continental United States. No detailed plan to prevent future incidents was discussed.[10] The article published in *El Mundo* added that "uninformed public opinion" generally gave the impression that few, if any, corrective measures would be taken, and that as a result, these violent clashes would continue. As a matter of fact, the day following this meeting, another clash occurred.

The following day, on Saturday, December 28, the local newspaper *El Mundo* reported the first attack of a group of soldiers on a local establishment. According to the published report, on Friday, December 27, 1940, at

around 10:00 p.m., between fifty and eighty continental soldiers stormed
and destroyed the 5 and 10 Beer Bar (Bar de Ceverza de 5 y 10 Centavos)
in Fernández Juncos Avenue, in San Juan, causing damage estimated at
$500. The soldiers belonged to the signal aircraft warning regiment sta-
tioned at Fort Buchanan. By the time the chief of the Puerto de Tierra police
station, Santiago Martínez, arrived, the soldiers were long gone; however,
one of the solders was identified and arrested.[11] The editorial comment by
the local daily *El Imparcial* was particularly bitter, suggesting that the name
"Isla de Diablo" should be included not only as a reference to Isla Grande
but to the entire city of San Juan, as "our women can no longer come to
shop in the capital without risking an assault . . . by one of the representatives of the Yankee Military Kultur." Meanwhile, other instances of unpro-
voked aggression by American soldiers and sailors against Puerto Rican
civilians (both men and women), occurred during the week and were
prominently reported in the local press; one of these involved a group of
socially prominent Puerto Ricans returning from a Christmas party at a late
hour of the night.[12]

According to a news brief published by the navy, "feelings are running
high as a result of another incident between American marines and Puerto
Rican workers." The incident took place early morning, February 21, 1941,
at the naval base at Isla Grande. The workmen alleged that they were fired
upon by a marine sentry and run over by a motorcycle driven by another
marine, who also subsequently drew his revolver and fired upon them. A
squad of marines with drawn bayonets was then called upon to put an end
to the disturbance. According to the navy's version of the affair, it started
when the sentry ordered those entering the base to stand in single file. The
workmen protested, as they would arrive late for work, and their paychecks
would be deducted for the lost time. Some attempted to enter through another gate, "and the ensuring confusion brought about the skirmish." More
than seven hundred workers assembled in front of the capitol in order to
protest what had happened.[13]

At about 4:00 p.m. on Saturday, May 31, 1941, in Barrio Monacillo,
where the Arundel Corporation was building houses for the sailors and a
hospital called San Patricio, Private Clifton R. Antwine shot Delgado
Guadalupe, a thirty-five-year-old worker from Guaynabo, killing him instantly. In a letter written to Interim Governor José M. Gallardo, Rear Ad-

miral Spruance stated the navy's version of this incident, a view which markedly differed from that recounted by Miguel Martínez of the Insular Police Force. According to the navy's account, as Carlos García de la Noceda, the paymaster for The Arundel Corporation and Consolidated Engineering was preparing the pay of the workers at the navy low-cost housing site at San Patricio, a large number of men pressed around the window of the small building where the payments were made. García became concerned as "the money box had been upset."[14] He thereupon asked Private Clifton R. Antwine to restore order. In making this effort, Private Antwine stated that Guadalupe attacked him with a heavy rock, and as a result, he received a severe concussion in the face. Antwine, who was armed, thereupon fired at Guadalupe, killing him.[15] However, Martinez's investigation, which resulted from interviewing five eye witnesses, states that Private Antwine was pushing and shoving the workers in a hostile manner. Since the ground was wet, Private Antwine slipped and fell, hitting his chin with the corner of the paymaster window. When he got up, he fired into the crowd, hitting and instantly killing Guadalupe.[16] As illustrated by these incidents, conflicts between the workers and military agencies were not limited to salary disputes. The following year, these conflicts intensified, and as a result, a number of strikes flared up.[17]

On January 19, 1942, a month after the Japanese attack on the American naval base at Pearl Harbor, and while American patriotism was running high, Puerto Rican workers went on strike, and all construction work was stopped at naval bases in Isla Grande, Vieques, and Roosevelt Roads in Ceiba.[18] A total of 4,000 workers went on strike, 2,000 of these assembling at the Sixto Escobar Park in San Juan in order to strategize their options.[19] Due to the intervention of the Department of Labor of the Insular Government, a meeting was held between the officials of the base and the striking laborers. The next day, an agreement was reached, and the workers returned to work.[20] However, the strikes continued. On February 23, strikes began in Vieques and Roosevelt Roads. In Vieques, 1,600 workers went on strike, while at the base of Roosevelt Roads in Ceiba, 2,900 workers took part in the strike. On February 25, a mediation commission was assembled to put an end to these labor protests. The following day, the strikers met with naval and local authorities. The strike concluded on March 2, and two days later, Arundel and Consolidated Engineering formally accepted the demands of workers, thereby increasing their wages an average of 12 to 18 percent and agreeing to overtime pay. Disparities in wages paid to continental and local workers were at the root of these strikes, the local Puerto Rican workers seeking equal pay with their continental counterparts.

As a result of these strikes, naval construction jobs began to pay 40 percent more than the sugar cane industry—the largest employer on the Island—approximately $2.25 per day.[21] However, labor disputes continued to be a repeated source of controversy. Even as the construction projects were floundering, on May 24, 1943, the Brotherhood of Electricians sent a letter to the Arundel Corporation on May 24 notifying them that a strike was imminent if the salary was not increased.[22] The grievances of the workers ranged from the insufficiency of the wages given the shortages and high prices of consumer goods, to lack of pay parity with continentals, and extended to the critical issue of work safety. Between December of 1941 and March of 1943, twenty-six workers died in accidents in the construction projects of the Arundel Corporation.[23]

Puerto Rico was not the only jurisdiction where U.S, contractors experienced labor conflicts. In Jamaica and Guyana, labor protests about disparities in pay along racial lines were quite frequent. Since locals were paid using a lower pay scale than stateside workers, who were compensated using the more generous U.S. labor rate, Jamaican and Guyanan workers went on strike. In Jamaica, the situation escalated to the point that U.S. troops had to be sent to restore peace.[24]

Drafting Puerto Rican Recruits

On May 1, 1939, the secretary of war, Harry W. Woodring, announced that he had issued orders establishing a new Military Department in the Caribbean area to be known as the Puerto Rican Department. The territory embraced by the new overseas department was not limited to Puerto Rico, as it also included the Virgin Islands under U.S. rule. The department was officially established on July 1, 1939, under the command of Brigadier General Edmund L. Daley,[25] who was stationed in Boston, Massachusetts, and commanded the First Coast Artillery District. Daley was assigned to head the new territorial division headquartered in San Juan. The objective of setting up the Puerto Rican Department was to decentralize the geographical area administered by the Second Corps Headquarters in Governor's Island, New York. This new territory functioned similarly to those already established in the Hawaiian Islands, the Philippines, and Panama.[26]

American troops started arriving in Puerto Rico soon after the German invasion of Poland on September 1, 1939. On September 14, Brigadier General Daley announced that 1,700 troops from Texas, California, New Jersey, Iowa, Vermont, Delaware, and Virginia would report for duty in the army's new Puerto Rico Department. These troops served to reinforce the infantry garrison already stationed on the island. After the transfer order was signed, Secretary Woodring made public the names of the army units assigned to Puerto Rico. These included field artillery, coastal defense, ordnance, signal, medical, and quartermaster units. In addition to the troops, a reinforced anti-aircraft gun battery from Fort Winfield Scott, California, was shipped from San Francisco.[27] Once the naval base at Isla Grande was commissioned on May 1, 1940, the navy was able to accommodate its contingent of sailors. The base, under the command of Captain V. C. Griffin, had a total capacity of 963 officers and 6,475 enlisted men. It was designed to service 48 seaplanes and 150 landplanes; though an additional 90 planes could be accommodated in an emergency.[28]

Registration of Puerto Ricans for the draft began on November 20, 1940, five weeks later than in the United States.[29] The Selective Service was established under Lieutenant Colonel Harry Besosa, and administered by 122 local boards. By 1941, 525,000 men, ages eighteen to sixty-four were registered. An army reception and induction center was set up at Fort Buchanan, a basic training station at Camp O'Reilly, and an advanced training center at Camp Tortuguero. An "interesting feature in the program" was the assigning of inductees to racial categories. Puerto Ricans were separated into "white" and "black." This distinction was indicated as a reference in all sorts of lists or reports kept by the army. Furthermore, quotas were set up. The ratios used at the time were "about four whites to one black." "Whites" were described as light-colored people of Latin origin, while "blacks" were said to be dark skinned and of a different racial origin, but it seems, not Latin. According to army records, by the end of 1941, "it had become apparent that Puerto Rican men inducted under U.S. standards were drastically inferior to continental troops. They were inferior physically, mentally, and in other ways." In order to "weed out the most undesirable men," the War Department authorized the commanding general of the Puerto Rican Department to release from active service "those Puerto Rican men who were ineffective or inefficient."[30] Under this authority, by late 1943, about 3,250 Puerto Ricans had been released to the enlisted reserve. The language utilized in the army reports racialized Puerto Ricans in such a way as to equate "darker" with "undesirable." Implicit assumptions about the supposedly inferior character of darker people, which made them supposedly unsuitable for combat in the armed forces, make it difficult to distinguish lack of specific skills from darker complexion. The conflation of racial categories and skill categories hinder the process of sorting out the actual problems the army may have confronted based on low literacy or lack of knowledge of the English language from racial classifications. Puerto Ricans were in fact considered unsuitable for specific tasks due to racist beliefs on the part of the officers from the continent.

As a result of this experience, the army instituted "higher standards for induction" in July 1942, and a 1,500-man draft objective was set up for September and October 1942. The army decided that these inductees could replace the continental troops stationed in the Caribbean. Due to this higher standard, the army contemplated the procurement of 16,000 additional troops, which would not be a problem given the huge number of registered men.[31] In spite of the fact that the army instituted bilingual training as a solution for educational deficiencies on the island, where it was estimated that 35 percent of the 2,000,000 people were illiterate,[32] Puerto Ricans regarded the army's "higher standards for induction" as discriminatory. What higher standard than Brigadier General Raul Esteves, a West Point graduate, commented Governor Tugwell to Secretary of the Interior Harold Ickes? Yet, despite his credentials, according to Tugwell "the regular Army distrusts him and does not want him. In fact, they are trying to get rid of him."[33]

Dr. José Padín, former commissioner of education and several times acting governor, stated in an interview with Colonel Charles G. Mettler of the Military Intelligence Field Office, on October 7, 1942, that there was a widespread feeling among Puerto Ricans that they were grossly discriminated against. As an example, he stated the limits placed on the number of Puerto Rican volunteers that the army was accepting. Dr. Padín added that Puerto Rican–born officers in the National Guard were being replaced by regular U.S. Army officers with the excuse that the army desired only to have regular officers in key positions, even to the exclusion of Puerto Rican–born graduates of the United States Military Academy. Dr. Padín was, of course, referring to Brigadier General Esteves, the first Puerto Rican to graduate from that prestigious institution.[34] The cry of "discrimination" continued, and was articulated in different forums. By October 1943, even the conservative Mayagüez Lions Club was complaining to the Selective Service of "alleged discrimination against Puerto Ricans regarding the much higher educational qualifications required for induction into the army in Puerto Rico than in the continental U.S."[35]

Apparently, lobbying efforts by Puerto Rico paid off, as *El Mundo* reported on January 13, 1944, that "Washington had instructed the local Selective Service not to require eighth grade education, but to draft men with as low as a fourth grade."[36] An editorial in the *World Journal*, published on March 29, stated that "the War Department is at long last giving Puerto Rican Americans the same opportunity as any other American—be he a Chinese speaking Chicagoan, a Japanese born Californian, or a Latin from Manhattan—to enter the U.S. Army and fight for the Nation."[37] The editorial claimed that "the underpaid, inadequately educated Puerto Rican who has little opportunity to improve himself" would benefit. A possible side benefit to this change in the recruiting standard is that on March 16, the navy selected fifty-five Puerto Rican women from Ponce for "processing of application and final consideration." This is a surprisingly high number, as the navy had previously only recruited one hundred women out of applicants totaling several times that number.[38]

Throughout the war years, Governor Rexford Tugwell continued to urge Lieutenant Coronel Besosa to accept more Puerto Ricans in the army, as a significant number were being rejected.[39] A study commissioned after the war ended, directed by Clarence Senior, research director at the University of Puerto Rico, entitled *Preliminary Analysis of Puerto Rican Selective Service Rejections*, confirms Governor Tugwell's concerns regarding the army's reluctance to accept Puerto Ricans. According to Senior's study, the general rejection rate for Puerto Rico was higher than for the United States. The rejection rates in the United States for the period between November 1940 and September 1941 was 52.8 percent for whites and 59.4 percent for blacks. Between April 1942 and December 1943, the rejection rates for whites decreased to 42.4 percent while that of blacks increased to 60.7 percent. The rejection rates for Puerto Ricans, though not for the same time period, are documented on Table II of that report. Unfortunately, a page is missing from the document in the archives. What we do know, however, is that from April 1944 to August 1946, a total of 163,141 Puerto Ricans were rejected by the army; of these, 136,445 were classified as "white" and 24,696 as "colored." Almost 50 percent were rejected due to "mental deficiency," which according to Senior, could be caused by the fact that the testing was done in English.[40] Fortunately, the *Puerto Rico Induction Program Report* provides some insight regarding these rates. According to this report, from 1941 to April 1945, 91 percent of Puerto Ricans that presented themselves to the Selective Service were rejected and 79.1 percent of those screened and tested were also rejected.[41] Clarence Senior documents that this rejection rate was much higher than that of either white or black continentals.

A more detailed analysis of the induction program shows that the acceptance rates dropped dramatically as the requirements were altered. In 1941, as regular U.S. Army standards were used, except for literacy in English, of the 6,003 presented, 5,094 men were accepted, for an acceptance rate of 84.8 percent. In 1942, the same standard applied until September, when the army put a higher standard in effect due to the "inferior quality of troops obtained under normal standards."[42] That year, of the 13,330 men presented, 7,540 were accepted, for an acceptance rate of 56.9 percent. By 1943, all inductions were under the higher standard, and of 32,173 men presented, 16,007 were accepted, for an acceptance rate of 49.8 percent. In 1944, the English literacy requirements were dropped, though regular U.S. Army standards were still required. Little screening was done at the Selective Service. As a result, an astonishing 124,255 men presented themselves to the Selective Service. Of these, 16,255 were accepted, for an acceptance rate of 13.1 percent. During the last months of the European conflict, January to April, as the same requirements continued to be adopted by the army, and the island's employment had not stabilized, 48,798 men presented themselves to the Selective Service, and 7,554 were accepted, for an acceptance rate of 15.4 percent.

According to army records, from 1941 to April 1945, 525,000 Puerto Ricans aged eighteen to sixty-four presented themselves to the Selective

Service, 224,559 were screened or examined, and 47,000 men were inducted. This number corresponded to an acceptance rate of 8.9 percent of all those that presented themselves to the Selective Service and 20.9 percent of all those screened and examined. It is interesting to note that due to the high unemployment rate on the island, the army labeled the induction program in Puerto Rico a "glorified WPA" (Works Progress Administration) or a "WPA in uniform."[43]

The Deployment of Puerto Rican Regiments

Initially, Puerto Rican troops were deployed on the island. In January 1943, for example, the Provisional Coast Artillery Regiment, composed in its entirety of native Puerto Rican troops, was assigned to Borinquen Air Field, in Aguadilla. This regiment, under the command of Major Stevens, was established "for the purpose of determining whether Puerto Rican troops were capable of taking over Coast Artillery duties." The regiment was a selective group of approximately 450 men. They had no trouble learning the Coast Artillery work, and they set a firing record that had never been equaled in the Antilles Department.

In June 1943, the newly formed 51st Coastal Artillery Regiment was filled with regular Puerto Rican troops. According to Major Stevens, these troops took a little longer to learn, but they proved to be willing and eager students. They were taught mathematics and English. In the opinion of Major Stevens, the Puerto Ricans were fully capable of handling Coast Artillery duties. Yet, stereotypes about Puerto Ricans on the part of Stevens also reveal his lack of knowledge and cultural distance from these men. In his report, Major Stevens stated that "Puerto Rican troops are very sentimental and home loving. When stationed in Puerto Rico, they want to go home every weekend." When they are stationed elsewhere, "they try various tricks in an effort to return to Puerto Rico." Major Stevens further states that Puerto Rican "feelings are very easily hurt and officers handling them must be careful in their remarks because Puerto Rican troops possess suicidal tendencies."[44]

The first detachment of troops from Puerto Rico arrived in Port of Spain, Trinidad, on September 4, 1943. They joined British and Americans already stationed in this British possession.[45] The troops of the 51st Coastal Artillery Regiment were moved to Trinidad during December of 1943. They were to perform regular Coast Artillery duties and join other Puerto Rican troops already stationed there. According to a memorandum written by Captain Marvin S. Bennett of the Office of Military Intelligence in Trinidad, the "white" Puerto Rican troops were well received in Trinidad and in other bases. This sentiment was expressed through newspaper articles as well as by the official reception the civilian authorities gave to the officers and men. Captain Bennett also stated in his memorandum that all base commanders were required to report any unbecoming behavior of the troops to the chief of staff of Military Intelligence.[46] Military Intelligence also kept an eye on past political connections with the Puerto Rican Nationalist Party, which had been the source of violent confrontations in Puerto Rico during the 1930s. According to a report by the Trinidad Artillery Coastal Command, there were a few Puerto Rican troops whose loyalty was being questioned because of their association with this political party. A check was therefore being made of their units, and an investigation of their background was requested from the G-2, Antilles Department, in order to determine their loyalty.[47]

By December of 1943, Puerto Ricans were fighting in Europe. Major General William E. Shedd, in his New Year's message to the troops under his command, praised the faithful and efficient performance of the Puerto Rican troops. He added that more Puerto Rican troops were likely to follow. According to an article published in the *World Journal*, the sending of more Puerto Rican units to Europe, and Major General Shedd's implied transfer of additional troops, was an indication that "the Army is fully satisfied that Puerto Ricans can hold their own against the enemy" and that they can provide valuable assistance with the planned invasion of the European continent. The *World Journal* added that the major general's message was perhaps the finest tribute paid by any high ranking officer thus far in this war to the Puerto Rican soldiers and officers. The local newspaper *El Mundo* reported that the Puerto Rican troops "have been anxious to join forces with our northern brothers and those of other nations who are fighting for the crusade of liberty," and now they will get a chance to do so.[48]

On February 2, 1944, Major General Shedd announced that the 65th Infantry had been ordered from Panama to the United States, and from there, they would be shipped to England in order to assist in the handling of the supplies for the incoming invasion. Shedd expressed his confidence in the ability, courage, and loyalty of these troops.[49]

An editorial published in the local newspaper *El Imparcial* stated that Puerto Ricans were going to be shipped to the Pacific Theater of operations to confront "hardened veterans of the Japanese Army." The editorial made note that the sacrifice of the Puerto Rican soldiers was greater than that of his stateside counterpart, as "he was fighting for the freedom which up until now has been denied to them."[50] As an example, on April 14, 1943, the same newspaper, *El Imparcial*, reported that the local House of Representatives was investigating a claim by the Puerto Rican laborers working for The Arundel Corporation in the construction of the naval base in Ensenada Honda at Ceiba that they were not allowed to drink the cold water that was prepared for the continentals. The workers added that they suffered all sorts of discrimination, and that if anybody protested, they were summarily fired, with no explanation given. The workers also claimed that while the continentals were paid $1.57 per hour to drive a truck, they on the other hand were paid $0.50 per hour and were required to work for ten continuous hours. The workers also complained about the segregated seating on the buses, as there were some seats reserved for Puerto Ricans and some for the continentals. If a Puerto Rican were to take the seat of a continental, he would be taken off the bus at the first opportunity and fired.[51]

A substantial number of Puerto Rican troops were stationed on Caribbean Islands as well as in Panama, in order to protect the canal. The 130th MP Aviation Company, consisting of 200 Puerto Rican officers and enlisted men, was stationed in Jamaica. They were under the command of Captain Doval, a forty-year-old officer who, according to Military Liaison Officer Captain K. F. Kahn, "is a Spanish type." Captain Kahn states that "the majority of the Puerto Ricans might be called the Spanish type, but some are quite negroid." He added that Puerto Ricans were trying to do a good job and that they performed their duties well. He concluded his report by stating that there had been no negative publicity on the presence of the Puerto Rican troops in the local Jamaican press, except for that published in the *New Negro Voice*.[52]

The Jamaicans were quite at odds with the segregation blatantly exhibited by the U.S. Army in that country. An article published in The *New Negro Voice*, a local Jamaican newspaper, stated that "American race prejudice is very queer. A visibly colored person who speaks in a foreign language is likely to be welcomed by Americans in places where the fairest of the persons with suspected Negro blood" would be barred. The article added that in the past two weeks a number of colored men were observed strolling in Kingston dressed in U.S. military uniforms. Many of them, of the racial type known locally as "sambo" were Puerto Ricans. The Jamaicans questioned if these colored men would be allowed to visit the local United Service Organization (a private non-profit organization that provided recreational and morale-building services to the U.S. military) "on an equal basis with other American soldiers."[53] Of course, this type of article was deeply resented by the U.S. Army. It claimed that the *New Negro Voice* was read only by the lower classes and by the more radical elements in Jamaica, and that no other local newspaper had carried similar articles since the arrival of the Puerto Rican troops. The army command hoped that the Puerto Ricans would not be privy to this article due to the small circulation of this newspaper and the fact that no copies of it were allowed on the base, as it feared the possibility that this information would create turmoil among the troops.[54]

One of the few times the performance of the Puerto Rican troops was not held in high regard by their commanding officers was when they were training with Panamanian forces. Lieutenant Colonel Dubois stated that among the Puerto Rican troops there was much unrest due to their desire to return to Puerto Rico on account of "homesickness." He added that the "mental attitude of inferiority complex among officers and enlisted men produces complaints that they are being discriminated against whenever a disciplinary action must be taken to enforce regulations." He urgently recommended the transfer of the 296th Regiment of the Combat Team to the continental United States for the completion of their training. Dubois believed that this unrest might lie in the fact that this regiment had fewer Puerto Rican officers, as these difficulties were not noted in the Costal Artillery Regiment, which had a higher percentage of native officers.[55] A report later stated "the impracticability of using the 296th Regiment of the Combat Team for its initial mission" due to general inaptitude and language difficulties. Such was the state of affairs that Lieutenant Colonel Dubois requested a study in order to inactivate the 296th Regiment of the Combat Team.

It is interesting to note that not all officers agreed with Dubois's assessment. Lieutenant Colonel Ruddel advised that the 296th be retained as a unit in order to give them an opportunity to enter combat. Colonel Collier stated that recruitment was still in progress in Puerto Rico and that the majority of the personnel selected was capable being trained as members of a combat unit. Major General E. W. Harding was of the opinion that reorganizing the 296th Regiment into service units, which would preclude its use in combat, would have a detrimental effect "on the attitude of the Puerto Rican populace toward the U.S."[56] He believed that with proper supervision and training, the unit could be made into an acceptable fighting force. All present recommended that no action be taken unless a formal request for inaction was received from General Douglas MacArthur's headquarters.

The new colonial culture introduced by the armed forces took the form of racial segregation and racist practices. The U.S. armed forces built segregated housing for continental and Puerto Rican troops, and its contracting company, the Arundel Corporation, built segregated housing for Puerto Rican and continental workers. These practices reproduced historically inherited differences, such as language and perceptions of race, differentiating Puerto Rican and continental workers. They also amplified the chasm between groups by layering, on top of these differences, structures of social inequality. The housing quarters were not just separate, reflecting differences in socialization based on language. They were also of unequal quality. Additionally, differences in pay scales between continental and local workers added to the sense of inferior treatment of the Puerto Rican population because, even in the case of workers within the same trade (e.g., carpenters or plumbers), pay scales were different. Additionally, the tensions between U.S. military and the Puerto Rican civilian population, the exclusionary practices in armed forces recruitment, and the racist assessment of Puerto Ricans once recruited or in service, left a bitter memory of segregation. In Vieques, these practices were combined with actual conflicts concerning resources, threatening the ability of the population to make a living. It is to this aspect that we turn in the next chapter.

CHAPTER 7

Involution, 1950–1953

During the 1950s, the traditional economy of Vieques, based on sugar cane agriculture and cattle ranching, was practically destroyed. Pineapple production also waned. The island was being used for target practice for diverse contingents of the armed forces, which came to Vieques for short periods and then left. A new service economy that catered to the consumption of the U.S. troops developed. It consisted of bars, restaurants, laundry services, and prostitution for the troops. As the transition from an agrarian economy to a service one unfolded, the historical problem of seasonal employment associated with the sugar industry actually worsened. The old plantation economy had been characterized by a long *tiempo muerto* of several months. In a good year, the sugar cane industry could provide employment for seven months, while during the other five, the dead season set in, with all its concomitant problems. This was true in Vieques as much as everywhere else where the sugar industry was the main source of employment. Viequenses referred to this *tiempo muerto* as *la bruja* (the witch). Surviving the *tiempo muerto* economically was called "*pasar la bruja*" or roughly, "enduring the witch."

The temporary war economy had provided a respite to working families who enjoyed full-time, year-round employment during the years 1941–1943. This ended when military construction ended in the summer of 1943. Between 1943 and 1946, unemployment blanketed Vieques. Between 1946 and 1948, the PRACO attempted to reconstitute some agrarian employment in Vieques but lost ground when the navy demanded to reoccupy the lands in 1948. The service economy of the 1950s, which set in when Vieques was transformed from an agricultural society to a reconcentrated town servicing the U.S. troops, had an even longer *tiempo muerto* than the old plantation economy. On some years, ten out of twelve months, the base generated no employment in Vieques. How did the residents survive with the island's sugar economy destroyed, the naval base providing scant employment, and the industrialization bonanza sweeping Puerto Rico largely bypassing the small island-municipio of Vieques? How did the economic dependence on the U.S. military institutions affect the relationship between the civilian population and the U.S.Navy?

U.S. World Hegemony and
Permanent Rearmament

The United States emerged victorious at the end of World War II as the economic and military hegemonic power of the capitalist world, possessing almost 40 percent of the world's industrial capacity within its continental-sized economy. America's reconstruction loans to Europe and Japan, whose economies were nearly destroyed in the war, were coupled with demands for opening up all previous colonial empires to free trade. As the unquestioned capitalist economy of the moment, economic hegemony functioned to reverse a time-honored protectionist tradition within the United States dating back to colonial times. At the same time, the independence of India from the British in 1947 precipitated movements for decolonization in Asia and Africa, which in some countries threatened not only to do away with the old empires, but with capitalism itself. Movements of national liberation were combined with socialist revolutions, in China against the Japanese colonialists, and in Vietnam against the Japanese, then the French, and then the United States colonial interventions.

The alliance of the United States and the Soviet Union against the Axis powers quickly shattered as competition for influence in the emerging decolonized nations replaced cooperation against a common enemy. In the late 1940s, this conflict crystallized into what came to be known as the Cold War between the United States and the Soviet Union, and the conflict endured for four decades, until the collapse of the Soviet Union in 1991. Far from producing disarmament, the aftermath of World War II resulted in a policy of permanent rearmament. Military spending functioned to sustain the economic hegemony wielded by the United States after World War II. In addition to adopting Britain's former role as the "workshop of the world," the United States simultaneously became the policeman of the world's economic systems, on constant alert against anti-capitalist revolutions and geopolitical challenges.

But the new empire was different from the previously dominant British one, and from pre-World War II U.S. imperialism. It was based on a constellation of military bases all over the world rather than on territorial rule over colonial peoples.[1] Puerto Rico is thus an exception in the U.S. imperial structure, a colonial anomaly in an otherwise fundamentally noncolonial imperialism.[2] At the end of World War II, with the onset of independence movements in the colonial world, the United States refashioned the old colonialism it had installed in Puerto Rico in the aftermath of the invasion of 1898 and gave the colonial relation a new makeover. This began with legislation by the U.S. Congress in 1947 allowing the residents of Puerto Rico to elect their own governor and culminated with the creation of the Commonwealth of Puerto Rico in 1952. Puerto Ricans would now enjoy their own constitution, an elected governor as opposed to a presidentially appointed one, and would retain U.S. citizenship. The old status of the island as an "unincorporated territory," subject to the power of the U.S. Congress but without being on track to becoming a state of the union, remained nevertheless. The status of "unincorporated territory" dates back to the Foraker Act of 1900 and a case in the U.S. Supreme Court, which challenged its constitutionality in 1901.[3]

The Supreme Court upheld that the United States could rule over Puerto Rico (and at that time, the Philippines) while at the same time demarcating the island as not part of the United States. In order to sustain this decision, the same set of justices that had ruled a few years earlier that separate was equal in the infamous *Plessy v. Ferguson* case, and had thus given legal sanction to segregation in the U.S. South, now ruled that the Philippines and Puerto Rico were indeed U.S. territories, only of a different sort. Puerto Rico, according to the logic of the court, was not foreign in an international sense, since it was under U.S. sovereignty, but it was nevertheless considered "foreign in a domestic sense" since the island had not been incorporated into the United States. The island was "merely appurtenant thereto as a possession," in the language of the court.[4]

Not all aspects of the U.S. constitution were applicable to U.S. possessions. This state of belonging to, but not being part of, the United States was essentially a legal doctrine justifying colonialism, and the court concocted, in order to justify it, the concept of "unincorporated territory," a concept not previously used for any of the territories that had joined the union. When U.S. expansionism shifted gears from the continental mass to islands overseas, from white settler colonialism in the continent to overseas empire after 1898, it also changed its legal forms and limited the rights of those now considered to be under the sovereign power of Congress. In the case of Filipinos and Puerto Ricans, they were declared "U.S. nationals" in 1904, that is, subject to the authority of Congress but not citizens. In 1917, Congress further differentiated between different types of colonial subjects, declaring that Puerto Ricans would henceforth be U.S. citizens, but not Filipinos, who retained the status of U.S. nationals. The federal courts would nevertheless operate in Puerto Rico and in many ways, paradoxically, the island would function as a state of the union. While all persons born in Puerto Rico were declared by the Jones Act of 1917 to be U.S. citizens, they could not vote for Congress or the U.S. president, as the island was not a state. The creation of the Commonwealth of Puerto Rico in 1952 did not change this lack of participation in the federal elections, and representation in Congress remains to this day limited to one member of Congress called a "resident commissioner," who has no vote. The institution of resident commissioner also dates back to the period immediately after 1898. Thus, the institution of the resident commissioner can be said to date back to the era of racialized statecraft of the epoch of *Plessy v. Ferguson* (1896). The relation between the Insular Government and the U.S. Navy would remain, as before, a highly skewed one based on unequal power, as the U.S. citizens of Puerto Rico and Vieques never really enjoyed the same set of rights in relation to the federal government that continentals did. They do not elect the executive and have no voting representation in the legislative branch of government. Thus, the changes introduced in Puerto Rico by the P.D.P. in 1940–1952, between the initiation of the agrarian reform and the creation of the Commonwealth of Puerto Rico, actually changed very little of the power dynamics between the U.S. Navy and the Insular Government. Puerto Ricans continued to live, as it were, under a set of institutions dating to the epoch of racialized statecraft of *Plessy v. Ferguson*.

In the 1950s, Vieques was a frequent site for deployment of troops engaged in practice war maneuvers and readiness training. It served as the last destination for troops being sent to combat zones in Korea, as it would serve later during the Vietnam War and others. The navy loved Vieques. It claimed that the island was the ideal location to simulate classical midtwentieth-century warfare, including amphibious landings, air assaults, submarine maneuvers, and ship to shore assaults. Throughout its useful life-time, the navy considered Roosevelt Roads, until its closure in 2003, as the "crown jewel" in the archipelago of naval island installations, scattered throughout the Western and Eastern Hemispheres, in the massive naval empire that was acquired during the World War II decade.

Navy and marine detachments were regularly sent to Roosevelt Roads for training. The navy would mobilize up to 100,000 troops at a time to the Caribbean for exercises, with amphibious landings on Vieques. Even a small percentage of the troops, when released for leisure, and eagerly seeking drink, food, women, and entertainment, was capable of overwhelming a municipality of roughly 10,000 inhabitants.

Emerging Service Economy

In September and October of 1951, the Atlantic Fleet Exercises (Lantflex) deployed 200 ships, 800 airplanes, and over 90,000 men from the navy and the marines for the largest amphibious exercises since the beginning of the Korean War.[5] As in most military towns, a lively new service economy developed that catered to the consumption of the U.S. troops, mainly featuring bars, restaurants, laundry services, and prostitution. Even if they did not all come ashore at the same time, the presence in the region of up to ten times as many military men as residents, meant that the streets were choked with large numbers of sailors and marines. This invasion of purchasing power brought a certain amount of prosperity to a few merchants, and some employment to local women who washed and ironed clothes for the troops, or engaged in the business of prostitution. While maneuvers brought in cash when the sailors were in town, they regularly augured trouble in the form of fights with local residents, excessive consumption of alcohol, and harassment of local women. When the training was completed, troops withdrew en masse as suddenly as they had arrived, leaving the streets empty and the cash registers quiet.

Enduring the Witch

As the abrupt transition from an agrarian economy to a service one unfolded, the problem of seasonal employment historically associated with the sugar industry actually worsened. A good year in the cane industry provided employment for seven months, while during the other five the fields were fallow, the payroll stopped, and *agregados* and their families depended upon subsistence crops to survive. Colloquially, surviving the idle season or *tiempo muerto* was called *pasar la bruja* (enduring the witch). But after the expropriations, the subsistence plots, which had been so crucial in maintaining household food production for survival during the dead season, disappeared.

The economy of the 1950s featured neither the full employment of the boom years of the war, nor the partial employment of the historically entrenched sugar industry. In fact, it was characterized by an even longer *tiempo muerto* than the old plantation economy. Ten out of twelve months, the base generated no employment in Vieques.[6] Without subsistence crops and without access to work, "enduring the witch" became a daunting challenge. Thus during the 1950s, the wicked witch that haunted Vieques was more wicked than the old witch of the sugar plantation epoch.

The Economy: Dependence on the Navy

Early in the 1950s, Viequenses still held hopes that the lands confiscated by the navy would be returned to them for agricultural use. Mayor Antonio Rivera and Methodist minister Rev. James K. Vincent were energetically advocating for the restoration of agricultural production and employment to the population. Reverend Vincent blamed the navy for the conditions of poverty prevailing in Vieques. He complained that before the navy took over two thirds of the island's land mass, the workers in Vieques earned over a million dollars in wages paid by the sugar mills. He argued that after the expropriations, per capita income was $52 a year and that 70 percent of the homes lacked basic sanitary facilities. According to Vincent the 11,700 inhabitants of Vieques "are kept fenced in like cattle,"[7] in contrast to the residents of Bikini Island, who he believed were relocated to a satisfactory and adequate place.[8]

Navy spokesperson Commander Pickett Lumpkin denied that the military presence was responsible for the poverty of Vieques, citing the previous land concentration prevailing in the island. Most of the 26,000 *cuerda*s taken by the navy had been monopolized by ten individuals for a long time.

In 1939, according to Lumpkin, before the navy took over the land, income stood at $1.00 weekly per family, not per person. In his version, the economy of Puerto Rico had greatly benefited from the maneuvers, which he claimed created more than $1 million in purchases between Vieques and Puerto Rico. According to Lumpkin, the poverty of Vieques predated the navy land expropriations, and therefore his federal agency was not responsible for it. Lumpkin pointed to the fact that the eastern zone of Vieques, where the firing range and maneuver zones were located, had not had sugar cane agriculture for twenty-five years. He paraded the fact that the navy had allowed the cattle ranchers of Vieques to graze their cattle on navy land (while failing to mention that it was the U.S. Navy that had expropriated the land of the very same ranchers). He even claimed that each expropriated family had been given a house and a *cuerda* of land "which they did not have before," and that the land was close to the road and had running water and electricity. This was of course patently false. The Picó Report of 1943 had been explicit on the actual dimensions of land granted to *agregado* settlements: "The present settlement at Santa María provides lots of only 50' x 40' which are entirely insufficient." This was, according to Picó, a "slum community."[9] While some families received a new home, most families were actually given the disassembled ruins of their demolished house, to reassemble themselves on their tiny lots. Some did not receive the building materials from their dismantled houses.

Lumpkin admitted that the huge military maneuvers might inconvenience the inhabitants, but that the "incalculable benefits derived by Vieques, Puerto Rico, and the Nation" overrode the nuisance of the maneuvers.[10] The dialogue in the press between the North American navy representative and the North American minister opened up space for further discussion in local North American circles and in Puerto Rico concerning Vieques. Admiral Barbey met with the Rotary Club of San Juan and suggested that they study the Vieques situation, while the annual meeting of the Methodist Church in Puerto Rico passed a resolution supporting the campaign of Reverend Vincent and Mayor Rivera for the restoration of agricultural land in Vieques.[11] The Methodist Church in Vieques claimed 1,500 active members and 1,300 sympathizers, according to an internal census of 1948.[12] It was therefore a considerable force in a community of approximately 10,000 inhabitants.

The residents of Vieques still believed that the navy's tenure on the island was temporary. On March 20, 1950, the municipal assembly requested that Vieques' representatives to Puerto Rico's legislature initiate a request to the U.S. Congress for the return of lands that the navy was not using. The same resolution requested that the Mosquito Pier and the local airport in Barrio Luján be opened to civilian use in order to promote tourism between Vieques, San Juan, and Saint Croix. The municipal assembly supported both Reverend Vincent and Mayor Rivera in their activism to restore the economy of Vieques.[13] The resident commissioner of Puerto Rico, Antonio Fernós Isern, was lobbying in Washington for the return of 2,000 *cuerdas* unoccupied by the navy in Vieques. Thus, while Mayor Rivera and Reverend Vincent requested the complete withdrawal of the navy, the resident commissioner aimed for the return of a parcel of land, most probably for PRACO now under the Land Authority. Fernós Isern made public statements about Puerto Ricans' U.S. patriotism, as exemplified when a call for a thousand volunteers for the 65th Infantry went out, and more than a thousand men showed up to enlist.[14] In the complex climate of the early 1950s, when the Popular Democratic Party of Puerto Rico was negotiating in Washington for the transition to the Commonwealth of Puerto Rico, or Estado Libre Asociado as it is known in Spanish, Fernós Isern combined his denunciations of the navy with pronouncements about Puerto Rico's commitment to the larger interests of the empire.

Meanwhile the United States Congress was authorizing monies, not for the return of lands to Puerto Rico, but for the navy to expropriate even more lands in Vieques. In September of 1950, the U.S. Congress authorized $330,000 for the purchase of 4,370 acres from cattle ranchers in the eastern part of Vieques. The ranchers went to the Federal Court in San Juan to seek remedy for insufficient funds tendered for acquisition of their lands. The press reported that the courts would decide the value of the land that the navy had been leasing on an irregular basis. If the purchases were carried out, the navy would be in a position of controlling 22,837 of the 32,240 acres, or 71 percent of land in the island. Navy spokespersons expected that the purchases would provide all the land they needed for their purposes, while the resident commissioner, for his part, expected to persuade the federal authorities to return lands in the western part of the island.[15]

The death of cane agriculture in Vieques meanwhile proceeded slowly, with some landowners still clinging to their old arrangement of shipping cane by barge to Humacao to be processed in Central Pasto Viejo of the Eastern Sugar Corporation. New problems emerged in the *zafra* (sugar harvest) of 1953, signaling the definitive decline of cane agriculture. In March of that year, Mayor Rivera lamented in the press that the sugar harvest was delayed by a labor stoppage in Central Pasto Viejo pier in Humacao while workers and management negotiated an agreement. The harvest ordinarily began in December and lasted until May. Half the season had already transpired. A fire in the cane holdings in a section of Vieques reorganized by PRACO, destroyed the crops of small farm proprietors. However, the gravest blow to the sugar industry was an unprecedented new regulation, requiring that cane shipped from Vieques to Humacao pass through U.S. Customs to be weighed. Fully recognizing the implications of this federal regulation regarding Vieques' status, Mayor Rivera bitterly complained that "as far as we know, Vieques continues to be part of the Commonwealth of Puerto Rico."[16] Further, the new regulations required cane to pass through customs during normal working hours, whereas traditionally it was weighed and shipped from the pier at Esperanza in Vieques to the pier at Central Pasto Viejo on three shifts, twenty-four hours per day.

The enforcement of the federal requirement that cane shipped by barge from Vieques to Humacao pass through U.S. Customs effectively reduced the cane shipments from 1,000 to 350 tons of cane per day. Shipping cane around the clock as before meant incurring heavy fees for off-hours weighing at the U.S. Customs Office and paying overtime to workers at both ends, increasing the cost to cane farmers. The forced reduction of flow and volume, in conjunction with the strike at the pier and the fire, put a bottleneck on the expected exportation of 70,000 tons of cane from Vieques. A small change in federal regulations thereby put the survival of the Vieques cane farmers at stake. The question of the mayor of Vieques reflected deep frustration about the supposed elimination of colonialism from Puerto Rico with the establishment of the Commonwealth of Puerto Rico in 1952. What good was this recently inaugurated Estado Libre Asociado, when it could not even facilitate commerce between two of its counties in the face of U.S. federal intervention?[17] Puerto Rico, as part of the United States, was subject to the uniformity and commerce clauses of the Constitution that prevent states from taxing the products of other states. If there was free trade between Puerto Rico and the United States, why was the flow of commerce impeded, by federal authorities, between two municipalities of the Commonwealth of Puerto Rico? The mayor of Vieques interpreted this intervention as a federal attempt to strangle the economy of Vieques to open the way for further expropriations and displacement of civilians by the U.S. Navy.

For Viequenses, it had been a hard decade since the cessation of the construction of the Mosquito Pier in the summer of 1943. Throughout, the residents of Vieques retained the hope that the navy operations were temporary, but the shift to the Cold War policy and the Korean War were hard facts that indicated just the opposite: the navy had come to stay. The population of Vieques declined between the U.S. Census of 1940 and that of 1950, from 10,362 to 9,228. The mayor tirelessly voiced the desire of the population of Vieques for a return to the old times when at least there was some employment in cane agriculture, but evidence continued to accumulate that the passing of the old Vieques was irreversible.

The Powder Keg Explodes

By 1953, multiple conflicts brewing in Vieques brought civilian life in the island to the brink of collapse. The sugar cane industry faded due to the expropriation of Central Playa Grande in the 1940s and to revised U.S. Customs policies in the 1950s restricting cane shipments between Vieques and the sugar mill in Humacao. There were few opportunities for work, but what was available required subservience to military personnel. The complex of bars, restaurants, and the existence of prostitution destroyed, in the perception of many, the more decorous social fabric of Vieques before the expropriations. It became obvious to the people living there that the navy planned to stay, and if anyone were to leave the island, it would be the Viequenses. However, the climate of anger and hostility toward the navy was tempered by economic dependence on the navy—precisely the entity that had destroyed the preexisting economic arrangements. This was an explosive formula.

Things started to go terribly wrong at the beginning of 1953, when yet another enormous mobilization of troops hit Vieques. Anthropologist Katherine McCaffrey has collected testimony from residents.

Rosa Moreno, a teenager in Vieques during the early fifties, recalled: "There were eight thousand people here. At night, the
sailors would get passes to come to town. There could be six-
thousand of them. They were fresh and would start fights.
Women and girls were afraid to go outside. My mother would
hide all of us inside, my sisters and brothers, and lock the door
and close the windows. The sailors would be roaming the
streets, banging on doors, asking for 'Margarita, Margarita.' My
mother wanted to protect her daughters. She also worried about
my brothers and my father, because they could be assaulted if
they tried to defend our honor."[18]

Life was disrupted in many ways by the navy presence, and not just by
the rowdy men in town. Sometime after sundown on March 20, 1953, four
young residents of Vieques surreptitiously entered Firing Range No. 1 on
the eastern end of Vieques. Despite posted "Danger" signs on the iron fence
that ringed the range, the residents entered urgently looking for a lost cow.
One of the residents accidently disturbed an explosive shell that detonated,
seriously injuring them all. They were rushed to the base hospital and air-
lifted to Rodríguez Hospital in San Juan for treatment, where twelve-year-
old Jesús Legrand died the next day,[19] and his brother Miguel and friends
Luis Campos and Frank Santiago began their long healing process. Jesús'
body was embalmed at a funeral home in San Juan and returned to Vieques
for burial. The young cadets who assisted the youths following the accident
took up a collection to help defray the costs of the funeral, but tensions
were at an all-time high between the residents and the military after this
incident.

Over the next two weeks, there were cases of a marine who pleaded
guilty to attacking Luis Ramírez, the son of wealthy Vieques merchant Don
Tomás Ramírez, after being asked to leave a private club. Ramírez's injury
required thirty stitches to close his wound; the sailor was fined $150. An-
other sailor was accused of launching a rock at a school teacher and hitting
him. According to a reporter in San Juan's daily *El Mundo*, yet another sergeant had killed a civilian after a personal argument over a woman two
weeks earlier.[20]

The final blow came on April 4, 1953, when four marines and four sailors arrived at El Bosque (The Forest) bar, located in Destino, a section of Barrio Puerto Ferro. The bar was owned by Afro-Viequense Julián Felipe Francis, affectionately known as Mapepe, then nearly seventy years old.[21]

Mapepe employed Catalina Cruz Rivera as a barmaid in his establishment. Her reported salary was $5 per day, paid by Mapepe. Eight drunken North American sailors and marines, some of whom had previously been drinking at the Venetian Bar, entered El Bosque Bar around nine o'clock in the evening. The rowdy marines apparently sought sexual favors from Catalina. Mapepe stepped in to stop the harassment when he feared that Catalina Cruz might be in danger. Some of the sailors claimed that Mapepe was wielding a machete.[22]

Mapepe's friend, seventy-three-year-old Julio Bermúdez, was gravely injured in the quarrel. Some sailors proceeded to ransack the bar, and Mapepe died twenty-four hours later from the injuries he suffered in the fight. The following day, Lieutenant Felix Guardiola of the Insular Police Department and navy officials opened an investigation in order to verify the details of this incident and to assign responsibility for Mapepe's death. Upon examining Mapepe's remains, the local medical examiner, Edgardo Ortiz Gordills corroborated that the skull was "mashed" and there were bruises on the brain.[23]

The indignation felt by the residents of Vieques due to the continued abuses by military personnel escalated to the point where they felt that either the marines should leave Vieques, or they should be given land in Puerto Rico to establish "another Vieques." According to Mayor Antonio Rivera, the only desire of the residents of Vieques was that the military maneuvers should end and that the soldiers should leave. Rivera lamented that due to the maneuvers, there was no peace in Vieques, and the locals lived in fear of continuous violence. Another concern enmeshed in the violence was the anxiety over safety in town, given that the target range was only a few miles away. Viequenses were acutely aware that a bomb had recently landed on civilian land in the neighboring island of Culebra and were concerned that this could also happen to them. "We want our land back so that we can live as we did in the past, which were good and peaceful times," reiterated the mayor. Rivera added that the military maneuvers had not benefited the population and that poverty had grown exponentially in Vieques.

The military had not even repaired the roads, which they constantly used, and only a few shopkeepers benefited from the military purchasing power. Following the murder, the navy declared the town of Isabel Segunda "off limits" to military personnel. Colonel F. B. Loomis, officer in charge of the Vieques division, indicated that he would continue to cooperate with Humacao District Attorney Benjamín Guerra Mondragón in order to clear up all of the facts related to the Mapepe case.[24]

Given the tense situation brewing in Vieques, Manuel Mellado Román, president of the Municipal Assembly of Vieques, submitted a unanimously approved resolution backing Mayor Rivera's comments regarding the intolerable conduct of some of the marines and navy men. Rev. John K. Vincent, a respected community leader in the island, added his words to the outrage felt by many Viequenses. He claimed that the actions taken by the navy in declaring Vieques "off limits" were arbitrary and undemocratic and resulted in a de facto economic boycott. According to Reverend Vincent, the navy was using its economic muscle to force the islanders into accepting unacceptable military behavior. Reverend Vincent added that Vieques was in need of Military Police in order to control the behavior of the troops but that these had been assigned to Puerto Rico, leaving Vieques with none. Because of the imposed economic embargo, there were many women suffering economic hardship, as they could no longer count on jobs washing and ironing the clothes of the military. Katherine McCaffrey recounts a conversation with Nilda Figueroa, an elderly woman who lived in the Montesanto resettlement and was an *agregado* when the navy arrived. She recalled washing and ironing for the sailors, charging $3.50 per dozen shirts, and earning as much as $17.50 per day. "When there was a maneuver, when the troops of gringos came, there was a lot [of work]. They came to my house with their clothes."[25]

"This has been the major [economic] contribution of the military personnel in Vieques," commented the Reverend Vincent, while adding that he supported Mayor Rivera's position on military shore conduct and demanding respect for the people of Vieques—a respect that could only be guaranteed with enforcement from the Military Police.[26] It should be noted that the mayor and the reverend were in fact requesting quite different solutions. While the North American reverend wanted military police to control the behavior of the troops on shore, the local mayor wanted the navy to leave Vieques altogether. In the short run, however, the mayor had to deal with the hardships that the off-limits policy represented to the commercial sector of Isabel Segunda.

Two days after the death of Mapepe, the legislature of Puerto Rico approved a resolution soliciting that two thousand acres of land currently under control of the navy be turned over to the government of Puerto Rico. It was believed this measure would provide some relief to Vieques. It was presented to the federal government by Antonio Fernós Isern, resident commissioner of Puerto Rico in Washington, but to no avail. The Municipal Assembly of Vieques, however, demanded that the entire 26,000 acres under navy control be returned to Vieques. The Municipal Assembly pointed out that Vieques had made sacrifices for the good of the nation, particularly during the war years, and that they needed the land back in order to revive their lethargic economy. In addition, the naval exercises benefited only a handful of bar owners and shopkeepers—25 of the 148 commercial establishments on the island according the Mayor Rivera— leaving the rest of the residents to fend for themselves. Paradoxically, some landowners benefited from the conjuncture of anti-navy sentiment after the death of Mapepe. On April 16, 1953, after the murder but before the trial of the accused, the Federal Court ruled that the navy had to double the compensation paid to seven expropriated Viequenses, the "major" cattle owners, for lands newly acquired by the navy in eastern Vieques—from $250,000 to $500,000.[27]

José and Emilio Christian were the nephew and great-nephew of Mapepe whom he had raised as his own children. They arrived from New York, where José worked as a federal employee, on April 15 to pay their last respects to their murdered stepfather. The local press reported that they met with Benjamín Guerra Mondragón and expressed their satisfaction with the investigation he was conducting. They were, however, disappointed that he did not receive support from the Viequenses who witnessed the crime. Julio Bermúdez, who was injured but survived the incident, and Catalina Cruz Rivera, who Mapepe was defending when he was killed, refused to testify, possibly out of fear of retaliation from the sailors. José and Emilio also expressed shock and disappointment that the bar was subjected to two break-ins after the death of their uncle.[28]

On April 28, Rear Admiral Austin K. Doyle, commander of the Tenth

Naval District, assured the residents of Vieques that the navy regretted this incident and that he would do everything in his power to prevent a similar situation from happening again. Nevertheless, Admiral Doyle's principal intervention was to oversee the transfer of the case from the civilian authorities to the navy, effectively removing Benjamin Guerra Mondragón from the case. The courts-martial of Bennett and Whitbeck lasted six days. Commander James A. Brough, legal counsel for the Tenth Naval District, presided over the hearings, which were held at the San Juan Naval Air Station and open to the public. Lieutenant Robert E. Dunne, member of the Naval Reserve, acted as district attorney, and Lieutenants Newell W. Wright and Robert B. Whitson of the Reserve acted as attorneys for the defense.[29]

The district attorney acknowledged that there were many conflicting accounts, making it extremely difficult to prosecute the case. This position made the defense's job much easier. It voiced that there was no malicious intent on the part of the accused. The defense claimed that there were no witnesses that could tie the accused to the murder, despite the fact that in addition to Julio Bermúdez and Catalina Cruz Rivera, there were a number of people sitting at the bar when the incident occurred.

We know of no civilians who were questioned during the courts-martial proceedings, despite the fact that thirty witnesses had appeared before the investigative board. It is possible that they were intimidated and feared reprisal for their testimony; on the other hand, even if they wanted to testify, they likely lacked the means to afford travel and accommodations, due to the distance from Vieques to the San Juan Naval Air Station where the courts-martial were held. Catalina Cruz Rivera took off for St. Croix during the investigative stage, and many locals exhibited a reluctance to answer questions during the investigation. In any case, no civilian contradicted the defense's claim that Staff Sergeant Bennet and Private First Class Whitbeck acted in self-defense by fighting off seventy-year-old Mapepe, who was brandishing a machete. The jury, comprised exclusively of white North American military personnel, deliberated for two hours and fifteen minutes. They found Staff Sergeant Bennett and Private First Class Whitbeck "not guilty" of voluntary manslaughter. All charges were dismissed.[30]

The contradictory stand of the population of Vieques towards the navy—at once hostile for destroying the previous economic arrangements, and amicable due to dependence on the purchasing power of the troops—is reflected in a previous Municipal Assembly statement that the marines and sailors were "men of order and respect" and that the Military Police had been efficient in preventing disagreeable incidents between them and the civilian population. During the courts-martial, Colonel Leonard Mason, working as a staff officer for General Erskine, commander of the Atlantic Fleet, met with Mayor Rivera to discuss the ugly incidents between the marines and the residents of Vieques. Colonel Mason apologized for the marines' recent behavior and told the mayor that the navy would guarantee the total security of the population during the next naval exercises. He stated that the marines would be taken to Isabel Segunda during the day and picked up by truck at night. Mayor Rivera claimed to have been very pleased with the cooperative attitude of the U.S. Navy and foresaw no additional problems. For the time being, dependence on the navy's economic power in Isabel Segunda secured a measure of peace in Vieques.[31]

The "Good and Peaceful Times of the Past"

The case of Mapepe serves as a reference point and as an emblem of this period in the minds of the residents of Vieques. The contradictions of the case were symptomatic of the dilemmas facing the population. Mapepe was killed in the establishment he owned, by the kind of men he normally befriended as customers and with whom he frequently socialized. His bar had prospered during the times of the naval maneuvers, and he was therefore able to pay a good wage to Catalina Cruz Rivera, who he stepped up to defend when she was endangered. The residents of Puerto Rico had supposedly negotiated a "compact" the year before by which they had granted their consent to the colonial relation to the United States through the establishment of the so-called Estado Libre Asociado or Commonwealth of Puerto Rico.[32] Yet this supposedly sovereign entity of U.S. citizens could not retain jurisdiction over the criminal behavior of military men in civilian territory, just as it could not prevent the U.S. Customs from impeding the flow of commodities between two of its municipalities. The men accused of Mapepe's murder were acquitted of all charges. Like everything else in Vieques, the town regarded the situation as an unsolved mystery. A local resident was dead, but no one was responsible.

The death of Mapepe came to symbolize everything that was wrong with the navy presence in Vieques. Without its own viable economy, constricted by the amount of land owned by the navy, the residents developed a meager service sector developed to serve the troops. In addition to the seasonal nature of employment, another problem with this economic configuration was the volume of troops that came to Vieques all at once for maneuvers, greatly outnumbering the civilian population. When they poured into town, the troops were an overwhelming force, swamping civilian life. True, they consumed in Vieques and kept restaurants, bars, and many laundresses employed, but the cost to the traditional notion of civilian life was high. It was because of the maneuvers that visions of a utopian past in Vieques began to emerge. Mayor Rivera articulated this vision when he argued that the people of Vieques "want our lands returned to us so that we may live as in the good and peaceful times of the past."[33]

The construction of a retrospective utopia, where local society was not disrupted by overwhelming military invasions, in which a certain "moral order"—now surely idealized—operated, focused sharply and exclusively on the absence of the less palatable aspects of life under the periodic invasion of hordes of drunken military men, while at the same time obfuscating the odious aspects of the old plantation society. As Rev. Justo Pastor Ruiz pointed out in his remarkable memoir of life in Vieques, in the old Vieques men sometimes went hungry: *un hombre se moría de hambre*. The emergent utopias, therefore, should not be construed as accurate historical representations of life in Vieques, but rather as expressions of discontent with the present of the 1950s. The elements that went into their formation are precisely the negation, or the absence, of what was odious in the daily life of the 1950s. The memory of the residents of Vieques, therefore, was a constructive endeavor fitted for present-day survival. Surely past times were better, and the recollections focused on what was better about the past. This essential structure of recollection became permanent and entrenched. Nazario Cruz Viera, interviewed in the *New York Times* in 2001, remembered that in the old Vieques before the expropriations, "We had everything. We lacked nothing." Cruz Cordero Ventura, interviewed by Samantha Burdman in 2002, remembered that where the navy established its western depots there were once communities with a church, where she made her first communion. Radamés Tirado (Mayor of Vieques 1976–1980) remembered his childhood: "I remember with the kids, I used to climb the hills, the

Cerro del Buey, and the Cerro Ventana, to go pick wild fruit. We picked wild fruit. One enjoys those things. We went to catch crawfish, we went fishing in the brooks. We had 28 brooks and now we have practically none. That's the free Vieques that I knew."[34]

The reconstruction of the memory of a utopian past went hand in hand with the recognition of the limitations of the power of the local governments, both at the municipal level and in the Commonwealth of Puerto Rico, to challenge the destructive aspects of the policies of the navy. In Vieques, the minister clamored for MPs to force the troops to behave with civility. The mayor and municipal assembly were less restrained, clamoring for the withdrawal of the navy. The Puerto Rican authorities of the commonwealth, however, spoke two ways. On the one hand, they sympathized with the residents of Vieques, while on the other they understood, but refrained from articulating, the limits of the colonial restructuring that had taken place with the establishment of the Commonwealth of Puerto Rico, whose name in Spanish suggests more powers than it actually enjoys in practice: Estado Libre Asociado. Thus, insular legislator Castaño introduced measures to limit the behavior of the troops in Vieques, while at the same time arguing, "We have never asked formally for the withdrawal of the sailors from Vieques, what has been requested is more respect for the people and the society of Vieques."[35]

By 1953, the fundamental features of the Vieques situation were established. The island's old economy, based on sugar cane agriculture, was destroyed due to expropriations and the application of U.S. customs regulations that constricted the flow of cane from Vieques to Humacao. Other agricultural attempts were curtailed with the demise of PRACO. Agrarian reform in the form of distribution of *parcelas* did not advance as in the rest of Puerto Rico. Unlike Puerto Rico, which began to industrialize rapidly, Vieques set out on a transition from agriculture to services. But the new service economy featured an even more dramatic dead season than the old agricultural cycle, with idleness ten out of twelve months of the year. A significant portion of the population lacked the subsistence plots, or an equivalent means of making a living, that had previously helped households to survive idle times. The displaced population knew that its dislocation was the product of U.S. Navy action, yet it had to rely for economic survival on the purchasing power introduced by sailors and marines during maneuvers. The purchasing power introduced by the troops was combined with drunkenness, the emergence of prostitution, and periodic outbursts of violence on the part of military personnel. These features of the new service economy violated established notions of decorum shared by broad layers of the local population. Historical resentment about the expropriations, therefore, was combined with current grievances against the violent behavior of the troops. Old resentment and new grievances, in turn, were intertwined with the fact that the local population had become economically dependent on troop purchasing power, an explosive mix that did not augur well for civilian-military relations in the future. In the meantime, the residents of Vieques had every reason to question the value of the newly established Commonwealth of Puerto Rico, an entity whose existence could guarantee neither the flow of commodities between Vieques and Humacao, a distance of six miles across the Vieques Sound, nor a justice system capable of retaining jurisdiction over those who murdered its residents. In sharp relief for all to see was the limit to the so called "decolonization" brought about by the creation of the Commonwealth of Puerto Rico.

Long-Term Effects

The expropriations in Vieques had a lasting and negative effect on the economy of the island and on its residents. As Puerto Rico moved forward, with a brand-new industrialization program to substitute its dependence on the sugar industry, Vieques was forgotten. During the decades following the expropriations in Vieques, Puerto Rico industrialized, standards of living improved significantly for its population, urbanization advanced, and levels of education of the population increased. But the positive effects of Puerto Rico's increasingly prosperous economy bypassed Vieques. The continuous bombings contaminated its soil and the minimal land on which the Viequenses lived was not enough to sustain them. The base did not provide substantial employment, while fishing and agriculture were primarily limited to subsistence activities.

While a detailed account of the fate of Vieques in 1953–2003 is beyond the scope of this book, we can point out some of the long-term consequences of the expropriations. We begin with specific conditions around 1950 because it was at that time that the fundamental partition of land that would characterize the island of Vieques was frozen. There were only minor changes to the amount of land owned by the navy and by residents of Vieques, respectively, in the six decades after 1950.

Long-Term Population Effects

The long-term effects of the expropriations on the population levels of Vieques cannot quite be described as catastrophic. The situation that emerged was rather one of stunted growth. The population of Vieques peaked in 1920, when the U.S. Census counted 11,651 persons living in the island. This was a result of the sugar boom of World War I, the famous "Dance of the Millions," which made the sugar planters of the Caribbean fabulously wealthy. The population of Vieques remained stable at 10,582 persons in 1930; 10,037 in 1935; and 10,362 in 1940. Even before the expropriations, Vieques could not support an increasing population, and each year a number of Viequenses emigrated, some to Puerto Rico, others to the neighboring island of St. Croix. In the mid-1940s, the majority of Puerto Ricans living in St. Croix were from Vieques.

Between 1930 and 1940, 26 percent of the population of Vieques emigrated (2,749 persons), most of them to St. Croix. In 1947, there were more than 3,000 Puerto Ricans living in St. Croix, principally from Vieques. Despite the fact that the economy of St. Croix had been experiencing a protracted contraction and long-term population decline, from about 26,681 persons in 1835 to 11,413 in 1930, the residents of Vieques migrated to St. Croix because the employment situation of Vieques was worse than in the U.S. Virgin Islands. A 1947 study described the population conditions as follows:

> Puerto Rican migration to an island in such a depressed condition would seem like "jumping out of the frying pan into the fire." The answer lies partly in the fact that sugar cane continues to be the main crop of the island, and that cane needs seasonal labor. The Danes formerly brought in workers for the cutting season from the nearby British islands. This practice continued until 1927. The immigration laws of the United States were applied to the Virgin Islands in that year and the cane growers had to look elsewhere for their labor. They found a situation made-to-order for them in the depressed conditions of the sugar industry on the island of Vieques. Sugar acreage and yield on that island of 51 square miles had been decreasing steadily since 1910 and people were looking for a chance to make a living elsewhere. Agents for the growers recruited sizable groups for transportation to St. Croix. Some of those who went on temporary jobs stayed. The tendency of Puerto Rican migration to St. Croix has been upward since that time.[1]

Before the navy arrived in Vieques, there was out-migration due to lack of employment. The expropriations affected an island that already had problems supporting the population level it had reached in 1920. There was a spike in population levels during the construction boom of 1941–1943, during which, by some accounts, the population of Vieques increased to perhaps 15,000, but this temporary increase had waned by the time of the census count of 1950. The long-term population trend reflects the stagnation of Vieques after 1940. At the end of the twentieth century, Puerto Rico's population was four times what it had been in 1900, but that of Vieques had only increased by 50 percent. (See Figure E.1.)

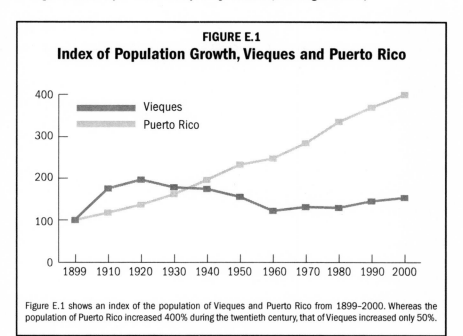

FIGURE E.1
Index of Population Growth, Vieques and Puerto Rico

Figure E.1 shows an index of the population of Vieques and Puerto Rico from 1899–2000. Whereas the population of Puerto Rico increased 400% during the twentieth century, that of Vieques increased only 50%.

Capital Assets, Employment, How to Make a Living

What kinds of assets were available to the residents of Vieques in 1950, after the expropriations? The taxation records of the municipality indicate that the wealth assessed in Vieques had several components: land, improvements to land, and movable or "personal" property, which included cattle and vehicles. The taxable value of the land in civilian hands decreased by 74 percent as a result of the expropriations: from $1,248,512 in 1940 to $328,772 in 1950. During the same period, the value of improvements to the land decreased by 32 percent: from $294,770 to $201,500. The value of personal property, which includes vehicles and cattle, increased by 2 percent between 1940 and 1945: from $368,300 to $375,780. This probably reflects the inventories of local merchants who sold goods to the troops and to workers who had employment in construction during the war. The value of personal property then dropped dramatically between 1945 and 1950 to $268,720 (a decrease of 27 percent). The drop between 1945 and 1950 probably reflects the decline in the commercial sector once construction activity ceased in Vieques and the war ended.

The net effect of the expropriations was a decrease in the amount of capital available to generate income. Since the decrease in property value was more extreme than the decline in population, total assets decreased from $186 to $86 per capita. This means that Viequenses were left in 1950 with less than half the assets per person compared to 1940, that is, with less than half the capacity to generate income.[2]

Before the expropriations, there were rural stores in the Vieques neighborhoods knows as *pulperías* and *colmados*, in addition to company stores in the sugar mills known as *tiendas de raya*. The sale of alcohol was not specialized, but took place instead together with the sale of foodstuffs and supplies. Between 1940 and 1945, the number of *pulperías* in the tax lists decreased from six to three, and the establishments that sold *Provisiones y Mercancía* decreased from three to two. Against this trend, in 1945, there appeared a number of establishments dedicated exclusively to the sale of alcohol: one *Bar y Hospedaje*, one *Cafetín y Rancho Chico*, ten *Cafetines*, one *Bar, Cafetín, y Mesa de Billar* [pool table], one *Bar*, and one *Cafetín y Establecimiento Comercial Independiente*. Not one of these businesses appears in the list of 1940. Their existence reflects the new purchasing power introduced by the military personnel in Vieques. A report by the Puerto Rico Planning Board noted in 1955 that in Vieques, there were many rum shops and a few restaurants. The number of rum shops was probably greater that in any other settlement of the same category in Puerto Rico. This was, according to the report, a response to the periodic concentration of military personnel in Vieques for military exercises.[3] The number of civilian automobiles registered in Vieques increased from forty-two in 1940 to seventy-four in 1945.[4] Many of these were used to transport the population from the military base to town and back. During the same period, prostitution thrived in Vieques. The neighborhood known as "El Cañón," near the old Vieques cemetery, became forbidden to the troops because the prostitutes practiced there.

During the Second World War, despite the catastrophic decline in land

and improvements to the land in civilian hands, the value of personal property remained relatively stable. The number of stores of all kinds remained stable, and their assessed value increased by 27 percent. The number of automobiles increased by 76 percent and their value by 278 percent between 1940 and 1945.[5] The number of bars, pool halls, restaurants, and hostels increased. The prosperous period of 1942–1943, during which the Mosquito pier was built, reduced the negative economic impact. There was a sector of the population for whom employment in military construction meant a good source of income, at least before the cessation of all construction in 1943.

After the second expropriations, unemployment became rampant. Most of the workers in Vieques had been in one way or another involved in the sugar industry. Among the fifty-three persons interviewed by the Proyecto Caribeño de Justicia y Paz, 32 (60 percent) had had jobs in the sugar industry or sectors related to it. Secondly, the wave of expropriations of 1947–1950 further reduced the civilian land area from 9,939 *cuerdas* in 1945 to 5,685 in 1950. Capital assets, including land, taxed by the municipality shrank from $1,911,582 in 1940 to $798,992 in 1950. (See Table E.1.) The military base never generated enough employment in Vieques but only temporary jobs during maneuvers.[6]

In 1950, the population was concentrated in the center of the island, without the agricultural economy that had existed before the war, without an alternative economy to replace what was lost, surrounded by a military base that generated no employment and barred access of the community to most of the seashore, mangroves, and coconut groves. Not only did landed assets and improvements to land decrease dramatically on account of the expropriations, and then some more on account of the second round of expropriations of 1947–1950, but the value of movable or "personal" property declined as well. The commercial sector of Vieques, which had been able to hold its own during World War II, had also collapsed by 1950. The taxation records point to scarcity of assets to make a living. This was compounded by the absence of the kind of insurance against hunger that *agregado* usufruct rights had provided before the expropriations. The rich tropical mangroves were off limits, and the coconut groves were destroyed by the navy during maneuvers in February of 1950.[7] Faced with such a catastrophic scenario, and lacking alternative sources of employment,

Viequenses took to the sea. A Vieques fisherman eloquently expressed the dilemma: "The only factory that has its door open to whoever wants to work is the sea."[8]

Puerto Rico and Vieques: Economic Contrasts

During the decades following the establishment of the commonwealth, Puerto Rico experienced phenomenal economic growth, particularly in the manufacturing sector. Puerto Rico's industrial revolution attracted world-wide attention, particularly among underdeveloped countries. Teodoro Moscoso, the Development Company's first administrator and foremost promoter, was named by President John Kennedy to head the Alliance for Progress, and the State Department displayed Puerto Rico as a shining example of what "capitalism and democracy" could accomplish together.[9]

The Industrial Incentives Act in 1947 awarded income tax exemptions to manufacturing firms willing to set up operations in Puerto Rico and attracted foreign capital.[10] Between 1948 and 1955, 409 additional companies established themselves on the island.[11] In addition, in 1947, the Development Company started the construction of the Caribe Hilton Hotel in order to promote stateside tourism on the island, with an investment of $6,500,000, initiating the development of a vibrant tourism industry that lasts to this day.[12]

During the 1950 and early 1960s, Puerto Rico had a substantial competitive advantage when compared to stateside manufacturing, and as such, this sector was responsible for most of the economic growth of the island. Puerto Rico maintained an annual growth rate of 6 percent yearly between 1948 and 1975, and the manufacturing sector grew by a whopping 10.1 percent yearly during the first five years of the 1970s.[13] Thus, while the larger island of Puerto Rico experienced agrarian reform and industrialization under the Popular Democratic Party and its much-vaunted Operation Bootstrap, Vieques, by contrast, languished under the effects of what might properly be called "Operation Navy." The developmental path of Vieques began to lag relative to the rest of Puerto Rico. (See Table E.2.)

The lack of job opportunities in the manufacturing, agricultural, and the cattle industries created an economic and social crisis on the island. The decline of the sugar industry was dramatic. Few industries moved to

Vieques. It is conceivable that Vieques could have sustained the impact of the expropriations if the Insular Government had targeted it as a site for industrial production like the other municipalities of Puerto Rico. But the constriction of economic life imposed by the navy made this task too difficult. In order to alleviate this crisis, on May 21, 1954, the Puerto Rican House of Representatives approved a resolution commissioning the local planning board to develop a permanent rehabilitation plan for Vieques.[14]

After the Industrial Incentives Act of 1947, the Development Company dedicated considerable efforts to attracting foreign capital to industrialize Puerto Rico. However, while Puerto Rico had inaugurated close to 400 new factories by 1954, Vieques had almost none. According to Vieques Mayor Antonio Rivera, the Developments Company's effort to promote Vieques as a potential manufacturing site was insufficient and inadequate. He pointed out that the only concession made to Caribbean Novelty Co., one of the first factories established in Vieques, was to offer it a free-rent building to operate for the first year. Caribbean Novelty, a subsidiary of an industrial firm from Long Island, New York, that manufactured women's underwear, started operations in June 17, 1954. It employed thirty-five workers and projected that this figure would increase to one hundred workers in the future. This, however, was not enough to offset the severe unemployment facing the island. Vieques mayor Antonio Rivera claimed that it was because of his efforts—not those of the Development Company—that this company established itself in Vieques. He added that it was necessary to promote these ventures in order to alleviate the local unemployment situation facing the Island.[15] Mayor Rivera did not limit his efforts to manufacturing. On November 16, 1954, he wrote to the administrator of the Development Company, Teodoro Moscoso, requesting his help in establishing a hotel that would also function as a school for hotel management. According to the mayor, due to the possibility that the military maneuvers might become permanent, a hotel of this nature would offer a great opportunity for the families of the members of the armed forces to visit Vieques.[16]

The study commissioned by the House of Representatives of Puerto Rico bore no fruit. By mid-1955, large portions of the population were migrating to Saint Thomas and Saint Croix in the U.S. Virgin Islands, and to Puerto Rico. Viequenses looked to the Land Authority as the only opportunity to revive its sagging agricultural economy. This public corporation promised to establish a pineapple-canning factory and to revitalize the agricultural and the cattle grazing industries, as the disappearance of PRACO left these industries in disarray. As related by Vieques merchant Paul Gonzalez, "Our economy only thrives during the military maneuvers. Once these disappear, Vieques looks like a cemetery. Vieques needs industries, not maneuvers."[17] Dr. Pedro Richardson, who had done numerous studies on Vieques for the government of Puerto Rico, commented that if the island's economic situation did not improve, Viequenses and their government would cease to exist.[18] Fortunately, by July 1955, the Land Authority reactivated the pineapple-canning factory established by PRACO, and 150 acres of pineapple were seeded.[19] It was expected that in the near future, 4,000 acres would be dedicated to the cultivation of this crop.[20] However, Wilfredo Santiago, special assistant to the executive director of the Land Authority, warned that the solution to the unemployment problem of Vieques required creating new industries and new sources of jobs. Agriculture could not provide sufficient opportunities to sustain an adequate lifestyle. Neither sugar cane nor cattle grazing, the two major industries in Vieques, provided sufficient income or job opportunities.[21]

The rise of the P.D.P. had been linked in the 1940s to its commitment to ending the historic power of the sugar companies over Puerto Rico. Thus, the sugar industry was on the wane everywhere, and agricultural production in general was declining in importance in Puerto Rico. However, when Governor Luis Muñoz Marín visited Vieques on March 22, 1957, Mayor Antonio Rivera and a panel of citizens who met with him claimed that sugar cane was the only viable alternative for the island, as the efforts by the Land Authority to develop the pineapple industry had failed.[22] As mentioned in a memorandum written to President Eisenhower by Mayor Rivera and a group of concerned citizens dated March 1, 1958, the lack of adequate transportation between Vieques and Humacao, were the sugar cane was processed, prevented cane farming from becoming profitable. Before the expropriations, marine commerce from Vieques traveled to Ceiba, a trip that took forty-five minutes to complete. After the construction of Roosevelt Roads, ships carrying supplies to Vieques were required to travel from Fajardo to Isabel Segunda, a two hour and fifteen minute trip. In addition, Viequenses complained that the military would not make its airport available for commercial use—not even for one flight a day—in order to mitigate the misery and hunger that was prevalent on the island. The memorandum was emphatic that the expropriations had made the situation in Vieques unbearable. It informed the president that many Viequenses had died defending the United States in both the Korean War and the Second World War. They therefore set forth that they should be allowed to live in peace and enjoy the economic growth so prevalent in Puerto Rico and the United States.[23] Two days after the Viequenses sent their memorandum to President Eisenhower, Governor Muñoz Marín, acknowledging the many problems facing Vieques, particularly those related to transportation, commissioned yet another study by the planning board.[24]

The economy of Vieques continued to slide. The island became dependent on its commercial sector, which was highly seasonal and catered to the U.S. troops that periodically came to Vieques for maneuvers and then left. The number of personnel stationed in Vieques permanently was minute, and it generated no multiplier effect on the local economy. The number of U.S. troops that came for maneuvers, by contrast, could be as high as 90,000. During the periods when the troops came to Vieques, they inundated the civilian area. They consumed at the bars and restaurants, and they hired the women of Vieques to wash and iron their clothes. Many families came to depend on the periodic bouts of income generation that the maneuvers generated. Prostitution also thrived. But these industries were considered indignities by most of the residents of Vieques who were used to work in agriculture. Conflicts between the troops and the local residents, fights in the bars, and complaints that the troops harassed the women in town plagued social life in Vieques. For example, when military personnel entered a private club in Vieques and asked to be served beer on February 8, 1959, and were told that the club did not serve beer to the public, they ransacked the club and attacked its president, initiating a melee which implicated fifty marines, fifty civilians, nineteen local policemen, and the a number of MPs, resulting in many wounded, two seriously.[25]

The decade of the 1960s brought more of the same for the Viequenses, with the exception that the navy tried to expropriate an additional 1,400 acres. This proposal would have left only about 1,700 acres for the population to live in, making a bad situation even worse. The navy made its intention to make civilian life unbearable in order to clear the island of residents when it opposed the development of tourism on the island as well as the use of its airport for other-than-military use. A navy spokesperson commented that Vieques was far removed from Puerto Rico and the United States, making it an ideal location to conduct military maneuvers.[26] Reacting to this news, Vieques Mayor Antonio Rivera requested that the local government intervene in order that Vieques obtain the use of the navy's airport for commercial use. He added that he did not understand how the United States could help its former enemies in Japan and Korea, assisting in their general well-being as well as in their economic development, while at the same time, causing so much damage to its own citizens. The navy, added Mayor Rodriguez, "should give us back the land it does not use."[27] Mayor Rivera also traveled to New Jersey in order to enlist the support on Puerto Ricans living on the mainland,[28] as well as to Washington and New York. Rivera hinted that he would establish picket lines in front of the San Juan Naval Base and at the Pentagon if he saw that his efforts had no effect. The only benefits the people of Vieques derived from the sacrifices endured, according the mayor, were the rum and sandwiches the marines purchased from the local merchants.[29] Reacting to these efforts, the month following Mayor Rivera's trip to the United States, Resident Commissioner Antonio Fernós Isern stated that he would request that the navy return free of charge Monte Santo and Santa Maria, formerly the most densely populated areas of Vieques.[30]

Given that these efforts were fruitless, Mayor Rivera placed his hopes, and redirected his efforts, toward the newly elected administration of the Democratic President John F. Kennedy.[31] Six months after the election of President Kennedy, Secretary of the Navy John B. Connally commented that he would consider transferring the military airport in Vieques to the government of Puerto Rico to be used for civilian purposes. During a meeting he sustained with Governor Muñoz Marín and Resident Commissioner Fernós Isern, both Muñoz Marín and Fernós suggested that the land on which the airport was built be returned to the government of Puerto Rico, as well as the valuable land used by the naval base in San Juan. No decisions were reached during these discussions.[32]

The navy's response to these conversations was swift. According to Captain Edward R. Hunt, of the Tenth Naval District, the navy needed to retain all of the territory it possessed in Vieques as it was the only place under naval command where similar operations could take place. Captain Hunt, in a presentation to the Navy League at the Caribe Hilton assisted by, among others, Admiral Allen Smith, commander of the Tenth Naval District, reminded his audience that the United States was facing a communist threat, and that its military forces must be prepared in order to combat this threat. Captain Hunt added that one of the reasons why Vieques was ideal for this type of maneuvers was that "it is relatively free of civilians."[33]

According to Mayor Rivera, the issue of the return of the expropriated lands in Vieques was now in the hands of Governor Muñoz Marín and President Kennedy, as there was nothing more he could do.[34] However, he did organize a picket in front of the naval base in San Juan as part of a passive resistance movement in order to draw attention to the plight of the residents of Vieques.[35] In the meantime, Governor Muñoz Marín discounted some reports that the negotiations with the navy had reached an "impasse." According to Muñoz Marín, the negotiations were continuing.[36] Yet, things were not running smoothly for him in Washington. Senator Richard B. Russell, head of the Armed Forces Committee of the Senate and a Democratic Senator from Virginia stated in a meeting with Admiral Smith and Governor Muñoz Marín that the navy should not return any land it currently used and, in addition, should not promote the development of tourism on the island. When asked if atomic weapons were stored in Puerto Rico, Senator Russell answered that he had no knowledge of this, but he thought that it was highly probable that the air force might have some.[37] The navy had plans to completely remove all population from Vieques. This sparked strong cultural resistance on the part of the residents. In a letter to President Kennedy, Puerto Rico's governor, Luis Muñoz Marín, argued that the residents of Vieques and their ancestors "have lived there for many generations. Their roots have grown around family, neighbors, schools, churches, houses, land, and jobs. The project involves forcible uprooting of these people—even removal of the bodies from the cemeteries because, we are told, the people of Vieques will not be allowed to return to visit the graves." The eviction of the population of Vieques, continued the governor, "is peculiarly subject to widespread denunciation and to hostile propaganda use. Puerto Rico has only recently emerged from colonial status. The United States is still charged by some people with colonial rule over Puerto Rico, a charge which is unjustified but can be made effective if given a dramatic symbol."[38] Muñoz's appeal to the empire was based on the notion of decolonization.

The complete eviction of the population of Vieques never happened.

On March 20, 1964, Mayor Rivera angrily reacted to some reports that the navy was considering the acquisition of 1,400 additional acres in Vieques.[39] He organized picket lines in front of the naval base and considered organizing groups to protest "this horrible injustice" at the White House and in Congress.[40] He, along with a group of thirty-three Viequenses, met with Governor Muñoz Marín in order to express their dismay at this new affront by the U.S. Navy,[41] who in turn requested a meeting with President Lyndon B. Johnson to discuss this matter.[42] Mayor Rivera, in the meantime, considered taking this case to the Federal Court. By filing an injunction, he hoped to be able to stop the navy's expropriation of these additional lands.[43]

Spokespersons for the Defense Department claimed that all information regarding Vieques was classified and therefore refused to comment about rumors regarding the impending expropriations.[44] The following day, May 5, 1964, Mayor Rivera was notified that the navy decided against further expropriations in Vieques.[45] He received a hero's welcome upon his return to Puerto Rico and finally to Vieques.[46] This is a turning point in the history of Vieques in that the plans to permanently remove all of the civilian population from Vieques, which apparently had been the preferred navy option since the late 1940s, and all further acquisition of land by the navy to that end, stopped after that date.

In 1970, the legislature of Puerto Rico commissioned a report on Vieques, which, among other things, included calculations of the growth of personal income in Puerto Rico, in San Juan, and in Vieques. This study demonstrated how far behind Vieques had fallen when compared to Puerto Rico and the severe impact the expropriation was having on the island. Between 1950 and 1969, Puerto Rico's internal income grew at a yearly rate of 9.4 percent, that of San Juan at a rate of 10.4 percent yearly, while that of Vieques lagged far behind, at 2.6 percent yearly.[47] Part of this was due to the fact that the population of Vieques actually declined from 9,228 in 1950 to 7,767 in 1970. But the increasing disparity in income is also present at the per-capita level.

Despite the catastrophic effect of the navy expropriations on the economy, median income either of persons or of families in Vieques was in the middle of the distribution if one considers all of the *municipios* of Puerto

Rico. In 1950, Vieques ranked 47th out of 77 *municipios*. In 2000, it was the second poorest *municipio* of Puerto Rico. (See Table E.3.) Thus, the relocation of the population to the center of the island in the 1940s and the preservation of the status quo over several decades produced long-term decline in Vieques relative to the rest of Puerto Rico. The massive protests against the navy in 1979,[48] and all opposition to the navy thereafter, took place within the economic parameters set by the partition of land established in the late 1940s and its economic consequences.

Attempts to establish some industries in Vieques after a so-called memorandum of understanding between the navy and the Insular Government in 1983 did not produce much improvement in Vieques, even though the agreement stipulated that the navy would make "every meaningful effort, working with Commonwealth agencies and groups, to obtain full employment on the island."[49] The agreement of 1983 was supposed to protect ecosystems, creat conservation zones, and shelter endangered species, to reduce noise, and to promote historic preservation. Very little of it was actually observed by the navy. In 1999, the navy illegally utilized armor piercing shells containing depleted uranium in Vieques, a few miles from the civilian population.[50] Upon impact, the shells pulverize, producing uranium-loaded dust that travels downwind to the civilian area of Vieques.

Health

Perhaps the longest lasting effect of the navy presence in Vieques will be the contamination produced by over five decades of military maneuvers and target practice, during which the eastern tip of Vieques was bombed from land, sea, and air.[51] The ecosystem has received high doses of cluster bombs, napalm, chaff, depleted uranium, and dozens of other pollutants that are harmful to human health. After the withdrawal of the navy, the central demand of the residents of Vieques has been cleanup of the toxics left behind by the military, and provision of health care for those who are sick from the pollution. At issue is whether the toxics introduced into the ecosystem by bombings during the maneuvers have had an impact on the health of the residents of Vieques, with the residents of Vieques loudly claiming that it has, and the Agency for Toxic Substances and Disease Registry claiming that "the residents of Vieques are not being exposed to harmful

levels of chemicals in the soil."[52] A study produced by the Commonwealth
of Puerto Rico demonstrated that Vieques has a 27 percent higher cancer
rate than the rest of Puerto Rico.[53] Showing that this higher cancer rate is
the product of military contamination is difficult scientifically. Biologists
have studied the presence of heavy metals in the plants in the civilian area[54]
and concluded that agriculture (except hydroponics) is not viable in any
area of Vieques.

The eastern part of Vieques (14,573 acres, or 40 percent of all island
land) was not returned to Puerto Rico after the navy left in 2003. The eastern part of Vieques has been listed in the Environmental Protection Agency
Superfund National Priorities list since 2005, and has been declared a
"wildlife refuge and wilderness area" at the same time. A wilderness refuge
is supposed to be a "landscape untrammeled by man" and "retaining its
primeval character and influence." There are few places on the planet more
touched by destructive human contact. The primary effect of the designa-
tion of the area as wildlife refuge is to bar humans from entering it, thus
relaxing the pressure on federal authorities to clean up, since by definition,
humans cannot be affected, as they cannot reach the area.[55]

Federal studies have not sufficiently explored the impact of pollution
and have been criticized for not analyzing sufficiently the pathways through
which pollutants travel from the bomb impact zone to the civilian area.[56]
Just to give one example, traces of uranium were detected in 97 percent of
the crabs in samples taken in all areas of the island, that is, not just the eastern impact zone.[57] The presence of unexploded ordnance in the eastern part
and underwater surrounding coastal areas guarantees that toxic substances
from unexploded bombs leak into the reefs and marine ecosystems and
spread from there to surrounding waters. The Agency for Toxic Substances
and Disease Registry (ATSDR) first found that decades of explosive deto-
nations by the navy on the Puerto Rican island of Vieques posed no health
hazards to residents and then backed away from these results in November
2009, after protests from community leaders, the scientific community, and
a probe by the Government Accountability Office, an investigative arm of
Congress.[58] At present, the residents of Vieques are awaiting the revised
findings by the federal ATSDR.

Appendix: Tables

TABLE 1.1
Monthly Imports of Food Products in Puerto Rico, 1940–1942

	Tonnage	Food	Population	Lb. of food per capita
1940	112,933	37,268	1,869,000	40
Jan.-Mar. 1942	91,153	41,930	1,950,000	43
Apr.-Dec. 1942	50,863	28,992	1,950,000	30
% Change (Apr.-Dec. 1942 relative to 1940)	-55%	-22%	+4%	-25%

Source: "The Puerto Rican Economy during the War Year of 1942," Jun. 1943. A.F.L.M.M., Sec. XII, Material de Proyecto de Recopilación de Documentos, Biblioteca Harry S. Truman. During the first few months of 1942, tonnage decreased by 55% and food imports by 22% when compared with 1940 levels. This created a critical shortage of food.

TABLE 1.2
Sales of Puerto Rico Cement, 1942 and 1944

Client	1942[1]	%	1944[2]	%
Corps of Engineers	$157,653	36	$153,500	39
The Arundel Corporation	108,750	25	0	0
Department of Transportation	80,732	18	0	0
P.R.R.A.[3]	21,480	5	1,876	1
Works Project Administration	11,575	3	0	
Insular Housing Department	10,072	2	425	0
War Emergency Project	0	0	47,053	12
Navy Department	0	0	20,972	5
Total Federal Clients	$390,262	89	$203,826	57
Total Insular Clients	47,730	11	167,392	43
Total Sales	**$437,992**	**100**	**$391,218**	**100**

Sources: 1. Contratos, Compromisos, y Embarques de la *Puerto Rico Cement* a partir del 31 de octubre de 1942. C.I.H., P.C.J.P. Col., Box #26, Fol. #25, Doc. #1A. 2. Contratos, Compromisos, y Embarques de la *Puerto Rico Cement* a partir del 31 de agosto de 1944. C.I.H., P.C.J.P. Col., Box #26, Fol. #28, Doc. #1. 3. Puerto Rico Reconstruction Administration. The construction of military bases required the bulk of all locally produced cement, thereby limiting its availability for other activities. During 1942, the peak of the construction activity, federal projects consumed 89% of the production of one of the two cement factories on the island, the state-owned Puerto Rico Cement. By 1944, this figure was reduced to 57%; the remaining 43% was sold to local businesses.

TABLE 1.3
Insular Governmental Income from Rum Tax Rebates, 1941–1947 (in $ millions)

Year	Government Income	Rum Tax Rebate	Tax Rebate as % of Government Income
1941	$53.0	$7.4	14
1942	75.6	18.0	24
1943	80.8	18.4	23
1944	147.0	71.4	49
1945	123.0	44.1	36
1946	129.1	27.6	21
1947	141.1	27.6	20
Total	**$749.60**	**$214.50**	**29**

Source: Hibben and Picó, *Industrial Development*, 208-209. Since federal taxes collected on locally produced rum were returned to Puerto Rico, the export of this product proved a second bonanza for the insular government, accounting for up 49% of its income in 1944, and an average of 29% between 1941 and 1947.

TABLE 2.1
Vieques Sugar Mills, 1907 and 1910

Name	Owner	Production in 1907 (tons)	Production in 1910 (tons)
Playa Grande	Benítez Sugar Co.	2,984	4,366
Esperanza	Víctor Mourraille	2,056	4,280
Santa María	Charles Le Brun	1,130	1,746
Arkadia	Arkadia Sugar Co.	1,500	2,437
Total Vieques		**7,670**	**12,829**

Source: "Government of Porto Rico, Treasury Department, Bureau of Property Taxes: Comparative Statistical Report of Sugar Manufactured in Porto Rico from the Crops of 1907, 1908, 1909, and 1910," National Archives Building, Washington, D.C., R.G. 350, Records of the Bureau of Insular Affairs, File #422. At the beginning of the twentieth century, Vieques had four sugar *centrales*: Playa Grande, Esperanza also known as Puerto Real, Santa María, and Arcadia. These *centrales* were small but profitable, due to the inclusion of Puerto Rico in the U.S. Customs system, giving its sugars free entrance to the U.S. market.

TABLE 2.2
Land Concentration in Vieques and Santa Isabel

Farms, by size	Vieques						Santa Isabel					
	% of Farms	% of all Farms	Area of Farms (cuerdas)	% of area of Farms	Improved Land	% Improved Land	# of Farms	% of all Farms	Area of Farms (cuerdas)	% of area of Farms	Improved Land	% Improved Land
Less than 3 *cuerdas*	7	7.87	13	0.06	13	0.09	5	31.25	10	0.11	10	0.11
3 to 9 *cuerdas*	37	41.57	184	0.87	150	0.99	4	25.00	19	0.20	19	0.20
10 to 19 *cuerdas*	15	16.85	205	0.97	150	0.99	2	12.50	23	0.24	20	0.21
20 to 49 *cuerdas*	2	2.25	564	2.66	381	2.52	2	12.50	60	0.63	21	0.22
50 to 99 *cuerdas*	7	7.87	482	2.27	294	1.95		0.00		0.00		0.00
100 to 174 *cuerdas*	8	8.99	1,035	4.88	946	6.26		0.00		0.00		0.00
175 to 259 *cuerdas*	6	6.74	1,258	5.93	1,059	7.01	1	6.25	175	1.84	130	1.37
260 to 499 *cuerdas*	3	3.37	1,055	4.97	590	3.91		0.00		0.00		0.00
500 to 999 *cuerdas*	2	2.25	1,320	6.22	385	2.55	1	6.25	876	9.21	776	8.16
1000 *cuerdas* or more	2	2.25	15,093	71.16	11,137	73.73	1	6.25	8,351	87.78	7426	78.05
Total	**89**	**100.00**	**21,209**	**100.00**	**15,105**	**100.00**	**16**	**100.00**	**9,514**	**100.00**	**8402**	**88.31**

Source: U.S. Department of Commerce, Bureau of the Census, *Fifteenth Census of the United States*, 219. Table 2.2 compares land tenure in Vieques and Santa Isabel in 1930. Santa Isabel in the main island of Puerto Rico was known as the fiefdom of the Aguirre Sugar Company and was frequently mentioned as a case of extreme land concentration during the 1930s. Land concentration in Vieques was extreme, as in Santa Isabel.

TABLE 2.3

Principal Landowners of Vieques in 1940–1941
and Their Properties in 1944–1945

Last Name	Name	*Cuerdas* 1940	No. Farms 1940	*Cuerdas* 1945	No. Farms 1945	*Cuerdas*: Difference (1)
Eastern Sugar	Associates	10,343	15	1,825	1	-8,518
Benítez	Dolores	3,636	2	0	0	-3,636
Benítez	Carlota y otros	3,636	2	0	0	-3,636
Benítez Bithorn	Carmen Aurelia	3,082	1	0	0	-3,082
Bithorn Benítez	María	3,082	1	0	0	-3,082
Benítez Santiago	Francisco y J.	1,191	2	0	0	-1,191
Benítez Bithorn	Carmen Amelia	554	1	0	0	-554
Bithorn Vda. Benítez	María	554	1	0	0	-554
Simons	Miguel	2,129	4	1,308	4	-821
Díaz Sabino	Esteban	678	16	0	0	-678
Rieckehoff	Ana	468	1	0	0	-468
Bermúdez	Juan	441	4	108	4	-333
Haristory	Justine y M.	347	1	0	0	-347
Díaz	Esteban	333	4	0	0	-333
Quiñones Almodóvar	Manuel	293	3	105	1	-188
Rivera Sucn.	Sixto A.	243	1	243	1	0
Rivera	Sixto A.	242	3	243	3	1
Ramírez	Tomás	210	2	315	3	105
González Mercedes	Jovito	190	2	0	0	-190
Quiñones Almodóvar	Natividad/otros	181	2	0	0	-181
Brignoni Vda. Pérez	Rosa	180	8	182	9	2
Brignoni Mercado	Juan	167	1	0	0	-167
Cruz Vélez	Eulogio	166	18	0	0	-166
Quiñones Sucn.	Epigmene	146	2	0	0	-146
Diaz Esteban y	Belén Carcaño	129	1	0	0	-129
Benites Castano	Carlos	124	1	0	0	-124

Value of Land 1940	Value of Land 1945	Land Value, Difference	Improvement Value 1940	Improvement Value 1945	Improvement Value Difference
662,210	121,010	-541,200	77,720	0	-77,720
2,720	0	-2,720	0	0	0
0	0	0	12,870	0	-12,870
20,300	0	-20,300	0	0	0
19,590	0	-19,590	0	0	0
0	0	0	6,080	0	-6,080
3,800	0	-3,800	10	0	-10
3,720	0	-3,720	10	0	-10
83,770	54,320	-29,450	12,230	610	-11,620
37,250	0	-37,250	5,190	0	-5,190
17,150	0	-17,150	150	0	-150
7,920	7,920	0	3,100	3,100	0
34,740	0	-34,740	2,150	0	-2,150
10,740	0	-10,740	10	0	-10
7,950	3,150	-4,800	0	0	0
19,600	19,600	0	50	50	0
13,740	13,740	0	100	100	0
6,300	10,500	4,200	0	0	0
9,110	0	-9,110	300	0	-300
10,000	0	-10,000	90	0	-90
12,240	12,350	110	140	140	0
11,620	0	-11,620	0	0	0
12,140	0	-12,140	2,070	0	-2,070
3,112	0	-3,112	530	0	-530
3,870	0	-3,870	100	0	-100
6,430	0	-6,430	0	0	0

continued on next page

TABLE 2.3 (CONTINUED)
Principal Landowners of Vieques in 1940–1941 and Their Properties in 1944–1945

Last Name	Name	Cuerdas 1940	No. Farms 1940	Cuerdas 1945	No. Farms 1945	Cuerdas: Difference (1)
Emeric	José	115	1	0	0	-115
Brignoni Mercado	Inés	110	1	110	1	0
Acevedo Guadalupe	Antolino	108	1	0	0	-108
Brignoni Huertas	José	108	1	0	0	-108
Fix Alais	A.	105	1	0	0	-105
Picó Mora	Arturo	105	1	6	1	-99
Fix	Nargaret D.	105	1	0	0	-105
Carle Dubois	Carlos	103	2	24	1	-79
Jaspard	Carlos	100	2	0	0	-100
Total		**33,705**	**110**	**4,469**	**29**	**-29,236**
Familia Benítez		15,736	10	0	0	-15,736
Familia Benítez (%)		47%	9%	0%	0%	54%
Eastern Sugar (%)		31%	14%	41%	3%	29%

Value of Land 1940	Value of Land 1945	Land Value, Difference	Improvement Value 1940	Improvement Value 1945	Improvement Value Difference
4,200	0	-4,200	80	0	-80
8,280	8,280	0	60	60	0
1,250	0	-1,250	0	0	0
1,260	0	-1,260	0	0	0
3,150	0	-3,150	0	0	0
4,200	600	-3,600	1,450	1,400	-50
3,150	0	-3,150	0	0	0
9,110	2,400	-6,710	1,070	1,330	260
8,480	0	-8,480	20	0	-20
1,063,102	253,870	-809,232	125,580	6,790	-96,670
50,130	0	-50,130	18,970	0	-18,970
5%	0%	6%	15%	0%	20%
62%	48%	67%	62%	0%	80%

1. The total for this column exceeds the total expropriated by the Navy because some landowners not included in this table actually acquired land between 1941 and 1945. The principal landowners of Vieques were members of the Benítez family, who owned 15,735 *cuerdas* of land out of a total of 36,032 *cuerdas* assessed for taxation, or 44% of the land of Vieques. Eastern Sugar Associates owned 10,343 *cuerdas* or 29% of the land in Vieques. Two large landowners controlled 73% of the surface of the island.

Source: A.G.P.R., D.H., Vieques, 1940-1950.

TABLE 3.1
Summary of Naval Land Acquisitions

	Approximate Acreage	Approximate Price	Price in $ per acre	Number of Parcels	Approximate Number of Parties
Naval Land Acquisition, 1941–1943					
Civil Action No. 2300	10,209	379,300	37	6	30
Civil Action No. 2443	97	18,200	188	18	55
Civil Action No. 2487	687	56,900	83	34	150
Civil Action No. 2604	1,234	66,600	54	6	15
Civil Action No. 2714	7,937	423,800	53	2	4
Civil Action No. 3211	13	1,200	92	1	10
Civil Action No. 3254	140	21,500	154	7	25
Civil Action No. 3361	696	74,000	106	42	200
Subtotal	**21,013**	**1,041,500**	**50**	**116**	**489**
Navy Land Acquisitions	4,340	530,400	122	9	40
1950, Civil Action No. 6108	4,340	530,400	122	9	40
Totals	**25,353**	**1,561,900**	**62**	**125**	**529**

Source: Department of the Navy, *Continued Use*, vol. 1, 2–200. The navy expropriated 10,209 acres or *cuerdas* from Juan Angel Tio and paid an average price of $37 per acre while the average price paid for the remainder of the land expropriated during this time frame was $60 per acre. All told, the navy expropriated 25,353 acres.

TABLE 3.2
Civilian Ownership of Farms in Vieques, by Barrio, 1940, 1945, 1950

Barrio	# of Farms in 1940	Cuerdas in 1940	# of Farms in 1945	Cuerdas in 1945	# of Farms in 1950	Cuerdas 1950
Florida	41	1,475	23	1,204	18	369
Llave	80	4,152	30	218	28	164
Mosquito	10	95	2	9	2	9
Puerto Diablo	24	7,539	23	3,921	18	2,791
Puerto Ferro	27	915	15	220	15	505
Puerto Real	193	2,418	165	4,238	155	1,689
Punta Arenas	7	13,369	–	–	–	–
Florida & Puerto Ferro	–	–	1	124	1	124
Florida-Puerto Real	2	3	–	–	–	–
Puerto Real & Llave	–	–	–	–	–	–
Puerto Real & Puerto Ferro	1	5,856	–	–	–	–
Unknown	2	210	–	–	6	34
Total	**387**	**36,032**	**259**	**9,934**	**243**	**5,685**

Source: A.G.P.R., D.H., Vieques, 1940–1950. Some farms spanned more than one barrio, and it was not possible to assign portions of farms to specific barrios. We retained the classification of the original documents. Urban land lots not included. In 1940, before the start of the expropriations, the entire island was owned by civilians. The data of 1945 summarize the effects of the first round of expropriations, as civilian ownership was reduced to 9,934 cuerdas, while the 1950 data illustrate the effects of the second round of expropriations. By this time, civilian ownership was further reduced, and only 5,685 cuerdas were in private hands.

TABLE 3.3
Population of Vieques, by Barrio

Barrio	1899[a]	1910[a]	1920[b]	1930[b]	1935[c]	1940[d]	1950[d]	1960[e]	1970[e]
Town (Isabel II)[1]	0	3,158	3,424	3,101	2,816	2,678	3,085	2,487	2,378
Florida[1]	2,645	565	603	775	659	1,253	2,638	1,989	2,381
Llave [1]	1,059	1,610	1,715	1,583	1,683	1,776	191	89	73
Mosquitos[1]	0	748	847	818	785	851	20	4	
Puerto Diablo [1]	0	854	584	505	687	548	894	693	709
Puerto Ferro[1]	879	638	1,041	839	776	570	723	507	884
Punta Arenas[1]	0	922	1,102	833	884	901	0		30
Puerto Real[2]	1,344	1,930	2,335	2,128	1,747	1,785	1,677	1,441	1,312
Total	**5,927**	**10,425**	**11,651**	**10,582**	**10,037**	**10,362**	**9,228**	**7,210**	**7,767**

1. Not counted separately in 1899. 2. Identified as Puerto Real Arriba and Puerto Real Abajo in 1899. As a result of the expropriations, the population of Vieques decreased from 10,362 in 1940 to 7,767 in 1970.

Sources: a. U.S. Department of Commerce, Bureau of the Census, *Thirteenth Census of the United States*, 1190; b. U.S. Department of Commerce, Bureau of the Census, *Fifteenth Census of the United States*, 131; c. Puerto Rico Reconstruction Administration, *Census of Puerto Rico*, 12; d. U.S. Department of Commerce, Bureau of the Census, *1950 Population Census Report*, quoted in Veaz, "Las expropiaciones," 202; e. Department of the Navy, *Continued Use*, vol. 1, 2:187.

TABLE 4.1
Lands Seized by the Navy during the First Expropriations (Different Estimates)

Source	Lands Expropriated (*cuerdas*)	Private Property, not Expropriated	Area of Vieques	% Expropriated
1	21,000	11,640	32,640	64%
2	21,860	11,822	33,682	65%
3	22,000	11,682	33,682	65%
4	23,500	10,015	33,515	70%
5	21,000	n/a	n/a	n/a
6	21,000	11,640	32,640	64%
7	26,097	9,935	36,032	72%

Sources: 1. Picó, "Report of the Committee." 2. *El Eco de Vieques*, Apr. 1947. 3. Pastor Ruiz, *Vieques antiguo*. 4. Picó, *The Geographic Regions*, 209-215. 5. Department of the Navy, *Continued Use*, vol. 1. 6. Rodríguez Beruff, *El archivo Luis Muñoz Marín*, 81. 7. Ayala, "Del latifundioazucarero," 20. Not all sources agree regarding the exact areas expropriated. Nevertheless, the differences are minor, and the sources all point to the devastating impact of the expropriations.

TABLE 4.2

Property Valuations and Income Reduction as a Result of the Expropriations in Vieques

Fiscal Year	Property Valuation	Municipal Income	Loss of Income Fiscal Year 1941–42	Insular Government Subsidy	Net Loss of Income
1941–42	$2,472,614.00	$46,244.54	–	–	–
1942–43	1,788,310.00	38,303.92	$ 7,940.62	–	$7,940.62
1943–44	1,420,126.00	33,718.97	12,525.57	–	12,525.57
1944–45	1,097,550.00	27,349.43	18,895.11	$11,553.00	7,342.11
1945–46	1,184,160.00	35,258.42	10,986.12	11,000.00	(13.88)
1946–47	943,440.00	22,279.95	23,964.59	10,900.00	13,064.59
1947–48	940,710.00	28,184.66	18,059.88	7,500.00	10,559.88
1948–49	970,180.00	30,382.28	15,862.26	9,047.00	6,815.26
Total		**$261,722.17**	**$108,234.15**	**$50,000.00**	**$58,234.15**

Sources: Office of the Treasurer, Apr. 21, 1948; Office of the Auditor, Apr. 28, 1949. A.G.PR., Fon. Office of the Governor, Tar. #96–20, Box #1044. Property-tax revenue amounted to $18,700 out of a municipal budget of $46,244 in fiscal year 1941–1942, that is, 40% of municipal revenue, before the expropriation of the Eastern Sugar Company. As a result of the expropriations, the municipality of Vieques lost $108,234.15 between 1941 and 1949. The Insular Government provided a subsidy of $50,000 between 1944 and 1949. However, the municipality of Vieques still had to make up for a loss of $58,234.15. Even after the subsidies from the insular government, Vieques lost 22% of its income between 1941 and 1949.

TABLE 4.3
PRACO Capitalization

PRIDCO[1]	$ 497,118
Land Authority[2]	1,457,029
Total Transferred	$ 1,954,147
Legislative Assignments	10,279,807
Total Capital	**$ 12,233,954**

1. Funds initially assigned to PRIDCO by Law #89. 2. Funds initially assigned to Land Authority by Law #90.

Source: PRACO Audited Financial Statements, Jun. 30, 1946. A.F.L.M.M., Sec. IV, President of the Senate, Ser. 2, Box #55, Doc. #1. The Puerto Rico Agricultural Corporation (PRACO) was created by Law No. 31 of Apr. 24, 1945. PRACO was assigned an initial capital of $12,233,954 to fulfill its objectives, most of it coming from legislative assignments. The Insular Government thus attempted to overcome the social crisis created in Vieques by the navy.

TABLE 4.4
Lands Administered by PRACO in Vieques

	Date	Acres
Leased from: Government of Puerto Rico[1]	Jan.-1946	12,807
Purchased from:		
· Natividad Quiñones de González	1946	722
· Eastern Sugar Associates	1947	3,161
· Smaller landowners	1946-1947	3,883
Total Lands Administered		**16,690**
Area of Vieques		33,000
% of Area of Vieques Administered by PRACO		**51%**

1. Lands expropriated by the navy in 1941–42. The navy transferred them to the Federal Department of the Interior, which retained the title but assigned them temporarily to the Government of Puerto Rico.

Sources: PRACO, Financial Statement Jun. 30, 1947, 26–27, A.F.L.M.M., Sec. IV, President of the Senate, Ser. 2, Fol. #55, Doc. #1; Picó, *The Geographic Regions*, 209–215. By 1947, PRACO became the largest landowner in Vieques and the manager of 16,680 *cuerdas*—51% of the land of the island.

TABLE 4.5
PRACO Land Acquisition in Vieques and in Puerto Rico

Seller	Date	Price	Assessed Value	Amount Overpaid	%
IN VIEQUES					
Tomás González	Mar. 14, 1946	$110,000	$77,300	$32,700	42%
Tomás González	Mar. 14, 1946	$14,000	Structure, no value	$14,000	N/A
Eastern Sugar Associates	Jun. 16, 1946	$386,500	$262,800	$123,700	47%
Purchases in Vieques		**$510,500**	**$340,100**	**$170,400**	**50%**
OUTSIDE VIEQUES					
Heirs of Angel Umpierre (Bayamón)	Dec. 31, 1945	$197,600	$162,600	$35,000	22%
Ernesto López Martínez	Dec. 31, 1945	$160,000	$144,600	$15,400	11%
Purchases Outside Vieques		**$357,600**	**$307,200**	**$50,400**	**16%**

Source: PRACO, Financial Statement, Jun. 30, 1947, 26-27, A.F.L.M.M., Sec. IV, President of the Senate, Ser. 2, Fol. #55, Doc. #1. Table 4.5 shows that PRACO paid prices 50% above assessed value in Vieques, in contrast to the prices paid in other areas of Puerto Rico, where it paid 16% above assessed value.

TABLE 4.6
Statistics from PRACO Financial Statements
(In $ thousands, Fiscal Year Ending June 30)

	1946	1947	1948[1]	1949	1950[2]
Government Assignments	$2,170	$3,355	$2,288	$2,288	$400
Sales	61	575		2,803	2,248
Cash	986	1,453	N/A	57	142
Annual Losses	(350)	(648)	(1,329)	(1,610)	(2,401)
Cumulative Losses		**(998)**	**(2,327)**	**(3,937)**	**(6,338)**
Number of Employees	398	2,150			
Employees in Vieques		1,113			

1. Figures for FY 1948 are estimates or they are from Auditing Report of 1949. 2. On July 1, 1950, PRACO was transferred to Puerto Rico's Department of Agriculture and Commerce. PRACO's Board of Directors was eliminated.

Source: A.F.L.M.M., Sec. IV, President of the Senate, Ser. 2, Fol. #55, Doc. #1. Out of the total 2,150 jobs PRACO generated in Puerto Rico, 1,113 or 52% were concentrated in Vieques in 1947. The cost of keeping a person working during fiscal year 1947 was $465—an amount that the government of Puerto Rico was willing to assume, showing the commitment of the Insular Government to alleviating the social crisis created in Vieques by the navy.

TABLE 4.7

Employment Trends in Relation to Expropriations and Military Construction

	1941–1943	1944–1945	1946–1948
Labor Force	2,794	2,794	2,794
Employed by the Navy	1,700	225	225
% Employed by the Navy	**61**	**8**	**8**
Employed by PRACO	0	0	1,113
% Employed by PRACO	**0**	**0**	**40**

Sources: Picó, "Report of the Committee," Table II; Hibben and Picó, Industrial Development, 47. Navy employment was minimal after the construction of the base in Vieques was completed.

TABLE 4.8

Comparison of PRIDCO and PRACO (Fiscal Year 1947)

Total Assets	Employees	Sales	Sales/Employee
PRACO $ 6.0 M	1,952	$361,000	$185.00
PRIDCO $10.9 M	845	$4,300,000	$ 5,056.00

Source: Hibben and Picó, Industrial Development, 151. While PRACO concentrated on job creation, PRIDCO concentrated on sales and profits.

TABLE 5.1
Owners of Cattle in Vieques, 1940, 1945, 1950

Year	Last Name	First Name	Value	%
1940	Eastern Sugar	Associates	$119,950	92. 7%
	Simons	Miguel	$5,340	4. 1%
	Bermudez	Juan y otros	$2,230	1. 7%
	BrignoniVda. de Pérez	Rosa	$800	0. 6%
	Cruz Vélez	Eulogio	$480	0. 4%
	Quiñones	Manuel	$250	0. 2%
	Pérez de Rivera	Julia	$120	0. 1%
	González	Tomás	$100	0. 1%
	Lopez Martínez	Ambrosio	$100	0. 1%
Total for 1940			**$129,370**	**100. 0%**
1945	Tio	Juan Angel	$94,870	73. 7%
	Cayere	Simons	$7,120	5. 5%
	Félix	Margaret D.	$4,890	3. 8%
	Ortiz Román Bermúdez	Juan Sucn.	$3,130	2. 4%
	González	Jovito	$2,910	2. 3%
	Aguiar	Federico	$2,610	2. 0%
	Ramírez	Tomás	$2,390	1. 9%
	Sáez	Rafael	$2,340	1. 8%
	Mellado	Manuel	$1,370	1. 1%
	Quiñones de González	Natividad	$1,060	0. 8%
	Tirado	Pablo	$880	0. 7%
	Díaz Felipe	Neris	$860	0. 7%
	BrignoniVda. de Pérez	Rosa	$800	0. 6%
	Rivera	Severino	$800	0. 6%
	Monell	Aeropagita	$670	0. 5%
	Quiñónez Ayala	Felipo	$580	0. 5%
	Cruz Vélez	Eulogio	$480	0. 4%
	Pérez de Rivera	Julia	$120	0. 1%

continued on next page

TABLE 5.1 (CONTINUED)
Owners of Cattle in Vieques, 1940, 1945, 1950

Year	Last Name	First Name	Value	%
1945 Cont.	López Martínez	Ambrosio	$100	0. 1%
	Rivera	Victoriano	$420	0. 3%
	Quiñónez	Manuel	$250	0. 2%
	Vélez Rodríguez	Manuel	$80	0. 1%
Total for 1945			**$128,730**	**100. 0%**
1950	Diaz Sobrino	Esteban	$12,120	22. 6%
	Biascochea & López		$11,870	22. 1%
	Ortiz Acevedo	Román	$3,980	7. 4%
	Cayere	Enrique	$3,650	6. 8%
	Biascochea	Alberto H	$3,630	6. 8%
	López Colón	Ignacio	$3,000	5. 6%
	González	Jovito	$2,910	5. 4%
	Ramírez	Tomás	$2,390	4. 5%
	Saez	Rafael	$2,340	4. 4%
	Aguiar	Federico	$2,080	3. 9%
	Mellado	Manuel	$1,620	3. 0%
	Díaz Felipe	Nerés	$880	1. 6%
	Tirado	Pablo	$880	1. 6%
	Rivera	Severino	$800	1. 5%
	Morell	Aeropagitas	$670	1. 3%
	Rivera	Victoriano	$370	0. 7%
	Quiñones Ayala	Felipe	$250	0. 5%
	Pérez de Rivera	Julia	$120	0. 2%
	López Martínez	Ambrosio	$100	0. 2%
	Vélez Rodríguez	Manuel	$80	0. 2%
Total for 1950			**$53,740**	**100. 0%**

Source: A.G.P.R., D.H., Vieques, 1940–1950. In 1940, the largest owner of cattle in Vieques was the Eastern Sugar Associates, controlling 93% of the total livestock. In 1945, it was Juan Angel Tio, with 74%. Cattle ownership appears a bit more dispersed in 1950. Official figures do not reflect the many smaller owners who grazed their cattle in Vieques.

TABLE 6.1
Percentage of Black Enlisted Men and Women

Service	July 1, 1949	July 1, 1954	July 1, 1956
Army	12.4	13.7	12.8
Navy	4.7	3.6	6.3
Air Force	5.1	8.6	10.4
Marine Corps	2.1	6.5	6.5

Source: McGregor, *Desegregation of the Armed Forces*, 395. In the aftermath of World War II, as desegregation advanced, the navy's percentage of black men and women actually dropped from 4.7 in 1949 to 3.6 in 1954 (compared with 12.4% and 13.7% for the army, respectively, in those years). While the percentage of blacks in the army approximated closely their percentage in the national population, that was not the case for the navy. Segregation in the navy not only was more entrenched than in the other branches of the armed services, but its dissolution advanced at a slower speed and with greater reluctance on the part of the leaders of that service.

TABLE E.1

Vieques: Assessed Value of Land, Improvements to Land, and Personal Property in 1940, 1945, 1950

Year	Land Value	Land Value (%)	Improvement Value	Improvement Value (%)	Personal Property Value	Personal Property Value (%)	Total Value
1940	$1,248,512	65%	$294,770	15%	$368,300	19%	$1,911,582
1945	$573,175	49%	$219,721	19%	$375,780	32%	$1,168,676
1950	$328,772	41%	$201,500	25%	$268,720	34%	$798,992

Source: A.G.PR., D.H., Vieques, 1940–1950. Capital assets, including land, taxed by the municipality shrank from $1,911,582 in 1940 to $798,992 in 1950. The military base reduced the income-producing assets of the population.

TABLE E.2
Vieques and Puerto Rico, Internal Income, Per Capita ($), 1950–1969

	1950	1960	1969	Growth Rates	
				1950 to 1960	1960 to 1969
Puerto Rico	$270	$574	$1,227	7.8%	8.8%
San Juan Region	$286	$644	$1,426	8.5%	9.2%
Fajardo Sub-Region	$304	$435	$813	3.6%	7.2%
Vieques	**$271**	**$291**	**$526**	**0.7%**	**6.8%**

Source: Oficina de Servicios Legislativos, *Condiciones socio-económicas*, 10. While the economy of the island of Puerto Rico grew at a pace of 7.8% between 1950 and 1960, and 8.8% between 1960 and 1969, in Vieques the growth rate was a minuscule 0.7% between 1950 and 1960.

TABLE E.3

Vieques Income in Relation to Income in Other Puerto Rican Municipalities

Year	Median Income, Persons 1950	Median Income, Households 1960	Median Income, Households 1970	Median Income, Households 1980	Median Income, Households 1990	Median Income, Households 2000
Puerto Rico		$1,082	$2,584	$5,348	$8,895	$14,412
San Juan	$781	$1,990	$3,469	$6,838	$10,539	$17,367
Vieques	$190	$792	$1,855	$3,143	$5,864	$9,331
Guaynabo	$641	$1,583	$4,375	$8,805	$15,041	$26,211
Vieques as % of PR		73%	72%	59%	66%	**65%**
Vieques as % of San Juan	24%	40%	53%	46%	56%	54%
Vieques as % of Guaynabo	30%	50%	42%	36%	39%	36%
Vieques Rank	**46th of 77**	**43rd of 75**	**46th of 76**	**76th of 78**	**77th of 78**	**77th of 78**
Percentile	40th	44th	41st	4th	3rd	3rd

Sources: The data for 1950 are from *Census of Population, 1950*, vol. 2, 53:25; data from 1960 through 2000 are from Puerto Rico Planning Board, http://www.jp.go-bierno.pr/. Vieques median income per person decreased as a percentage of the median income of the island as a whole. In fact, in 1950, Vieques median personal income was ranked 46th out of the 77 municipalities on the island. In 2000, it was ranked next to last.

Notes

Introduction

1. McCaffrey, *Military Power and Popular Protest*, is a brilliant analysis of the protests against the navy in 1979; *Murillo, Islands of Resistance*, offers an overview of the struggle to get the navy out of Vieques in 1999–2001; Barreto, *Vieques, the Navy and Puerto Rican Politics*, is strong on the importance of the Vieques issue to the Puerto Rican communities of the United States.
2. See the *Annals of the American Academy of Political and Social Science* 285 (Jan. 1953), with articles by Rexford Tugwell, J. K. Galbraith and Carolyn Shaw Solo, Teodoro Moscoso, Luis Muñoz Marín, Harvey S. Perloff, and others. A. Fernós-Isern's article in this volume was entitled "From Colony to Commonwealth."
3. See Ayala, *American Sugar Kingdom*.
4. The great Caribbean historian Eric Williams once remarked that the plantation regime was "an unstable economy based on a single crop which combined the vices of feudalism and capitalism with the virtues of neither." Eric Williams, *The Negro in the Caribbean*, 13, quoted in Mintz, *Sweetness and Power*, 23.

Chapter 1

1. A standard source is Moore, *A Careless Word*; we have used the figures constructed by T. Horodysky in www.usmm.org on the basis of Moore and many other sources. See www.usmm.org/shipssunkdamaged.htm and www.usmm.org/casualty.html. Accessed Feb. 20, 2008.
2. Bird, *Report on the Sugar Industry*, 42.
3. "The Puerto Rican Economy during the War Year of 1942," 1–6. A.F.L.M.M., Sec. XII, Material de y sobre Luis Muñoz Marín, Proyecto de Recopilación de Documentos, Biblioteca Harry S. Truman.
4. Merchant Marine website: www.usmm.org/shipssunkdamaged.html.
5. Tugwell, *The Stricken Land*, 360–361.
6. "Loose Lips Sink Ships," a public poster campaign, admonished all citizens to keep silent concerning any information about troop movements. The scenario supposed that German agents would be lurking about, ready to report this information to submarine captains, resulting in the death of civilians' loved ones. Another side of the campaign for silence was that it was designed to prevent public morale from flagging during the U-boat assaults. The prevention of public discourse would minimize sharing information.
7. Tugwell, *Stricken Land*, 361.
8. Ibid., 362.

9. See U-boat.net: http://uboat.net/allies/merchants/listing.php. Accessed Nov. 23, 2010.
10. U.S. Department of the Interior, *The Puerto Rican Economy during the War Year of 1942*, 3–5, 13.
11. Ibid.
12. Carta Informativa Americana, Carta No. 15, Apr. 14, 1942. A.F.L.M.M., Sec. IV, Presidente del Senado, Fdr. # 7, Doc. # 5.
13. Milkman, *Gender at Work*, 13.
14. Luis Muñoz Marín (President of the Puerto Rican Senate) to William H. Davis (Chairman, War Labor Board), Oct. 20, 1942. A.F.L.M.M., Sec. IV, Presidente del Senado, Fdr. # 6, Doc. # 16; Tugwell, *Stricken Land*, 220.
15. "The Puerto Rican Economy during the War Year of 1942," 18.
16. Luis Muñoz Marín to William H. Davis, Chairman, War Labor Board. Aug. 30, 1942. A.F.L.M.M., Sec. IV, Presidente del Senado, Fdr. # 6, Doc. # 16.
17. Filipo L. de Hostos to Senator Harry S. Truman. Sep. 30, 1942. A.F.L.M.M., Sec. XXII, Material de y sobre Luis Muñoz Marín, Proyecto de Recopilación de Documentos. Biblioteca Harry S. Truman.
18. Tugwell, *Stricken Land*, 222–223.
19. "Berlin Claims 3 Tankers," *New York Times*, Feb. 17, 1942.
20. "Dutch West Indies Get U.S. Troop Aid," *New York Times*, Feb. 12, 1942.
21. "Standard to Expand Oil Plant in Aruba," *New York Times*, Jan. 6, 1942.
22. C. H. Calhoun, "Aruba Is Shelled," *New York Times*, Feb. 17, 1942.
23. "Bolder Than Northern Raids," *New York Times*, Feb. 17, 1942.
24. "Aruba Traffic Resumed," *New York Times*, Feb. 28, 1942.
25. Associated Press, "Nazi Threat to Puerto Rico Recalled by Raid on Aruba," *New York Times*, Feb. 17, 1942.
26. "Ninth Tanker Is Sunk," *New York Times*, Feb. 20, 1942.
27. Ireland, *Battle of the Atlantic*, 80; Costello and Hughes, *The Battle of the Atlantic*, 200–207.
28. Ibid., 204.
29. "Lack of Ships Now a Major Problem," *New York Times*, May 17, 1942; Carta Informativa Americana, Carta No. 20, Jun. 23, 1942. A.F.L.M.M., Sec. IV, Presidente del Senado, Fdr. # 7, Doc. # 3.
30. "Lack of Ships Now a Major Problem," *New York Times*, May 17, 1942.
31. Luis Muñoz Marín to Paul Gordon (Department of the Interior), Aug. 17, 1942. A.F.L.M.M., Sec. IV, Presidente del Senado, Fdr. # 7, Doc. # 1.
32. Ayala and Bernabe, *Puerto Rico in the American Century*, 142–144.
33. Ibid., 185.
34. "Assails Tugwell As 'Like Hitler,'" *New York Times*, May 2, 1944. The bureaucratization of the Socialist Party, and its alliance with the Republicans, is a complex historical issue. At the time of the general strike of sugar cane workers in 1934, the Socialist Party, and the Puerto Rico Secretary of Labor, a functionary of the Socialist Party, functioned primarily to suppress the workers, not to support them, as one would expect of a party of labor. See Taller de Formación Política, *¡Huelga en la caña!*
35. In other colonies where plantations prevailed, meeting food demands was a problem. The plantation economy of Java underwent stress during the war precisely because typically plantations are not self-sufficient in food. In mid-1943, under duress caused by Allied attacks, and unable to export rubber, the Japanese ordered the conversion of plantation lands to food production in Sumatra to allow for self-sufficiency in the face of Allied blockade. The Sumatran rural proletariat proceeded to affirm squatter rights. See Stoler, *Capitalism and Confrontation in Sumatra's Plantation Belt*, 96–97.

36. For the limitations of the agrarian reform, see Ayala and Bernabe, *Puerto Rico in the American Century*, 184–187.
37. "Comercio de arroz no ha podido sustanciar petición," *El Mundo*, Apr. 16, 1942.
38. "Puerto Rico Capital Lacks Bread," *New York Times*, May 24, 1942, 13; "Protest in Puerto Rico," *New York Times*, May 24, 1942, 13; "Puerto Rico May Get Food by Air," *New York Times*, Jun. 6, 1942, 27.
39. "Se proyecta racionar el arroz a los detallistas," *El Mundo*, Apr. 16, 1942. "El gobernador proclama racionamiento de arroz," *El Mundo*, Jul. 17, 1942.
40. "La OAP fija precios máximos específicos para varios artículos," *El Mundo*, Nov. 13, 1942.
41. Ortiz Cuadra, *Puerto Rico en la olla*, 65.
42. "Lista de precios específicos la prepara la OAP," *El Mundo*, Oct. 19, 1942; "Precios para el consumidor," *El Mundo*, Oct. 25, 1942: 5; "La WPA proporcionará alimentos a 137,687 niños," *El Mundo*, Nov. 13, 1942.
43. "La distribución de arroz en Río Piedras," *El Mundo*, Nov. 25, 1942.
44. "Congelado el arroz para establecer sistema de cuotas," *El Mundo*, Dec. 12, 1942; "Cuota semanal arroz dos libras por persona," *El Mundo*, Dec. 15, 1942.
45. Ortiz Cuadra, *Puerto Rico en la olla*, 65–66.
46. "Tesorería ha logrado disminuir contrabando de cigarrillos en P.R.," *El Imparcial*, Nov. 25, 1941, 5.
47. Luis Muñoz Marín to Hon. Harry S. Truman. Jul. 30, 1945, A.F.L.M.M. Sec. IV, Presidente del Senado, Fdr. #1.
48. Guillermo Arroyo, Chief of Police, to Luis Muñoz Marín, Aug. 8, 1945. A.F.L.M.M., Sec. IV, Presidente del Senado, Fdr. #1, Doc. #27.
49. "The Puerto Rican Economy during the War Year of 1942," 25.
50. "Urge se permita exportación de ron en barriles," *El Mundo*, Nov. 18, 1942.
51. Santiago Caraballo, "Guerra, reforma y colonialismo," 59.
52. Rodríguez Beruff, *Strategy as Politics*, 355.
53. P.A.A.C., Minutes of the Board of Directors, Nov. 29, 1939, 16. The Consolidated Engineering Company, established in 1867, was responsible for designing, constructing, and maintaining the shore facilities needed to support the U.S. Navy around the world.
54. The main operating airport on the island was the Pan American aerodrome in Isla Grande, which had been in operation since 1928, and was used for international flights. Rodríguez Beruff, *Strategy as Politics*, 355.
55. P.A.A.C., Minutes of the Board of Directors, Nov. 29, 1939, 16.
56. See chapters 3 to 7 of this book.
57. Armando Morales, Jefe, División Terrenos Públicos y Archivos, Puerto Rico Department of the Interior, "Memorandum al Comisionado Interino; Asunto: Propiedades de El Pueblo de Puerto Rico que han sido cedidas al Gobierno de los Estados Unidos para la DEFENSA NACIONAL," Jan. 8, 1941. A.G.P.R., Fon. Obras Públicas, Ser. Asuntos Varios, Leg. 398, Box 241, 2.
58. Morales, "Memorandum," 2.
59. Dispatch from Officer in Charge of Construction, Naval Air Station, San Juan to Judge Advocate General, "Info: Budocks," Feb. 28, 1940. *A.G.P.R.*, Fon. Obras Públicas, Ser. Asuntos Varios, Leg. 398, Box 240.
60. H. W. Johnson, Officer in Charge of Construction to José Enrique Colom, Commissioner of the Interior of Puerto Rico, Feb. 28, 1940, A.G.P.R., Fon. Obras Públicas, Ser. Asuntos Varios, Leg. 398, Box 240.
61. P.A.A.C., Minutes of the Board of Directors, Feb. 26, 1940, 152.
62. For the Battle of San Juan, see Dr. Cayetano Coll y Toste, *Boletín Histórico de Puerto*

Rico, Tom.13, 180–221.

63. P.A.A.C., Minutes of the Board of Directors, Mar. 15, 1940, 158.
64. P.A.A.C., Minutes of the Board of Directors, May 25, 1941 and Jun. 17, 1941, 263–271.
65. Rodríguez Beruff, *Política militar y dominación*, 158–160.
66. P.A.A.C., Minutes of the Board of Directors, Nov. 26, 1943, 491.
67. P.A.A.C., Joint contractors for Bureau of Yards and Docks Contract NOy–3680, Undistributed Earnings, Dec. 31, 1943.
68. In 1947, this base was transferred to the air force and named *Ramey Air Force Base*. Rodríguez Beruff, *Política militar y dominación*, 158–160.
69. For the established view see Dietz, *Economic History of Puerto Rico*, 184–188, nd Santana Rabell, *Planificación y política*, 143; for the transformative effect of federal expenditure on Puerto Rico see Bolívar Fresneda, *Guerra, banca y desarrollo*, Chapter 1.
70. H.A.B.P.P.R., Annual Report, Jun. 30, 1940, 1
71. "Contratos, compromisos, y embarques de la Puerto Rican Cement a partir del 31 de Octubre de 1942," in C.I.H., Col. P.C.J.P., Box # 26, Fdr. # 25, Doc. # 1A .
72. Teodoro Moscoso to Francisco M. Susoni, President of the House of Representatives. Mar. 21, 1946. A.F.L.M.M., Sec. IV, Presidente del Senado, Fdr. # 380, Doc. # 23.
73. Ibid.
74. H.A.P.R.W.R.A., *Electric Revenue Bonds*, Jan. 1, 1947, 6, 21.
75. One of the ships transporting production equipment to Bacardi Corporation of America was sunk by German U-Boats. Peter Foster, *Family Spirits: The Bacardi Saga*, 69.
76. Miguel A. Santín, "Siguen afluyendo millones al Tesoro de Puerto Rico: Rentas federales producen $2,196,311 en 2 meses," *El Mundo*, Dec. 3, 1941, 9.

Chapter 2

1. Sued Badillo, *Los caribes*, questions the distinction between "Caribs" and "Tainos" introduced by the Spanish and British colonizers. In his argument, the maligning of the natives of the eastern Caribbean as distinct from the supposedly "friendly" Taino was a device introduced in order to justify their enslavement.
2. Torres, "La isla de Vieques," 452.
3. Ibid., 455.
4. Ibid., 456.
5. Ibid., 457.
6. Blackburn, *The Overthrow of Colonial Slavery*, 5, 163.
7. For the counterpoint between peasants and plantations in the Caribbean, see Sydney W. Mintz, "From Plantations to Peasants in the Caribbean," and "Slavery and the Rise of Peasantries." Juan A. Giusti Cordero, "Labor, Ecology, and History," is a masterful discussion of the interaction between peasants and plantations in Puerto Rico itself. For the struggle of slaves to maintain food production in a Caribbean plantation context, see Dale Tomich, "The Other Face of Slave Labor."
8. Morales Carrión, *Puerto Rico*.
9. Scarano, *Sugar and Slavery*.
10. O'Reilly, "Memoria."
11. Scarano, *Sugar and Slavery*; Sonesson, *Puerto Rico's Commerce*.
12. Rabin, "La influencia francesa en Vieques."
13. Rabin, *Compendio de lecturas sobre la historia de Vieques*, 72.

14. Bonnet Benítez, *Vieques en la historia*, 126.
15. Ayala, *American Sugar Kingdom*, 113.
16. Pastor Ruiz, *Vieques antiguo*, 174; Iglesias Pantín, Luchas Emancipadoras, Tom. 2, 148–5, has details about the death of three strikers killed by the police and has the list of the workers sentenced to prison in Vieques.
17. "La Central Puerto Real está en manos de 'receivers,'" *El Mundo*, Jul. 9, 1921; Bonnet Benítez, *Vieques en la historia*, 126.
18. About the web of interlocking directorates of the U. S. sugar corporations in Puerto Rico, the financial groups they represented, and the sugar refineries with which they were vertically integrated, see Ayala, *American Sugar Kingdom*, 74–120.
19. Fernández y García, *El libro de Puerto Rico*, 544; Bonnet Benítez, *Vieques en la historia*, 126.
20. Gilmore, *The Porto Rico Sugar Manual*, 192.
21. A Puerto Rican cuerda is equal to 0.9712 acres. Throughout this book, we have used both cuerdas and acres, according to the source being cited, without converting them. They are almost equivalent.
22. Picó, *The Geographic Regions*, 209–211.
23. Taller de Formación Política, ¡*Huelga en la caña*!
24. Picó, *The Geographic Regions*, 210–211.
25. Ibid., 209.
26. In *Black Reconstruction in America*, 55–84, W. E. B. Du Bois famously described what happened after Lincoln's emancipation proclamation in the U.S. South as "the general strike."
27. Figueroa, *Sugar, Slavery, and Freedom*.
28. The idea of "pure plantation economy" is here borrowed from Best, "The Mechanism of Plantation Type Societies."
29. Ayala, *American Sugar Kingdom*, 230–247.
30. We built a database with the records of all property assessments in Vieques in 1940, 1945, and 1950. The database is based on A.G.P.R., Departamento de Hacienda, Tasaciones, Vieques (1940, 1945, 1950). The *Archivo General de Puerto Rico* contains the records of all municipal tax assessments from 1905 until 1955. The assessments are organized by *municipio*, in handwritten volumes that measure approximately 15" by 21", and include the following variables: (1) Name of the owner (which allows the researcher to determine the gender of the owner) (2) Type of property (e.g., farm, urban lot, personal property) (3) Location of the property (*barrio* in the case of farms, street and no. in the case of urban lots) (4) Area in *cuerdas*. A Puerto Rican *cuerda* is equal to 0.9712 acres. (5) Assessed value of the land (6) Type of improvements to the land (7) Assessed value of improvements (8) Type of personal property (e.g., trucks, cars, cattle) (9) Assessed value of personal property. The data was photocopied at the *Archivo General Puerto Rico*, entered into a computerized database, and analyzed using Statistical Package for the Social Sciences. The complete database is available for download in Excel format in www.sscnet.ucla.edu/soc/faculty/ayala/vieques/. Our figures from the tax records may contain properties that were sold, subdivided, reassessed, or transferred and therefore taxed twice under different owners in the same year. That is why the total acreage taxed is slightly higher than the actual acreage of Vieques.
    This database will be cited hereafter as A.G.P.R., D.H., Vieques, 1940–1950.
31. The classic critique is Bird, *Report on the Sugar Industry*.
32. For the tobacco industry, see Levy, "The History of Tobacco Cultivation in Puerto Rico"; for decreasing land concentration after 1898, see Ayala and Bergad, "Rural Puerto Rico during the Early Twentieth Century Reconsidered."

33. Puerto Rico Reconstruction Administration, *Census of Puerto Rico (1935)*, 124.
34. Department of the Navy, *Continued Use*, vol. 1, 2: 199.
35. Ley de Tierras (Law 26 of 1941), Title V, quoted in Edel, "Land Reform in Puerto Rico," Part I: 40.

Chapter 3

1. See Rodríguez Beruff, *Las memorias de Leahy*.
2. Costello & Hughes, *The Battle of the Atlantic*, 189.
3. A.G.P.R., D.H., Vieques, 1940–1950.
4. Pastor Ruiz, *Vieques antiguo*, 196.
5. Interview with Aurelio Tio, by Vivian Carro and Lisa Wheaton, Feb. 1979. In V.H.A., Col. P.C.J.P.
6. Carro and Wheaton, Interview with Aurelio Tio.
7. Bergad, *Coffee and the Growth of Agrarian Capitalism*; Bergad, "Coffee and Rural Proletarianization."
8. Edel, "Land Reform in Puerto Rico," Part II, 32; Dietz, *Economic History of Puerto Rico*, 201.
9. Carro and Wheaton, Interview with Aurelio Tio. Translation by Vivian Carro.
10. Bonnet Benítez, *Vieques en la historia*, 126–27; Tio, Prólogo a *Vieques en la historia*, xii–xiii; Langhorn, *Vieques: History of a Small Island*, 59; Pastor Ruiz, *Vieques antiguo*, 207.
11. On the "total" character of plantations see Best, "The Mechanism of Plantation Type Societies," and Beckford, *Persistent Poverty*.
12. Proyecto Caribeño de Justicia y Paz, "Entrevistas a los expropiados."
13. Giusti Cordero, "Labor, Ecology, and History."
14. Department of the Navy, *Continued Use*, vol. 1, 2: 213.
15. McCaffrey, "Culture, Power, and Struggle," 77–78.
16. David Gonzalez, "Vieques Voters Want the Navy to Leave Now," *New York Times*. Jul. 30, 2001.
17. Associated Press, "One Who Remained," *New York Newsday*, Jul. 30, 2001; Ayala, "Interview with Doña Severina Guadalupe."
18. Pastor Ruiz, *Vieques antiguo*, 206.
19. Proyecto Caribeño de Justicia y Paz, "Entrevistas a los expropiados."
20. U.S.N.–S.M.A.., "Technical Report and Project History Contract NOy-3680: Section 22 St. Thomas, Roosevelt Roads, San Juan, St. Lucia, Antigua, Culebra," NOy-3680 Administrative Data NOy-3680: contract; Factual Survey Vol. I General Report, re: The Arundel Corporation and Consolidated Engineering Company, Incorporated, Mar. 22, 1943, 177.
    NOy-3680 was a navy construction contract with the Arundel Corporation.
    The power of eviction was precisely what the landowners had historically wielded over the *agregados*. The *parcelas* program of the P.D.P. was aimed at giving the rural labor force the minimal freedom of a piece of land to build a house and grow some subsistence crops, without fear of eviction.
21. Look Lai, *Indentured Labor, Caribbean Sugar.*
22. A navy report mentions that there were some exceptions. "It also appears that tenants were in some cases made parties in the court actions." Department of the Navy, *Continued Use*, vol. 1, 2: 200. However, no documentation is provided and not a single case is mentioned.

23. Department of the Navy, *Continued Use*, vol. 1, 2: 204.
24. Unless otherwise noted, this section is based on Proyecto Caribeño de Justicia y Paz, "Entrevistas a los expropiados."
25. Hessman, "Opposed Landings," 14.
26. Department of the Navy, *Continued Use*, vol. 1, 2: 199.
27. The Superior Court of Puerto Rico has a *Sala de Expropiaciones* to deal with private owners who seek further compensation when the government uses its right of eminent domain. The term *expropriation* is not in any way meant to convey lack of compensation, but rather the compulsory character of the "sale" to the state. Thanks to Prof. Juan Giusti Cordero of the University of Puerto Rico for this information.
28. The second expropriations of 1947–1948 are explored in detail in chapter 5.
29. This situation was still prevalent in 1979 at the time of the interviews. As a result of the struggle in that period, the navy began the process of transferring rights to the Commonwealth of Puerto Rico, which in turn titled some owners, although not all. Some communities are still seeking legal titles. See Giusti Cordero, *Informe histórico preliminar.*
30. Proyecto Caribeño de Justicia y Paz, "Entrevistas a los expropiados."
31. "Emergencia de guerra, y nosotros estamos pie con pie al lado de la nación americana. porque teníamos temor—Alemania, Hitler, era peligroso." Samantha Burdman, Interview with Nazario Cruz Viera.
32. All textual quotes are from Proyecto Caribeño de Justicia y Paz, "Entrevistas a los expropiados."
33. Picó, *Report of the Committee*, 2, 3.
34. Department of the Navy, *Continued Use*, vol. 1, 2: 193.
35. *Barrios* are minor civil subdivisions of *municipios*. The taxation records indicate the *barrio(s)* where the taxed property was located.
36. The first round of expropriations lasted from Nov. 1941 until Sep. 1943, according to Veaz, "Las expropiaciones de la década del cuarenta," 187. According to Pastor Ruiz, *Vieques antiguo*, 207, "It is estimated that of 33,682 arable cuerdas, the base took 22,000." The navy figure is from Department of the Navy, *Continued Use*, vol. 1, 2: 193.
37. Department of the Navy, *Continued Use*, vol. 1, 2: 201.
38. Department of the Navy, *Continued Use*, vol. 1, 2: 190.
39. Pastor Ruiz, *Vieques antiguo*, 206.
40. Department of the Navy, *Continued Use*, vol. 1, 2: 201.
41. Agricultural Experiment Station, "Report on the Possibilities," 1.
42. Pastor Ruiz, *Vieques antiguo*, 199.

Chapter 4

1. Dr. Leoncio T. Davis (Mayor of Vieques) to Vicente Géigel Polanco (President of the Legislative Committee responsible for Municipal Reforms). Dec. 22, 1941. A.F.L.M.M., Sec. IV, President of the Senate, Box # 2669, Doc. # 1.
2. Pastor Ruiz, *Vieques antiguo*, 206.
3. Picó, "Report of the Committee," 1.
4. Ibid.
5. Pastor Ruiz, *Vieques antiguo*, 206.
6. Memorandum Endorsement from E. J. King, Commander in Chief, U.S. Fleet and Naval Operations to Vice Chief of Naval Operations. Jul. 12, 1942. 98, A1 Building Program

(8/41–10/44). Ser. V, Subject Title 1936–1947. Records of the Strategic Plan Division, Operational Archives, U.S. Navy History Division, Navy Yard, in C.I.H., Col. P.C.J.P., Box 8, Let. 1, No. 6.

7. Representing Vieques were: the mayor, Dr. Leoncio T. Davis; Antonio Rivera Rodríguez, vice president of Liberal Party Committee; Juan J. Colón, president of the Popular Democratic Party Committee; and Jovito González, representing the sugar cane growers.

The first mention of a committee to study conditions in Vieques and file a report appears in a memo from Julio A. Pérez, secretary to the President of the Senate, to Luis Muñoz Marín. Feb. 23, 1943. A.F.L.M.M., Sec. IV, President of the Senate 1941–1948, Vieques, Ser. 9, Box #506–3, Doc. #11.

The Partido Liberal was a descendant of the Partido Unión, one of the autonomist parties in Puerto Rico. In the 1930s, the tendency within the Partido Liberal led by Luis Muñoz Marín, was expelled and went on to establish the Popular Democratic Party in 1938. See Ayala and Bernabe, *Puerto Rico in the American Century*, 143.

8. Julio A. Pérez, A.F.L.M.M., Sec. IV, President of the Senate 1941–1948, Vieques, Ser. 9, Box #506–3, Doc. #11.

The members of the committee were: Juan Luis Boscio, Fernando Villamil, Emilio Serra, Frederick P. Bartlett, Ralph Will, José Acosta Velarde, Raúl Gándara, Max Egloff, and Lt. Thomas Kiarsten. The name of Teodoro Moscoso, the prominent leader of the Puerto Rico Industrial Development Corporation (PRIDCO), appears crossed out from the list of possible candidates to this committee. We can only speculate that Luis Muñoz Marín thought Moscoso was too busy managing the newly developed Puerto Rico Industrial Development Company (PRIDCO). Max Egloff and Frederick P. Bartlett were personal friends of Governor Tugwell, who had previously worked with him in the United States. Tugwell brought them to Puerto Rico to work as coordinators of the Office of the Governor. Tugwell, *Stricken Land*, 182. Until Jun. 1943, Bartlett was the manager of Region XI of the National Resources Planning Board in San Juan. Archivo General de Puerto Rico (A.G.P.R.), Fon. Public Works, Ser. Varios Issues, Leg. # 398, Box # 214.

9. Telegram from Muñoz Marín to Antonio Rivera, Juan J. Colón Hernández, and Jovito González. Feb. 26, 1943. A.F.L.M.M., Sec. IV, President of the Senate, Box #2666, Doc. #15.

10. Telegram to Dr. Leoncio T. Davis from Muñoz Marín, Mar. 1, 1943. A.F.L.M.M., Sec. IV, President of the Senate, Box # 506–3, Doc. #13.

11. Letter to Dr. Rafael Picó from Muñoz Marín. Mar. 1, 1943. A.F.L.M.M., Sec. IV, President of the Senate, Box # 506–3, Doc. #28. The Picó Committee was named by the President of the Senate and it was a Special Committee of the Senate.

12. According to the Census of 1940, the average household in Vieques had 4.5 occupants, as opposed to the average family in Puerto Rico, which had 5.3. The 700 expelled families represent, therefore, 3,150 individuals, or 30 percent of a population of 10,362.

13. Picó, "Report of the Committee," 1.

The navy utilized the argument about the poverty of the rural population before the expropriations time and again, to minimize the disaster caused by its presence in Vieques. See, for example, "Barbey sugiere al Club Rotario estudie la situación en Vieques," *El Mundo*, Mar. 4, 1950.

14. Picó, "Report of the Committee."

15. Picó, "Report of the Committee," 5–8.

16. Letter to Rexford G. Tugwell from Muñoz Marín, Mar. 19, 1943. A.F.L.M.M., Sec. IV, President of the Senate, Box # 506–3, Doc. # 3. The letter is written in Spanish, despite

the fact that Tugwell did not speak Spanish, while Luis Muñoz Marín had perfect command of the English language.

17. Nine Letters to various federal agency heads, Apr. 6, 1943. A.F.L.M.M., Sec. IV, President of the Senate, Box # 506–2, Docs. # 28, 29.

18. Muñoz Marín (President of the Puerto Rican Senate) to Teodoro Moscoso (General Administrador, Compañía de Fomento), Apr. 13, 1943. A.F.L.M.M., Sec. IV, President of the Senate, Box # 382, Doc. # 36.

19. Picó, "Report of the Committee," 3.

20. *Laws of Puerto Rico*, Law Number 83 approved on May 11, 1943, 195–196.

21. Office of the Treasurer, Apr. 21, 1948; Office of the Auditor, Apr. 28, 1949. A.G.P.R., Fon. Office of the Governor, Tar. # 96–20, Box # 1044.

22. Luis Muñoz Marín (President of the Puerto Rican Senate) to Dr. Rafael Picó (President of the Puerto Rico Planning Board), Dec. 24, 1943. A.F.L.M.M., Sec. IV, President of the Senate, Box # 419, Doc. # 1.

23. Letter to Muñoz Marín from E. Geigel Polanco, Dec. 28, 1943. A.F.L.M.M., Sec. IV, President of the Senate, Box #420, Doc. #31. Benjamin Thoron worked in the federal Interior Department and subsequently with the Division or Territories. Tugwell, *The stricken land*, 182, 389.

24. Pagán, *Historia de los partidos políticos*, 223.

25. Pastor Ruiz, *Vieques antiguo*, 205.

26. Roy Schroder (Director of the Federal Works Agency, Puerto Rico and Virgin Islands Headquarters) to Luis Muñoz Marín, Jul. 5, 1943. A.F.L.M.M., Sec. IV, President of the Senate, Box #286, Doc. #15.

27. Letter from Rafael Picó to Muñoz Marín, Jul. 15, 1943. A.F.L.M.M., Sec. IV, President of the Senate, Box #286, Doc. #1.

28. The holdings of Eastern Sugar Associates spanned 11,000 in the east of the island, of which 8,000 were expropriated. See Picó, *The Geographic Regions*, 211; U. S. Department of the Navy, *Continued Use*, vol. 2: 199.

29. Pastor Ruiz, *Vieques antiguo*, 209.

30. Financial Statements, audited by the Comptroller of Puerto Rico, Apr. 26, 1945 to Jun. 30, 1946. A.F.L.M.M., Sec. IV, President of the Senate, Box #55, Doc. #1.

31. When the law creating PRACO was approved, the war had ended in Europe, and a year had transpired since the approval of Law 89 and Law 90.

32. Farm Security Administration, Bureau of the Budget, Emergency Crop and Loan, Office of Defense Transportation, Office of Price Administration, Works Projects Administration, Food Distribution Administration, Agricultural Adjustment Administration.

33. Roy Schroder (Director of the Federal Works Agency, Puerto Rico and Virgin Islands Headquarters) to Luis Muñoz Marín, Jul. 5, 1943. A.F.L.M.M., Sec. IV, Box #286, Doc. #15.

34. Pantojas García, *Development Strategies*, 44; Hibben & Picó, *Industrial Development*, 36.

35. A. W. Maldonado, *Teodoro Moscoso*.

36 Pico, *The Geographic Regions*, 210–213; El Eco de Vieques, Apr. 1947.

37. Picó, *The Geographic Regions*, 209–215.

38. PRACO, Financial Statement, Jun. 30, 1946. A.F.L.M.M., Sec. IV, President of the Senate, Ser. 2, Box #55, Doc. #1.

These figures match perfectly those from the tax assessments. The wife of Tomás González, Natividad Quiñones de González, appears in the tax records as the owner of a farm of 347 *cuerdas* in *barrio* Florida, valued at $20,950, with buildings valued at $500, and also as the owner of a lighthouse located on 375 *cuerdas* in the same barrio, valued at $21,490, for a total of 722 *cuerdas*, valued at $42,440. A.G.P.R., D.H., Vieques, 1940–1950.

39. Ayala & Carro, "Expropiations and Displacement of Civilians in Vieques, 1940–1950," Table 10.1.

40. Picó *The Geographic Regions*, 215.

41. PRACO, Financial Statement, Jun. 30, 1947. A.F.L.M.M., Sec. IV, President of the Senate, Ser. 2, Box #55, Doc. #1.

42. A.F.L.M.M., Sec. IV, President of the Senate, Ser. 14, Box #28, Doc. #1.

43. PRACO, Audited Financial Statement, Jun. 1946–1950. A.F.L.M.M., Sec. IV, President of the Senate, Ser. 2, Box #55, Doc. #1; A.G.P.R., Governor's Office, Tar. # 96–20, Box # 838. There are auditing reports for 1946, 1947, 1949, y 1950. The auditing report for 1948 is missing.

44. PRACO, Audited Financial Statement. Jun. 30, 1947. A.F.L.M.M., Sec. IV, President of the Senate, Ser. 2, Box #55, Doc. #1.

45. Losses of $998,000 during 1947 divided by 2,150 employees.

46. PRACO, Audited Financial Statement, Jun. 30, 1947. A.F.L.M.M., Sec. IV, President of the Senate, Ser. 2, Box #55, Doc. #1.

47. Rodríguez Beruff, *El archivo Luis Muñoz Marín*, 88.

48. Picó, *Discursos de Muñoz Marín 1934–1948*, vol. 1: 275–295.

49. According to the financial statement of FY 1947, sales were $575,000, including transfers between companies. Hibben & Picó, *Industrial Development*, 151.

Chapter 5

1. Pico, *The Geographic Regions*, 210–213; *El Eco de Vieques*, Apr. 1947.

2. Office of the Treasurer, Apr. 21, 1948; Office of the Auditor, Apr. 28, 1949. A.G.P.R., Fon. Office of the Governor, Tar. # 96–20, Box # 1044.

3. McCabe, "Objeta plan de la marina en Vieques," *El Mundo*, Jun. 5, 1947.

4. On Aug. 1947, U. S. Congress passed a law authorizing Puerto Ricans to elect their own governor, and in 1948, Puerto Ricans elected Luis Muñoz Marín. The old colonial reality persisted, however, as evidenced by the House Committee Report that stated: "The changes which would be made by the enactment of H. R. 3309 would not alter Puerto Rico's political or fiscal relationship to the united States. Congress does not surrender any of its constitutional authority to legislate for Puerto Rico or to review insular laws. Neither would this legislation prove an obstacle to a subsequent determination by the Congress of the permanent political questions." H. Rep. 455, 80th Cong., 1st Sess., 1947 Cong. Code and Administrative News 1588, quoted in Trías Monge, *Puerto Rico: the Trials*, 105–106, 207.

5. Letter from Muñoz Marín to Julius A. Krug (Secretary of the Interior), May 13, 1947. A.F.L.M.M., Ser. IV, President of the Senate, Fdr. #13, Doc. #13.

6. A.F.L.M.M., Sec. V, governor of Puerto Rico, Ser. 8, Fdr. #57.

7. McCabe, "Objeta plan de la marina en Vieques," *El Mundo*, Jun. 5, 1947.

8. McCabe, "Objeta plan."

9. Tugwell, *The Stricken Land*, 322. According to North American sociologist Maxine W. Gordon, "the U.S. Armed Forces' policy towards Puerto Ricans (even the 76.5% white) differed in no significant way from its policy towards Negroes": "Cultural Aspects of Puerto Rico's Race Problem," *American Sociological Review*, 15(3) (Jun. 1950), 387.

10. Carb, "Barbey expone razones para selección de Vieques," *El Mundo*, Jun. 6, 1947.

11. The sugar quotas were a product of the Great Depression. In 1934, the Jones Costigan

Act established a system of sugar quotas for the domestic beet farmers, cane farmers of Louisiana, and for Hawaii, Philippines, and Puerto Rico, in an attempt to overcome overproduction. See Ayala, *American Sugar Kingdom*, 239–40.

12. Barbey's words were reported in Spanish, and we have retranslated them into English: "Aseguró entonces que la isla se habría de beneficiar grandemente, en el sentido económico, pero que 'si de esos proyectos no se derivara beneficio económico alguno, por encima de todo está la seguridad nuestra frente a la seria situación que vivimos.'" Santana, "Barbey explica expropiación de Vieques," *El Mundo*, Oct. 16, 1947.

13. Picó, "Report of the Committee."

14. Santana, "Ganaderos de Vieques están en contra," *El Mundo*, Jan. 13, 1948.

15. "Veterano favorece la toma de Vieques," *El Mundo*, Oct. 24, 1947.

16. Cruz Cruz, "Una comisión de Vieques irá donde Barbey," *El Mundo*, Oct. 28, 1947.

17. Ibid.

18. The speakers were Deusdedit Marrero, Juan Santos Rivera, Leonard Schlafer, and Juan Antonio Corretjer. Students from the University of Puerto Rico spoke after the PCP: José A. Benítez, Juan Mari Bras (who was later secretary general of the Puerto Rican Socialist Party in the 1970s [C. A. & J. B.]), José Gil Lamadrid, and José Rodríguez Benítez. Cruz Cruz, "Una comisión de Vieques irá donde Barbey," *El Mundo*, Oct. 28, 1947.

19. "Veterano favorece la toma de Vieques," *El Mundo*, Oct. 24, 1947.

20. Van Vranken, "Piñero discute hoy el caso de isla de Vieques," *El Mundo*, Oct. 1, 1947.

21. Van Vranken, "Sullivan estudia ampliar plazo para la evacuación de Vieques," *El Mundo*, Oct. 2, 1947; Picó, "Report of the Committee." The decrease, according to the auditor of Puerto Rico, was 41 percent. See page 90 and Table 4.2.

22. Van Vranken, "Marina rechazó una petición en el caso de la Isla de Vieques," *El Mundo*, Oct. 5, 1947.

23. "Varios envíos de madera hacia isla Vieques," *El Mundo*, Nov. 16, 1947.

24. "Se llegó a un acuerdo en el caso de Vieques," *El Mundo*, Nov. 6, 1947.

25. In addition to the landowners, the petition included a list of owners of houses and house occupants located on these private lands: Gabriel Márquez, Francisco Lebrón, and Ramón Ortiz were owners of houses. Esteban Coto, Eleuterio Bermúdez, Pablo García Ventura, Francisco Trufiño, Germán García Ventura, Oliva Solís vda. de González, Leocadio Acosta, Fundador Davis, Eleuterio Encarnación Félix, Gregorio Encarnación, Ramón Alicea, Ramón Conde, and Jorge Santiago were listed as occupants of houses. The government of Puerto Rico was listed in the suit because it owned Cayo Carene (a key) in Vieques.

26. Sánchez Cappa, "Marina inicia expropiación en Vieques," *El Mundo*, Nov. 22, 1947.

27. Gálvez Maturana, "Otros países podrán usar base Vieques," *El Mundo*, Dec. 4, 1947.

28. A.F.L.M.M., Sec. V, Governor of Puerto Rico, Ser. 8, Fdr. #57. According to Picó, *The Geographic Regions*, 210–213, the amount of land returned to the navy was 13,000 acres. "CA tendrá que devolver tierras usa en Vieques," *El Mundo*, Dec. 11, 1947, reported (erroneously) 20,000 acres.

29. *Colonos* were cane farmers who delivered cane to the sugar mills. They could be owners or renters, they could be family farmers, or they could be capitalist farmers hiring many workers.

30. A.G.P.R., D.H., Vieques, 1940–1950.

The figures for cattle ownership refer to taxation records that list only cattle. Taxation records that indicate, for example, "trucks, cattle, implements" are not included, because they do not assign a specific value to the cattle apart from the other assets. The Eastern Sugar Associates was the second-largest landowner of Vieques before 1940, and Juan

Angel Tio was the largest landowner and the owner of Central Playa Grande before it was expropriated by the navy in Nov. 1941.

31. The estimated value of the cattle varies immensely, from a high of 300,000 reported by the ranchers to the press when they were seeking compensation from PRACO, to a low of $128,730 in the tax assessments of 1945. A.G.P.R., D.H., Vieques, 1940–1950.

32. Letter to James P. Davis from Paul Edwards, Dec. 30, 1947. A.F.L.M.M., Sec. IV, President of the Senate, Fdr. #370, Doc. #9.

33. Alberto Biascochea, Enrique Cayere, Esteban Díaz, Jovito González, and Tomás Ramírez. "Dan prórroga a vecinos de isla Vieques," *El Mundo*, Dec. 13, 1947.

34. "Dan prórroga."

35. "Junta de la CA liquidará cuido ganado Vieques," *El Mundo*, Jan. 6, 1948.

36. Davis was mayor of Vieques between 1936 and 1943.

37. Ellsworth was president of the board of directors of PRACO from Apr. 26, 1945 to Jan. 1948. A.F.L.M.M., Sec. IV, President of the Senate, Ser. 14, Box #28, Doc. #1.

38. Santana, "Ganaderos de Vieques están en contra de dividir con la CA," *El Mundo*, Jan. 13, 1948.

39. "CA liquidará cuido de reses en 48 horas," *El Mundo*, Jan. 7, 1948.

40. "Compañía agrícola fija forma de liquidar ganado que cuidaba," *El Mundo*, Jan. 10, 1948.

41. "Marina llegó a un acuerdo con los viequenses," *El Mundo*, Dec. 18, 1947; "La Marina cede terreno para el ganado en Vieques," *El Mundo*, Dec. 30, 1947.

42. Santana, "Ganaderos de Vieques están en contra de dividir con la CA," *El Mundo*, Jan. 13, 1948.

43. Ramón M. Díaz, "Barbey promises to help cattlemen if they desert Agricultural Company," *El Imparcial*, Jan. 6, 1948. A.F.L.M.M., Sec. V, Government of Puerto Rico, Fdr. #57, Doc. #17.

44. Santana, "Ganaderos Vieques opuestos a que pasen tierras al Gobierno," *El Mundo*, Aug. 4, 1948.

45. Combas Guerra, "Boricuas hacen excelente labor en maniobras," *El Mundo*, Feb. 19, 1948.

46. Financial Statements, audited by the Comptroller of Puerto Rico, Apr. 26, 1945, to Jun. 30, 1946. A.F.L.M.M., Sec. IV, President of the Senate, Ser. 9, Box #55, Doc. #1; A.G.P.R., Oficina del Gobernador, Tar. 96–20, Box #838.

The press continued to report PRACO transactions until 1954, but in fact PRACO formally disappeared. On July 1, 1950, PRACO was transferred to the Puerto Rico Department of Agriculture and Commerce. PRACO's board of directors was eliminated.

47. A glance at the leadership of the Asociación de Pequeños Ganaderos de Vieques indicates that it was the same organization previously referred to as Asociación de Ganaderos Menores de Vieques.

48. Santana, "Marina alega dio oportunidad ganaderos Vieques en subasta," *El Mundo*, Jul. 7, 1951.

49. "Juez federal resuelve caso expropiación: valora medio millón 4,500 cuerdas tomadas isla Vieques," *El Mundo*, Apr. 17, 1953.

Chapter 6

1. Morris J. McGregor, *Integration of the Armed Forces, 1940–1965* (Washington, D.C.: Center of Military History, United States Army, 1981), 72–73.

2. U.S.N.–S.M.A., "Technical Report and Project History Contract NOy-3680: Section 22 St. Thomas, Roosevelt Roads, San Juan, St. Lucia, Antigua, Culebra," NOy3680 Administrative Data NOy-3680: contract; Factual Survey Vol. I General Report, re: The Arundel Corporation and Consolidated Engineering Company, Incorporated, Mar. 22, 1943, 31.
3. U.S.N.–S.M.A., "Technical Report and Project History," 178.
4. Ibid.
5. Ibid.
6. Ibid., 175.
7. Letter from Lieutenant-Commander Virgil Baker to the Chief of Naval Operations. Mar. 6, 1919. File #404, Naval Stations (1919), Records of the General Board of the Navy Yard, Naval Historical Center, in C.I.H., Rodríguez Beruff Col., Box #8, Fdr. #5, Doc. #5.
8. P.A.A.C., Minutes of the Board of Directors, 100–496.
9. "Brief of News in Puerto Rico," Dec. 20, 1940, in C. I. H., Rodríguez Beruff Col., Box #16, Fol. #3, Doc. #1F.
10. "A los marinos se les castiga con severidad," *El Mundo*, Dec. 28, 1940, 1, 22.
11. "Soldados americanos asaltan y destruyen un bar," *El Mundo*, Dec. 28, 1940.
12. "Brief of News in Puerto Rico," Dec. 28, 1940, in C.I.H., Rodríguez Beruff Col., Box #16, Fol. #3, Doc. #1E.
13. "Brief of News in Puerto Rico," Feb. 24, 1941, in C. I. H., Rodríguez Beruff Col., Box #16, Fol. #3, Doc. #1C.
14. Letter from Rear Admiral Spruance to José M. Gallardo, Interim Governor, Jun. 3, 1941, in C.I.H., Rodríguez Beruff Col., Box #16, Fol. #3, Doc. #1A.
15. Letter from Rear Admiral R. A. Spruance, in C.I.H., Rodríguez Beruff Col., Box #16, Fol. #13, Doc. #1B.
16. Memorandum from Miguel Martínez, Chief of the District of the Insular Police, to the Commander of the Insular Police, Jun. 1, 1941, in C.I.H., Rodríguez Beruff Col., Box #16, Fol. #13, Doc. #1B.
17. Giusti Cordero, "La Huelga Cañera de 1942," 88.
18. Ibid., 85.
19. "Minutes of the Board of Directors," P.A.A.C., 1939–1943, 100-496.
20. Giusti Cordero, "La Huelga Cañera de 1942," 96.
21. See chapter 4.
22. "Electricistas de Arundel irán a la huelga si no se les aumenta su salario," *El Imparcial*, Jun. 1, 1943, 2.
23. U.S.N.–S.M.A.., "Technical Report and Project History Contract NOy-3680: Section 22 St. Thomas, Roosevelt Roads, San Juan, St. Lucia, Antigua, Culebra," NOy3680 Administrative Data NOy-3680: contract; Factual Survey Vol. I General Report, re: The Arundel Corporation and Consolidated Engineering Company, Incorporated, Mar. 22, 1943, Fdr. 41 of 43.
24. García Muñiz, *La estrategia de Estados Unidos*, 54.
25. Daley was an elderly officer who had been called into active service due to the European military crisis. He remained in Puerto Rico until Mar. 1941, when he was named commander of the V Army Corps based at Camp Beauregard, near Alexandria, Louisiana. The V Corps was deployed in Belfast, Ireland, in early 1942. However, General George Marshall decided to retire all over-age officers, including Daley, at the time of the deployment in Europe. Rodríguez Beruff, *Strategy as Politics*, 357.
26. War Department or Ministry, G-2 Regional Files, 1933–1944, Islands, Puerto Rico Record of the War Department, General and Special Staffs, R.G.–165, Box #2113, N.A., "Puerto Rican area designated as new Military Department," S–200, May 1, 1939, in in C.I.H., Rodríguez Beruff Col., Box #21, Fol. #4, Doc. #3–B.

27. "Ordered to Puerto Rico: 1,700 Units of Army are Mainly Artillery Units," *New York Times*, Sep. 15, 1939, in C.I.H., Rodríguez Beruff Col., Box #21, Fol. #4, Doc. #3–A.
28. San Juan, Puerto Rico (1942), Questionnaire dated Aug. 31, 1942 to Oct. 22, 1942, Box #78, Ser. VIII, Subject Files: 1939–1957, Records of the Field Liaison and Records Sec. (OP–141–H), Base Maintenance Division, Office of the N.C.O., 1930–1945, Operational Archives, U.S. Navy History Division, N.A., in C.I.H., Rodríguez Beruff Col., Box #8, Fol. #13, Doc. #2.
29. Rodríguez Beruff, *Strategy as Politics*, 363.
30. "Puerto Rico Induction Program," R.G. 165, Records of the War Department, General and Special Staffs, Box #182, Apr. 15, 1945, N.A., in C.I.H., Rodríguez Beruff Col., Box #23, Fol. #12, Doc. #2.
31. "Puerto Rico Induction Program," Apr. 15, 1945, N.A., in C.I.H., Rodríguez Beruff Col., Box #23, Fol. #12, Doc. #2.
32. John Beaufort, "Army Orders in Puerto Rico Given in English and Spanish," *Christian Science Monitor*, Apr. 7, 1943, in C.I.H., Rodríguez Beruff Col., Box #21, Fol. #4, Doc. #2A.
33. FDR Library, R.G. Tugwell papers, Container #27, Fdr. Ickes, Letter from Rexford G. Tugwell to Harold Ickes, Oct. 30, 1941, in C.I.H., Rodríguez Beruff Col., Box #1, Fol. #1, Doc. #5.
34. Military Intelligence Field Office, Miami, Florida, Oct. 7, 1942, Interview with Dr. José Padín, in C.I.H., Rodríguez Beruff Col., Box #46, Fol. #3, Doc. #5; FDR Library, R.G. Tugwell papers, Container #27, Fdr. Ickes, Letter from Rexford G. Tugwell to Harold Ickes, Oct. 30, 1941, in C.I.H., Rodríguez Beruff Col., Box #1, Fol. #1, Doc. #5.
35. System of Recruitment or Conscription, G-2, Regional File, 1933–1944, Island of Puerto Rico, R.G. 165, Records of the War Department, General and Special Staffs, Box #2113, Declassified Apr. 2, 1952, N.A., in C.I.H., Rodríguez Beruff Col., Box #21, Fol. #4, Doc. #1C.
36. System of Recruitment or Conscription, Declassified Apr. 2, 1952, N.A., in C.I.H., Rodríguez Beruff Col., Box #21, Fol. #4, Doc. #1C.
37. System of Recruitment or Conscription, Declassified Apr. 2, 1952, N.A., in C.I.H., Rodríguez Beruff Col., Box #21, Fol. #4, Doc. #1G. During World War II, about 120,000 people of Japanese ancestry, most of them U.S. citizens (62 percent), were interned in concentration camps.
38. System of Recruitment or Conscription, Declassified Apr. 2, 1952, N.A., in C.I.H., Rodríguez Beruff Col., Box #21, Fol. #4, Doc. #1G.
39. FDR Library, Tugwell Papers, Container #18, Fdr. Diary, Jan.–Mar. 1944, 4, 13, 15, 20, in C.I.H., Rodríguez Beruff Col., Box #1, Fol. #1, Doc. #4.
40. United States Department of the Interior, Division of Territories and Island Possessions, Puerto Rico, May 18, 1937 to Jan. 5, 1949. "Preliminary Analysis of Puerto Rican Selective Service Rejections," Nov. 29, 1946, N.A., in C.I.H., Rodríguez Beruff Col., Box #16, Fol. #3, Doc. #3 (A-M).
41. "Puerto Rico Induction Program," R.G. 165, Records of the War Department, General and Special Staffs, Box #182, Apr. 15, 1945, N.A., in C.I.H., Rodríguez Beruff Col., Box #23, Fol. #12, Doc. #2, 5, 6.
42. "Puerto Rico Induction Program," R.G. 165, Records of the War Department, General and Special Staffs, Box #182, Apr. 15, 1945, N.A., in C.I.H., Rodríguez Beruff Col., Box #23, Fol. #12, Doc. #2, Table 1.
43. "Puerto Rico Induction Program," R.G. 165, Records of the War Department, General and Special Staffs, Box #182, Apr. 15, 1945, N.A., in C.I.H., Rodríguez Beruff Col., Box #23, Fol. #12, Doc. #2, 5, 6.

44. Interview with returning officer concerning experiences in Puerto Rico and Trinidad, Apr. 22, 1944. System of Recruitment or Conscription, G-2, Regional File, 1933–1944, Island of Puerto Rico, R.G. 165, Records of the War Department, General and Special Staffs, Box #2113, Declassified Apr. 2, 1952, N.A., in C.I.H., Rodríguez Beruff Col., Box #21, Fol. #4, Doc. #1L.

45. Associated Press Extract. Fortifications, General G-2 Regional Files, 1933–1944, Islands, Puerto Rico, Records of the War Department, General and Special Staffs, R.G. #165, Box #2113, N.A., in C.I.H.,Rodríguez Beruff Col., Box #21, Fol. #8, Doc #9B.

46. Memorandum from Captain Marvin S. Bennett regarding the white Puerto Rican Troops in the Trinidad Sector and Base Command. Nov. 8, 1943. Fortifications, General G-2 Regional Files, 1933–1944, Islands, Puerto Rico, Records of the War Department, General and Special Staffs, R.G. #165, Box #2113, N.A., in C.I.H., Rodríguez Beruff Col., Box #21, Fol. #8, Doc #9D.

47. Annex Number 4 to the G-2 Periodic Report, Jan. 12, 1944. Fortifications, General G-2 Regional Files, 1933–1944, Islands, Puerto Rico, Records of the War Department, General and Special Staffs, R.G. #165, Box #2113, N.A., in C.I.H., Rodríguez Beruff Col., Box #21, Fol. #8, Doc #9 A.

48. System of Recruitment or Conscription, Declassified Apr. 2, 1952, N.A., in C.I.H., Rodríguez Beruff Col., Box #21, Fol. #4, Doc. #1J.

49. "Puerto Rican Units Helps to Handle AEF Supplies," *New York Times*, Feb. 9, 1944, Fortifications, General G-2 Regional Files, 1933–1944, Islands, Puerto Rico, Records of the War Department, General and Special Staffs, R.G. #165, Box #2113, N.A., in C.I.H., Rodríguez Beruff Col., Box #21, Fol. #8, Doc #9 E, F.

50. Editorial, *El Imparcial*, Mar. 13, 1944. Fortifications, General G-2 Regional Files, 1933–1944, Islands, Puerto Rico, Records of the War Department, General and Special Staffs, R.G. #165, Box #2113, N.A., in C.I.H., Rodríguez Beruff Col., Box #21, Fol. #8, Doc. #9 F.

51. "Arundel no permite que los puertorriqueños tomen agua fría; es para los continentales," *El Imparcial*, Apr. 14, 1943, 5.

52. Interview with Captain K. F. Kahn, Military Liaison Officer, Jamaica, Mar. 27, 1944. Fortifications, General G-2 Regional Files, 1933–1944, Islands, Puerto Rico, Records of the War Department, General and Special Staffs, R.G. #165, Box #2113, N.A., in C.I.H., Rodríguez Beruff Col., Box #21, Fol. #4, Doc #4G.

53. *New Negro Voice*, Mar. 3, 1944. Fortifications, General G-2 Regional Files, 1933–1944, Islands, Puerto Rico, Records of the War Department, General and Special Staffs, R.G. #165, Box #2113, N.A., in C.I.H., Rodríguez Beruff Col., Box #21, Fol. #8, Doc #9 C.

54. Periodic Report, Jamaica Base Command, Mar. 3, 1944. Fortifications, General G-2 Regional Files, 1933–1944, Islands, Puerto Rico, Records of the War Department, General and Special Staffs, R.G. #165, Box #2113, N.A., in C.I.H., Rodríguez Beruff Col., Box #21, Fol. #8, Doc #9 C.

55. State of Unrest between Insulars and Panamanians in Puerto Rico. Jan. 28, 1945, in C.I.H., Rodríguez Beruff Col., Box #23, Fol. #12, Doc #1A.

56. Inaction Study of the 296th RTC and Activation Units. Jul. 3, 1945, in C.I.H., Rodríguez Beruff Col., Box #23, Fol. #12, Doc. #1C.

Chapter 7

1. The empire of bases is magnificently discussed by Chalmers Johnson in his excellent trilogy on the American empire: *Blowback: The Costs and Consequences of American*

Empire (2000); The Sorrows of Empire: Militarism, Secrecy, and the End of the Republic (2004); and *Nemesis: The Last Days of the American Republic* (2006).

2. Ayala and Bernabe, *Puerto Rico in the American Century*, 1.
3. *Downes v. Bidwell*, 182 U.S. 244 (1901).
4. See Ayala and Bernabe, *Puerto Rico in the American Century*, 26–27.
5. "Unos 2,000 infantes visitarán cuidad San Juan diariamente," *El Mundo*, Sep. 29, 1951, 5.
6. Pastor Ruiz, *Vieques antiguo*, 206.
7. "Marina afirma ha dado ayuda a Isla Vieques," *El Mundo*, Feb. 28, 1950, 14. The population figure is the one offered by this source.
8. Reverend Vincent was of course ignorant of the true plight of the Bikinians. The Bikini islanders actually suffered tremendous hardship on account of their relocation to the islands of Rongerik, then to Kwajalein, then to Kili. The architect of their relocation was Horacio Rivero, the first Puerto Rican to become an admiral in the U.S. Navy. At one point in 1952, the government had to perform emergency food drops to offset deteriorating conditions for Bikini islanders. See David Vine, *Island of Shame*, 63–67.
9. Picó, "Report of the Committee," 3.
10. "Marina afirma ha dado ayuda a Isla Vieques," *El Mundo*, Feb. 28, 1950, 1, 14.
11. "Barbey sugiere el Club Rotario estudie la situación en Vieques," *El Mundo*, Mar. 4, 1950.
12. Benjamín Santana, "Don Vicente ministro metodista de Vieques que usa un avión para su obra y para ayudar a la comunidad," *El Mundo*, Mar. 5, 1950, 9.
13. Carmelina Paz de Quiñónes, "Vieques pide se le permita uso de tierras," *El Mundo*, Mar. 27, 1950, 4.
14. Benjamín Santana, "Fernós ayudará a solucionar problema de tierras en Vieques," *El Mundo*, Aug. 30, 1950, 4.
15. James F. Cunningham, "La Marina se dispone adquirir una nueva parcela en Vieques," *El Mundo*, Sep. 20, 1950, 3.
16. Juan Luis Márquez, "Alcalde acusa grave situación en Isla Vieques," *El Mundo*, Mar. 15, 1953, 12.
17. The U.S. Census utilizes *municipios* in Puerto Rico in lieu of counties.
18. McCaffrey, *Military Power and Popular Protest*, 54
19. "Una bomba causa muerte a menor," *El Mundo*, Apr. 23, 1953.
20. Benjamín Santana, "Alcalde teme que 'algo serio' ocurra en la Isla de Vieques," *El Mundo*, Apr. 8, 1953, 1, 12.
21. Santana, "Alcalde teme," 1, 12; Benjamín Santana, "Apoyan actividad alcalde Vieques en su protesta contra la Armada," *El Mundo*, Apr. 13, 1953, 1, 15.
    Julián Felipe Francis was also known by a variety of other names, including Felipe Francis, José Christian, and Juan Felipe Francis. Some articles report his age as seventy-eight while others at seventy or sixty-eight. Some spell his nickname as "Mapé" while others spell it as "Mapepe."
22. Eddie Vázquez Otero, "Hoy proseguirá corte marcial caso de Vieques," *El Mundo*, May 23, 1953, 1, 16.
23. Vázquez Otero, "Hoy proseguirá," 1, 16; "Dueño cafetín muere en trifulca marinos," *El Imparcial*, Apr. 17, 1953, 7.
24. Santana, "Alcalde teme," 1, 12; "Declaran a Vieques 'fuera de limites,'" *El Mundo*, Apr. 9, 1953.
25. McCaffrey, *Military Power and Popular Protest*, 47–49
26. Benjamín Santana, "Apoyan actitud alcalde Vieques en su protesta contra la Armada," *El Mundo*, Apr. 13, 1950, 1, 15.

27. "Piden que Fernós gestione tierras," *El Mundo*, Apr. 10, 1953; "Alcalde Vieques dice que ahora hay tranquilidad y trabajo," *El Mundo*, Apr. 29, 1953, 25; Benjamín Santana, "Asamblea Vieques pide a Marina que devuelva sus tierras allí," *El Mundo*, Apr. 17, 1953, 21; "Juez federal resuelve caso expropiación," *El Mundo*, Apr. 17, 1953, 30.
28. Benjamín Santana, "Lamentan civiles Isla Vieques no cooperan aclaración crimen," *El Mundo*, May 15, 1953, 2.
29. "Marina lamenta los incidentes acaecidos en la Isla de Vieques," *El Mundo, Apr. 28, 1953, 7; Eddie Vázquez Otero, "Jurado exonera los 2 marinos caso Vieques," *El Mundo*, May 25, 1953; Eddie Vázquez Otero, "Hoy proseguirá corte marcial caso de Vieques," *El Mundo*, May 23, 1953, 16; "Van a acusar dos marinos caso Vieques," *El Mundo*, May 2, 1953, 1, 16, 28.
30. Vázquez Otero, "Jurado exonera."
31. "Van a acusar dos marinos caso Vieques," *El Mundo*, May 2, 1953, 1, 16, 28; Juan Luis Márquez, "Discuten plan con infantes sobre Vieques," *El Mundo*, May 13, 1953, 16.
32. See Ayala and Bernabe, *Puerto Rico in the American Century*, 162–178.
33. Santana, "Alcalde teme," 1, 12.
34. David Gonzalez, "Vieques Voters Want the Navy to Leave Now," *New York Times*, Jul. 30, 2001; Samantha Burdman, "Interview with Cruz Cordero Ventura," Aug. 20, 2002; Ibid.
35. "Representante respalda actitud asumida por alcalde Vieques: Alude a comerciantes que le desautorizaron al pronunciarse contra actos de los marinos," *El Mundo*, Apr. 27, 1953.

Epilogue

1. Senior, *The Puerto Rican Migrant in St. Croix*, 7, 1–2.
2. This calculation does not take into account the assets of the navy. The payroll of the navy to civilians in 1941–1943 was spectacular, but it subsided after that date. The decrease, however, is more extreme than the figures reveal, if one considers that houses, particularly the cluster in Isabel Segunda, which were not income generating assets, are included as "improvements" in the tax records.
3. Junta de Planificación de Puerto Rico, *Plan de desarrollo* (1955), 14.
4. A.G.P.R., D.H., Vieques, 1940, 1950.
5. Automobiles were not listed in the tax records of 1950.
6. One of the complaints expressed by Puerto Rico's resident commissioner, Carlos Romero Barceló, in 1999 was precisely that the navy presence in Vieques, unlike other military bases, did not generate prosperity: "If Vieques is indeed safe, why hasn't the navy headquartered troops to live there? Why hasn't the navy made it a home port with the economic prosperity and commitment that such an action would entail?" Carlos Romero Barceló, "Testimony before the Committee."
7. McCaffrey, "Culture, Power, and Struggle," 122; Harris, *Puerto Rico's Fighting 65th Infantry*, 20.
8. Quoted in McCaffrey, "Culture, Power, and Struggle," 149.
9. Ross, *The Long Uphill Path*, Foreword. This is an enthusiastic source. A special issue of the *Annals of the American Academy of Political and Social Science* (Jan. 1953) was devoted to Puerto Rico and was equally enthusiastic. For some of the limitations of Operation Bootstrap, not visible at the time of the boom, see Ayala and Bernabe, *Puerto Rico in the American Century*, 267–315.
10. Ross, *The Long Uphill Path*, 61–77.
11. Ibid., 129.

12. Bolívar Fresneda, "Un sueño irrealizado," 204–209.
13. Echenique, *El desarrollo económico de Puerto Rico*, 5.
14. José M. Ufret, "Ordenan estudio plan rehabilitación Vieques," *El Mundo*, May 21, 1954, 13.
15. "Establecen industria en Vieques," *El Mundo*, Jun. 17, 1954, 4.
16. Pedro Hernández, "Pide hotel de turismo en Vieques," *El Mundo*, Nov. 16, 1954, 16.
17. F. Cancel Hernández, "Falta de industrias, crisis en Vieques obliga a emigrar," *El Mundo*, May 25, 1955, 1, 18.
18. "En Vieques. Expresan esperanzas en programa de AT," *El Mundo*, May 28, 1955, 15.
19. F. Cancel Hernández, "Autoridad de Tierras. Revive enlatado piñas en la Isla de Vieques," *El Mundo*, Jul. 4, 1955, 21.
20. "Esperanza para Vieques," *El Mundo*, Jul. 6, 1955, 6.
21. F. Cancel Hernández, "Autoridad de Tierras. Revive enlatado piñas en la Isla de Vieques," *El Mundo*, Jul. 4, 1955, 21.
22. Juan Martínez Chapel, "Muñoz en Vieques. Habitantes le exponen problemas a gobernador," *El Mundo*, Mar. 22, 1957, 1.
23. "Memorándum a Ike. Alcalde Vieques plantea presidente situación isla," *El Mundo*, Mar. 1, 1958, 29.
24. "Muñoz tratará situación Vieques," *El Mundo*, Mar. 3, 1958, 5.
25. A. Jiménez Lugo, "Heridos graves motín en Vieques. Surgió pelea entre civiles, infantes marina. Diez recibieron heridas leves," *El Mundo*, Feb. 10, 1959, 1, 12; Victor M. Padilla, "Informa policía. Todo normal en Vieques tras motín con infantes," *El Mundo*, Feb. 11, 1959, 1, 16
26. "Dice marina EU objeta fomentar turismo Vieques," *El Mundo*, May 2, 1960, 1, 28.
27. Hector J. Mejías, "Pedirá Muñoz intervenga en su lucha con marina EU," *El Mundo*, May 4, 1960, 15.
28. "Planteará problemas de Vieques en New Jersey," *El Mundo*, May 26, 1960, 5.
29. Darío Carlo, "Alcalde Rivera Rodríguez. Sale a plantear problemas de Vieques a autoridades federales en Washington," *El Mundo*, May 30, 1960, 14.
30. Sam Brady, "Fernós hará gestiones pro Vieques. Tuvo conferencia con el Alcalde," *El Mundo*, Jun. 13, 1960, 1, 18.
31. "Caso Vieques será llevado a Demócratas. Alcalde espera den más ayuda," *El Mundo*, Nov. 22, 1960, 1, 16.
32. "Isla Grande también. Marina estudia traspaso aeropuerto Vieques a ELA," *El Mundo*, Jun. 24, 1961, 1, 12.
33. Joaquín O. Mercado, "Marina objeta ceder parte Vieques a ELA," *El Mundo*, Jun. 30, 1961, 1, 10.
34. A. Jiménez Lugo, "Contesta a la armada. Alcalde Rivera puso en manos de Kennedy y Muñoz problema de las tierra de Vieques," *El Mundo*, July 1, 1961, 1, 12.
35. Darío Carlo, "Alcalde Vieques, COPU montarán piquete base," *El Mundo*, Aug. 1, 1960, 1, 15.
36. "Muñoz descarta impase en caso Vieques y Marina," *El Mundo*, Aug. 25, 1961, 1, 20.
37. Darío Carlo, "Algunas atómicas. Senador Russell en pro marina siga en Vieques," *El Mundo*, Oct. 21, 1961, 1, 10.
38. Luis Muñoz Marín to John F. Kennedy, Dec. 28, 1961, in www.vieques-island.com/navy/kennedy.html, consulted on Dec. 28, 2010.
39. Darío Carlo, "Adquisición tierras por la armada. Alcalde ve 'nuevo atropello' contra pueblo Vieques," *El Mundo*, Mar. 21, 1964, 1, 20. In some articles, the amount of land to be expropriated was said to be 4,300 acres.
40. A. Quiñones Calderón, "Protesta expropiaciones. Vieques hará piquetes contra la marina E.U.," *El Mundo*, Apr. 16, 1964, 1, 51.

41. A. Quiñones Calderón, 'Alcalde plantea hoy caso de Vieques en fortaleza. Grupo tratará expropiación por la marina," *El Mundo*, Apr. 22, 1964, 1, 10.

42. A. Quiñones Calderón, "Ve necesidad uso máximo tierras aquí," *El Mundo*, Mar. 23, 1964, 1, 14.

43. A. Quiñones Calderón, "Alcalde Vieques llevaría caso corte federal," *El Mundo*, Apr. 24, 1964, 1, 12.

44. "Autoridades EU rehusan comentar. Alcalde planteará caso Vieques en Washington," *El Mundo*, May 5, 1964, 43.

45. A. Quiñones Calderón, "Noticia llena de júbilo a Isabel II," *El Mundo*, May 6, 1964, 1, 14.

46. A. Quiñones Calderón, "Agradece respaldo de la prensa. Dan gran recibimiento a alcalde de Vieques a su regreso a la Isla," *El Mundo*, May 7, 1964, 1, 20.

47. Legislatura de Puerto Rico, *Condiciones socio-económicas del Municipio de Vieques*, 10.

48. See McCaffrey, *Military Power and Popular Protest*.

49. United States Navy, *Memorandum of Understanding*.

50. Associated Press, "Radioactive Shells Fired in Puerto Rico: Officials Say Navy Didn't Tell Them of Mistake," *Chicago Tribune*, May 29, 1999: 26; Michelle Faul, "Puerto Rico Officials Say US Didn't Tell of Shelling Error," *Boston Globe*, May 29, 1999: A3; Michelle Faul, "Navy Admits Firing Shells with Uranium on Island," *Houston Chronicle*, Jun. 3, 1999: 13.

51. There is a growing literature. McCaffrey, "Environmental Struggle after the Cold War," provides a good recent summary.

52. See www.atsdr.cdc.gov/HAC/PHA/reports/isladevieques_02072003pr/summary.html, accessed Dec. 29, 2010.

53. Figueroa, Suárez, De La Torre, Torres, and Pérez, *Incidencia y mortalidad de cáncer en Vieques, 1990–2004*.

54. Massol-Deyá, Pérez, Pérez, Berríos, and Díaz, "Trace Elements Analysis in Forage Samples from a US Navy Bombing Range"; Massol-Deyá and Díaz, 'Trace Element Composition in Forage Samples from a Military Target Range, Three Agricultural Areas, and One Natural Area in Puerto Rico."

55. Lindsay-Poland, "Vieques: Refuge for Whom?"

56. Wargo, *Green Intelligence*, chapters 5–8.

57. National Oceanic and Atmospheric Administration, National Ocean Service, Office of Response and Restoration, and Ridolfi, Inc., *Final Data Report for the Vieques Island Biota Sampling Project* (Jul. 2006), Table 3.2.
    www.response.restoration.noaa.gov/book_shelf/1141_Tables_all_Vieques.pdf.

58. Mireya Navarro, "Reversal Haunts Federal Health Agency," *New York Times*, Nov. 30, 2009; Mireya Navarro, "Toxic Substances Agency Draws Fire," *New York Times*, May 20, 2010.

Bibliography

Agricultural Experiment Station, University of Puerto Rico. "Report on the Possibilities of Utilizing Navy Lands in Vieques Island for a Resettlement Project." Mimeographed Report 23, Oct., 1943.

Archivo General de Puerto Rico, Departamento de Hacienda, 1940–1950. Registros de Tasación sobre la Propiedad, Vieques. This source is cited as A. G. P. R., D.H., 1940–1950.

Ayala, César J. *American Sugar Kingdom: The Plantation Economy of the Spanish Caribbean, 1898–1934.* Chapel Hill: University of North Carolina Press, 1999.

Ayala, César J. "Del latifundio azucarero al latifundio militar: las expropiaciones de la marina en la década del cuarenta." *Revista de Ciencias Sociales* (University of Puerto Rico) No. 10 (Jan., 2001), 1–33.

Ayala, César J. "From Sugar Plantations to Military Bases: The U.S. Navy's Expropriations in Vieques, Puerto Rico, 1940–45." *Centro—Journal of the CUNY Center for Puerto Rican Studies* 13(1) (Spring, 2001), 22–44.

Ayala, César J., and Laird Bergad. "Rural Puerto Rico during the Early Twentieth Century Reconsidered: Land and Society, 1899–1915." *Latin American Research Review* (37)2 (Apr., 2002), 65–99.

Ayala, César, and Rafael Bernabe. *Puerto Rico in the American Century: A History since 1898.* Chapel Hill: University of North Carolina Press, 2007.

Ayala, César J., and José Bolívar. "Entre dos aguas: economía, sociedad, e intervención estatal en Vieques, 1942–1948." *Revista de Ciencias Sociales.* San Juan, Puerto Rico (Winter, 2004), 52–79.

Ayala, César J., and Viviana Carro. "Expropriations and Displacement of Civilians in Vieques, 1940–1950." In *Puerto Rico under Colonial Rule: Political Persecution and the Quest for Human Rights,* edited by R. Bosque Pérez and J. Colón Morera. Albany: S.U.N.Y. Press, 2005, 173–205.

Ayala, César. Interview with Doña Severina Guadalupe, Isabel Segunda, Vieques. Apr. 11, 2001.

Barreto, Amílcar Antonio. *Vieques, the Navy, and Puerto Rican Politics.* Gainesville: University of Florida Press, 2002.

Beckford, George. *Persistent Poverty: Underdevelopment in the Plantation Economies of the Third World.* Oxford: Oxford University Press, 1970.

Bergad, Laird. *Coffee and the Growth of Agrarian Capitalism in Nineteenth Century Puerto Rico.* Princeton: Princeton University Press, 1983.

209

Bergad, Laird. "Coffee and Rural Proletarianization in Nineteenth Century Puerto Rico, 1840–1898." *Journal of Latin American Studies* 15(1) (1983), 83–100.

Best, Lloyd. "The Mechanism of Plantation Type Societies: Outlines of a Model of Pure Plantation Economy." *Social and Economic Studies* 17(3) (1968), 283–326.

Bird, Esteban A. *Report on the Sugar Industry in Relation to the Social and Economic System of Puerto Rico*. San Juan: Puerto Rico Reconstruction Administration, 1937.

Blackburn, Robin. *The Overthrow of Colonial Slavery: 1776–1848*. London: Verso, 1988.

Bolívar Fresneda, José. *Guerra, banca y desarrollo: el Banco de Fomento y la industrialización de Puerto Rico*. Forthcoming. San Juan: Fundación Luis Muñoz Marín, 2011.

Bonnet Benítez, Juan Amédée. *Vieques en la historia de Puerto Rico*. San Juan, Puerto Rico: F. Ortiz Nieves, 1976.

Burdman, Samantha. *Donde Uno Nace: The Expropriations of Vieques, Puerto Rico*. Senior Thesis, video: Trustees of Dartmouth College, 2002.

Coll y Toste, Cayetano. *Boletín Histórico de Puerto Rico*. Tom. 13, 1926. Reprinted by Ateneo Puertorriqueño, San Juan: Editorial Lea, 2004.

Costello, John, and Terry Hughes. *The Battle of the Atlantic*. London: Collins, 1977.

Department of the Navy. *Continued Use of the Atlantic Fleet Weapons Training Facility Inner Range (Vieques): Draft Environmental Impact Statement*. Tippetts-Abbett-McCarthy-Stratton: Ecology and Environment, 1979.

Dietz, James. *Economic History of Puerto Rico: Institutional Change and Capitalist Development*. Princeton: Princeton University Press, 1986.

Du Bois, W. E. B. *Black Reconstruction in America: An Essay Toward a History of the Part which Black Folk Played in the Attempt to Reconstruct Democracy in America, 1860–1880*. New York: Atheneum, 1977 [c1962].

Echenique, Miguel. *El desarrollo económico de Puerto Rico: una estrategia para la próxima década: informe preparado para el Consejo Financiero del gobernador*. San Juan: Editorial Universitaria, Universidad de Puerto Rico, 1976.

Edel, Mathew D. "Land Reform in Puerto Rico," *Caribbean Studies*, Part I (Oct., 1962), 22–60, and Part II (Jan., 1963), 28–50.

Estades Font, María Eugenia. *La presencia militar de los Estados Unidos en Puerto Rico, 1898–1918: Intereses estratégicos y dominación colonial*. Río Piedras, Puerto Rico: Huracán, 1988.

Fernández y García, Eugenio, ed. *El libro de Puerto Rico*. San Juan: El Libro Azul Publishing Co., 1923.

Figueroa, Luis A. *Sugar, Slavery, and Freedom in Nineteenth-Century Puerto Rico*. Chapel Hill: University of North Carolina Press, 2005.

Figueroa, Nayda R., Erick Suárez, Taína De La Torre, Mariela Torres, and Javier

Pérez. *Incidencia y mortalidad de cáncer en Vieques, 1990-2004*. San Juan: Departamento de Salud, Estado Libre Asociado de Puerto Rico, 2009.

Foster, Peter. *Family Spirits: The Bacardi Saga*. Toronto: Macfarlane Walker & Ross, 1990.

García Muñiz, Humberto. *La estrategia de Estados Unidos y la militarización del Caribe: ensayo sobre el desarrollo histórico de las fuerzas de seguridad y la presencia militar de Estados Unidos en el Caribe angloparlante*. Río Piedras, Puerto Rico: Instituto de Estudios del Caribe, Facultad de Ciencias Sociales, Universidad de Puerto Rico, 1988.

García Muñiz, Humberto. *Los Estados Unidos y la militarización del Caribe*. Río Piedras, Puerto Rico: Instituto de Estudios del Caribe, Universidad de Puerto Rico, 1988.

García Muñiz, Humberto. "U. S. Military Installations in Puerto Rico: Controlling the Caribbean." In *Colonial Dilemma: Critical Perspectives on Contemporary Puerto Rico*, edited by Edgardo Meléndez and Edwin Meléndez. Boston: South End Press, 1993, 53–65.

García Muñiz, Humberto, and Jorge Rodríguez Beruff, eds. *Security Problems and Policies in the Post-Cold War Caribbean*. New York: St. Martin's Press, 1996.

García Muñiz, Humberto, and Jorge Rodríguez Beruff. "U. S. Military Policy toward the Caribbean in the 1990s." *Annals of the American Academy of Political and Social Science* 553 (May, 1994), 112–124.

Gilmore, A. B. *The Porto Rico Sugar Manual, Including Data on Santo Domingo Mills*. New Orleans: A. B. Gilmore, 1930.

Guisti Cordero, Juan. "La Huelga Cañera de 1942. Crónica de una Huelga General." *Fundamentos* (Revista de Estudios Generales de la Universidad de Puerto Rico) 5–6 (1997–1998), 82-96.

Giusti Cordero, Juan. *Informe histórico preliminar: Asociación Pro-Títulos de Monte Santo et al.* vs. *Estado Libre Asociado et al.* Civil Núm. KPE 96–0729 (907) Tribunal de Primera Instancia, Sección Superior de San Juan, Jun. 8, 1999.

Giusti Cordero, Juan A. "Labor, Ecology, and History in a Caribbean Sugar Plantation Region: Piñones (Loíza), Puerto Rico 1770–1950." Ph.D. diss., SUNY-Binghamton, 1994.

Giusti Cordero, Juan A. "La marina en la mirilla: una comparación de Vieques con los campos de bombardeo y adiestramiento en los Estados Unidos." In *Fronteras en conflicto: Guerra contra las drogas, militarización y democracia en el Caribe, Puerto Rico y Vieques*, edited by Humberto García Muñiz and Jorge Rodríguez Beruff. San Juan: Red Caribeña de Geopolítica, 1999, 133–201.

Gordon, Maxine W. "Cultural Aspects of Puerto Rico's Race Problems." *American Sociological Review* 15(3) (Jun., 1950), 382–392.

Government of Puerto Rico. *Special Commission on Vieques. 1999. Study of the Situation of the Island-Municipality with Regards to the U.S. Navy's Activities*. (www. comisionvieques. govpr. org).

Griffith, David, and Manuel Valdés Pizzini. *Fishers at Work, Workers at Sea: A Puerto Rican Journey through Labor and Refuge.* Philadelphia: Temple University Press, 2002.

Harris, W. W. *Puerto Rico's Fighting 65th Infantry: From San Juan to Chorwan.* San Rafael, California: Presidio Press, 1980.

Hessman, James D. "Opposed Landings: Vieques, the Navy Comes under 'Constant Bombardment.'" *Sea Power Magazine* (Mar., 1979), 12–16.

Hibben, Thomas, and Rafael Picó. *Industrial Development of Puerto Rico and the Virgin Islands of the U.S.: Report of the U.S. Section, Caribbean Commission.* Port of Spain (Caribbean Commission) and San Juan (Puerto Rico Planning Board), 1948.

Hochstuhl, William C. *German U-Boat 156 Brought War to Aruba February 16, 1942.* Oranjestad, Aruba: Aruba Scholarship Foundation, 2001. Reprinted from Aruba Esso News Special Edition, Feb. 16, 1942.

Iglesias Pantín, Santiago. *Luchas emancipadoras.* Tom. 2. San Juan: n. p., 1962.

Ireland, Bernard. *The Battle of the Atlantic.* Barnsley, South Yorkshire: Leo Cooper, 2003.

Johnson, Chalmers A. *Blowback: The Costs and Consequences of American Empire.* New York: Metropolitan Books, 2000.

Johnson, Chalmers A. *The Sorrows of Empire: Militarism, Secrecy, and the End of the Republic.* New York: Metropolitan Books, 2004.

Johnson, Chalmers A. *Nemesis: The Last Days of the American Republic.* New York: Metropolitan Books, 2006.

Junta de Planificación de Puerto Rico. *Plan de desarrollo para la isla de Vieques.* San Juan: Junta de Planificación de Puerto Rico, Mar., 1955.

Lai, Walton Look. *Indentured Labor, Caribbean Sugar: Chinese and Indian Migrants to the British West Indies, 1838-1918.* Baltimore: Johns Hopkins University Press, 2004.

Langhorn, Elizabeth. *Vieques: History of a Small Island.* Vieques: Vieques Conservation and Historical Trust, 1987.

Levy, Teresita A. "The History of Tobacco Cultivation in Puerto Rico, 1899–1940." Ph.D. diss., City University of New York, 2007.

Lindsay-Poland, John. "Refuge for Whom?: Vieques and the Uses of a Bombing Area." Paper Presented at the Congress of the Latin American Studies Association, San Juan, Puerto Rico, Mar., 2006.

Maldonado, A. W. *Teodoro Moscoso and Puerto Rico's Operation Bootstrap.* Gainesville: Unversity of Florida Press, 1997.

Massol Deyá, Arturo, and Elba Díaz. "Trace Element Composition in Forage Samples from a Military Target Range, Three Agricultural Areas, and One Natural Area in Puerto Rico." *Caribbean Journal of Science* 39(2) (2003), 215–220.

Massol-Deyá, Arturo, Dustin Pérez, Ernie Pérez, Manuel Berríos, and Elba Díaz. "Trace Elements Analysis in Forage Samples from a US Navy Bombing Range

(Vieques, Puerto Rico)." *International Journal of Environmental Research and Public Health* 2(2) (Aug., 2005), 263–266.

McCaffrey, Katherine T. "Culture, Power, and Struggle: Anti-Military Protest in Vieques, Puerto Rico." Ph.D. diss., City University of New York, 1999.

McCaffrey, Katherine T. *Military Power and Popular Protest: The U.S. Navy in Vieques, Puerto Rico.* New Brunswick: Rutgers University Press, 2002.

McCaffrey, Katherine T. "The Struggle for Environmental Justice in Vieques, Puerto Rico." In *Environmental Justice in Latin America: Problems, Promise, and Practice,* edited by David V. Carruthers. Cambridge, Mass.: MIT Press, 2008, 263–285.

McCaffrey, Katherine T. "Environmental Struggle after the Cold War: New Forms of Resistance to the U.S. Military in Vieques, Puerto Rico." In *The Bases of Empire: The Global Struggle against U.S. Military Posts,* edited by Catherine Lutz. New York: New York University Press, 2009, 218–242.

McGregor, Morris J. Integration of the Armed Forces, 1940–1965. Washington, D.C.: Center of Military History, United States Army, 1981, 72–73.

Milkman, Ruth. *Gender at Work: The Dynamics of Job Segregation by Sex during World War II.* Urbana and Chicago: The University of Illinois Press, 1987.

Mintz, Sidney W. "Slavery and the Rise of Peasantries." In *Roots and Branches: Current Directions in Slave Studies,* edited by Michael Craton. Toronto: Pergamon Press, 1979.

Mintz, Sidney W. "From Plantations to Peasants in the Caribbean." In *Caribbean Contours,* edited by Sidney Mintz and Sally Price. Baltimore: Johns Hopkins University Press, 1985, 127–153.

Mintz, Sidney W. *Sweetness and Power: The Place of Sugar in Modern History.* New York: Viking, 1985.

Moore, Arthur R. *A Careless Word—A Needless Sinking: A History of the Staggering Losses Suffered by the U.S. Merchant Marine, both in Ships and Personnel during World War II.* Kings Point, N.Y.: American Merchant Marine Museum, 1985.

Morales Carrión, Arturo. *Puerto Rico and the Non-Hispanic Caribbean: A Study in the Decline of Spanish Exclusivism.* Río Piedras, Puerto Rico: University of Puerto Rico Press, 1952.

Murillo, Mario. *Islands of Resistance: Puerto Rico, Vieques and U.S. Policy.* New York: Seven Stories Press, 2001.

Oficina de Servicios Legislativos, División de Economía. *Estudio sobre: Condiciones socio-económicas del Municipio de Vieques.* San Juan, P.R.: Legislatura de Puerto Rico, Oficina de Servicios Legislativos, División de Economía, 1970.

O'Reilly, Alejandro. "Memoria de D. Alejandro O'Reylly sobre la isla de Puerto Rico, año 1765." In *Crónicas de Puerto Rico,* edited by Eugenio Fernández Méndez. Río Piedras: Editorial de la Universidad de Puerto Rico, 1969, 238–269.

Ortiz Cuadra, Cruz Miguel. *Puerto Rico en la olla: ¿somos aún lo que comimos?* Madrid: Ediciones Doce Calles, 2006.

Pagán, Bolívar. *Historia de los partidos políticos puertorriqueños, 1898–1956.* Tom. 2. Barcelona: Imprenta M. Ponceja, 1972.

Pantojas García, Emilio. *Development Strategies as Ideology: Puerto Rico's Export Led Industrialization Experience.* Boulder: Lynne Rienner, 1990.

Pastor Ruiz, J. *Vieques antiguo y moderno.* Yauco, Puerto Rico: Tipografía Rodríguez Lugo, 1947.

Picó, Fernando, ed. *Discursos de Muñoz Marín 1934–1948*, vol. 1. San Juan: Fundación Luis Muñoz Marín, 1999.

Picó, Rafael. *Report of the Committee for the Investigation of Conditions in the Island of Vieques.* Archivo Luis Muñoz Marín (Trujillo Alto, Puerto Rico), Series 9, Fdr. 506–3 (Mar. 18, 1943).

Picó, Rafael. *The Geographic Regions of Puerto Rico.* Río Piedras, Puerto Rico: University of Puerto Rico Press, 1950.

Proyecto Caribeño de Justicia y Paz. "Entrevistas a los expropiados de Vieques. Vieques, Puerto Rico." Archivo del Fuerte del Conde de Mirasol, Vieques, 1979.

Puerto Rico Policy Commission. *Report of the Puerto Rico Policy Commission.* San Juan: Puerto Rico Policy Commission, 1934.

Puerto Rico Reconstruction Administration. *Census of Puerto Rico: 1935, Population and Agriculture.* Washington, D.C.: United States Government Printing Office, 1938.

Rabin, Robert. "La influencia francesa en Vieques." *Revista Universidad de America* 2 (2) (Dec., 1990), 58–61.

Rabin, Robert. *Compendio de lecturas sobre la historia de Vieques.* Vieques: Museo Fuerte Conde de Mirasol, 1994.

Rodríguez Beruff, Jorge. *Política militar y dominación: Puerto Rico en el contexto latinoamericano.* Río Piedras, Puerto Rico: Huracán, 1988.

Rodríguez Beruff, Jorge. *El archivo Luis Muñoz Marín: La ventana para el estudio de la historia puertorriqueña.* San Juan: Fundación Luis Muñoz Marín, 2000.

Rodríguez Beruff, Jorge. *Las memorias de Leahy.* San Juan, Puerto Rico: Fundación Luis Muñoz Marín, 2002.

Rodríguez Beruff, Jorge. *Strategy as Politics: Puerto Rico on the Eve of the Second World War.* San Juan: Editorial, Universidad de Puerto Rico, 2007.

Romero Barceló, Carlos. Testimony before the Committee on Armed Services, U.S. Senate, Oct. 19, 1999. www.senate.gov~armed_services-statemnt-1999–991019cr. pdf.

Santana Rabell, Leonardo. *Planificación y política: Un análisis crítico.* San Juan: Editorial Cultural, 1984.

Santiago Caraballo, Josefa. "Guerra, reforma y colonialismo: Luis Muñoz Marín, las reformas del P.D.P. y su vinculación con la militarización de Puerto Rico en el contexto de la Segunda Guerra Mundial." Ph.D. diss., University of Puerto Rico, 2005.

Scarano, Francisco. *Sugar and Slavery in Puerto Rico: The Plantation Economy of Ponce, 1800–1850*. Madison: University of Wisconsin Press, 1984.

Senior, Clarence. *The Puerto Rican Migrant in St. Croix*. Río Piedras, Puerto Rico: University of Puerto Rico Social Science Research Center, 1947.

Sonesson, Birgit. *Puerto Rico's Commerce, 1765–1865: From Regional to World-wide Market Relations*. Los Angeles: UCLA Latin American Center Publications, 1999.

Stoler, Ann Laura. *Capitalism and Confrontation in Sumatra's Plantation Belt, 1870–1979*. New Haven: Yale University Press, 1985.

Sued Badillo, Jalil. *Los caribes, realidad o fábula? Ensayo de rectificación histórica*. Río Piedras: Editorial Antillana, 1978.

Taller de Formación Política. *¡Huelga en la caña!* Río Piedras: Huracán, 1982.

Tío, Aurelio. Prólogo a *Vieques en la historia de Puerto Rico*, por Juan Amédée Bonnet Benítez. San Juan, Puerto Rico: F. Ortiz Nieves, 1976.

Tomich, Dale. "The Other Face of Slave Labor: Provision Grounds and Internal Marketing in Martinique." In *Caribbean Slave Society and Economy: A Student Reader*, edited by Hilary McD. Beckles and Verene A. Shepherd. Kingston, Jamaica: Ian Randle, 1991, 304–318. Reprinted in Verene A. Shepherd and Hilary McD. Beckles, eds., *Caribbean Slavery in the Atlantic World*. Princeton: Markus Wiener Publishers, 2000.

Torres, Bibiano. "La isla de Vieques." *Anuario de Estudios Americanos* (Seville) 12 (1955), 449–466.

Trías Monge, José. *Puerto Rico: The Trials of the Oldest Colony in the World*. New Haven: Yale University Press, 1997.

Tugwell, Rexford. *The Stricken Land: The Story of Puerto Rico*. Garden City, N.Y.: Doubleday & Company, Inc., 1947.

U.S. Department of Commerce, Bureau of the Census. *Thirteenth Census of the United States: Volume III, Population 1910, Reports by States, with Statistics for Counties, Cities and Other Civil Divisions: Nebraska-Wyoming, Alaska, Hawaii, and Porto Rico*. Washington, D.C.: Government Printing Office, 1913.

U.S. Department of Commerce, Bureau of the Census. *Fifteenth Census of the United States: 1930. Outlying Territories and Possessions*. Washington, D.C.: Government Printing Office, 1932.

U.S. Department of Commerce, Bureau of the Census. *1950 Population Census Report*. Washington, D.C.: Government Printing Office, 1952.

U.S. Department of Commerce, Bureau of the Census. *Census of Population, 1950, vol. 2, Characteristics of the Population, Parts 51–54, Territories and Possessions*. Washington, D.C.: Government Printing Office, 1953.

U.S. Department of the Interior, Office of Statistics, Office of the Governor, La Fortaleza, P.R., and Division of Territories and Island Possessions. *The Puerto*

Rican Economy during the War Year of 1942. Washington, D.C., 1943.

United States Congress, House Committee on Armed Services. Hearings before the Panel to Review the Status of the Navy Training Activities in the Island of Vieques. Washington, D.C.: Government Printing Office, 1989.

United States Navy. *Memorandum of Understanding Regarding the Island of Vieques*. Washington, D.C.: Government Printing Office, 1983.

Veaz, Maribel. "Las expropiaciones de la década del cuarenta en Vieques." *Revista del Colegio de Abogados de Puerto Rico* 56 (2) (Apr.–Jun., 1995), 159–213.

Vine, David. *Island of Shame: The Secret History of the U.S. Military Base on Diego García*. Princeton: Princeton University Press, 2009.

War Department, Office Director Census of Porto Rico. *Report on the Census of Porto Rico, 1899*. Washington, D.C.: Government Printing Office, 1900.

Wargo, John. *Green Intelligence: Creating Environments That Promote Human Health*. New Haven: Yale University Press, 2009.

Williams, Eric. *The Negro in the Caribbean*. Washington, D.C.: Associates in Negro Folk Education, 1942.

Index

9 781558 765382